The African Experience in Literature and Ideology
▼▼▼

D1563870

ABIOLA IRELE

The African Experience
in Literature and Ideology

▼▼

INDIANA UNIVERSITY PRESS
Bloomington and Indianapolis

The paper used in this publication meets the minimum requirements of American National Standard for Information Sciences—Permanence of Paper for Printed Library Materials, ANSI Z39.48-1984.

∞™

Manufactured in the United States of America

Library of Congress Cataloging-in-Publication Data
Irele, Abiola.
    The African experience in literature and ideology / Abiola Irele.
        p.   cm.
    Reprint. Originally published: London ; Exeter, N.H. : Heinemann, 1981.
    ISBN 0-253-33124-2 (alk. paper). — ISBN 0-253-20569-7 (pbk. : alk. paper)
    1. African literature (French)—History and criticism.   2. African literature—History and criticism.   3. Literature and society—Africa.   4. Negritude (Literary movement)   I. Title.
PQ3980.I74   1990
840.9'896—dc20   89-24586
                                                            CIP

1 2 3 4 5 94 93 92 91 90

In Memoriam

Janheinz Jahn

1918-1973
▼▼

Contents

▼▼

Sources

▼▼▼

Critical Positions
1. 'Studying African Literature.' Paper presented at Conference on 'Text and Context in Africa', Afrikastudiecentrum, Leiden, September 1976. Published in proceedings, Mineke Schipper-de-Leeuw (ed.) *Text and Context in Africa*, special no. *African Perspectives* – 1977, No. 1 (Leiden: Afrikastudiecentrum, 1977).
2. 'The Criticism of Modern African Literature.' Paper presented at Conference on African Literature in English, University of Ife, Ile-Ife, December 1968. Published in C. Heywood (ed.) *Perspectives on African Literature* (London: Heinemann Educational Books, 1971).
3. 'African Literature and the Language Question.' Paper presented at Conference on 'Le Critique africain et son peuple comme producteurs de civilisation', Yaoundé, April 1973. Published in proceedings under same title (Paris: Présence Africaine, 1977).

Négritude and Nationalism
4. 'What is Négritude?' Paper presented at Conference on 'Political Theory and Ideology in African Society', Centre for African Studies, University of Edinburgh, February 1970. Revised and published under the title 'Négritude – the Philosophy of African Being' in *Nigeria Magazine* Nos. 122–123, Lagos, 1977 (special number, World Festival of Black and African Arts).
5. 'Négritude and African Personality.' Original paper presented in French at 'Colloque sur la Négritude', Dakar, March 1971, and published in proceedings, same title, Présence Africaine, Paris, 1972. English version presented at Inaugural Conference of Nigerian Society for International Affairs, University of Ibadan, September 1971. (First publication here).
6. 'Pan-Africanism and African Nationalism.' Review article of V. Bakpetu Thompson, *Africa and Unity – the Evolution of Pan*

Africanism (London: Longman, 1969), and published in *Odu*, New Series, No. 6, Ife, October 1971.

Literary Studies

7. 'Literature and Ideology in Martinique: René Maran, Aimé Césaire, Frantz Fanon.' Paper presented at Conference on 'The Meaning of Africa to Afro-Americans', State University of New York at Buffalo, April 1969. Published in *Research Review*, Vol. 5, No. 3, January 1970, Institute of African Studies, University of Ghana, Legon.

8. 'French African Narrative Prose and the Colonial Experience': published as Introduction to *Lectures Africaines* (London: Heinemann Educational Books, 1969).

9. 'Faith and Exile: Cheikh Hamidou Kane and the Theme of Alienation' in *Le Français au Nigeria*, Vol. 7, No. 3, Ibadan, December 1972.

10. 'Traditional and the Yoruba Writer: D. O. Fagunwa, Amos Tutuola, Wole Soyinka.' Paper presented at weekend seminar on Yoruba Language and Literature, University of Ife, December 1969. Revised and published in *Odu*, New Series, No. 11, January 1975.

11. 'The Season of a Mind: Wole Soyinka and the Nigerian Crisis', published in *Benin Review*, Number One, Benin City, June 1974.

Preface to the Indiana Edition
▼▼

The reprinting of a book, one imagines, is always a cause for satisfaction for its author. At the same time, it can occasion a certain unease as a fresh reading of the work reveals to him with a special clarity the defects of his writing. Moreover, his thinking on certain questions often progresses in such a way as to create a distance between, on the one hand, new positions which—with further reflection and the passage of time—one may have arrived at on these questions, and on the other, the particular direction or emphasis of one's earlier formulations. The compulsion to revise, to rewrite and sometimes even to repudiate one's earlier work is ever present with an author.

I must confess here to mixed feelings of this order on the occasion of the reprinting of this book. Yet, as I consider the present collection, first published in 1981, I realize that it constitutes in its own way a personal statement on African literature which it would be futile for me now to attempt to modify either in whole or in part. I have therefore not undertaken a revision of any of the essays in the book, preferring to let the collection stand as a testimony to my particular perspective on the subject at the time the book first appeared. I can only hope that the statement it makes, such as it is, has retained much of its interest, perhaps even of its validity, to merit its being presented once more to the public.

However, current developments within the corpus of African literature, and the intense theoretical debates that have ensued concerning its criticism, make it necessary for me to return to certain issues arising from these essays, in order to place them within the perspective of the present moment of their republication. As anyone who has taken an interest in the subject is aware, the literary scene in Africa has evolved considerably in the past decade, with not only the appearance of new themes in the work of the older writers but also, and especially, the emergence of a new generation of writers whose work is giving a wholly new direction to literary expression on the continent. This phenomenon, to which I could only make a passing reference in my earlier introduction, has involved profound changes both in the handling of themes and of the formal modes of expression in African literature. It is a subject that in itself requires the kind of extensive examination, founded upon a modified critical perception in tune with these developments, that only another work can adequately treat. I need only to refer to the fate of an observation I make in an essay in this collection about French African fiction to suggest the scale of the critical readjustments that must animate such an examination: the splendid refutation of my incautiously categorical statement about the limited possibilities of an African recasting of the French language which Amadou Kourouma provides in his remarkable novel, *Les Soleils des Indépendances.*

An issue intimately related to these developments is that concerning the ideological premises of African expression in its early stages. These are now being challenged more and more, and have even been superseded to some extent. I have not been indifferent to the debates on this issue, and they have made me aware how much the essays in this collection reflect the essentialist tenets of an earlier generation of African writers and black ideological leaders preoccupied with the problem of identity in their contestation of the colonial order. I believe I owe it to readers of this reprint to state that my position on this question has evolved somewhat. Indeed, I have had occasion to re-examine this question in what may be considered a new light, as shown in my inaugural lecture at the University of Ibadan, *In Praise of Alienation,* the title of which is, I imagine, sufficiently indicative of my present orientation on this question.

On one further issue arising from these essays, I have however been slower to modify my stance. This concerns the whole question of literary value and critical procedures in their application to African literature. I can only reiterate here the point I made in my earlier introduction about the uncertain status of literary judgements and the way they are conditioned by historical and cultural circumstances. I am all the more reassured about the position I have taken on this matter in that the point I endeavoured to make has now received a comprehensive development in Barbara Herrnstein Smith's admirable study *Contingencies of Value,* a work that seems to me to support and confirm with rigorous logic what I could only state as a bald intuition.

I am nonetheless aware that her magisterial intervention does not close the debate, especially on the general front of literary theory, where the endeavour to chart a personally congenial course has to contend with formidable forces. I refer here of course to the prevailing trends in contemporary theories of literature proposed to us by Western scholarship, with their affirmation of the primacy of form in literature and their insistence on the autonomy of the literary work as a coherent system of signs requiring no reference to an external reality beyond the text for its proper apprehension. Current literary theory represents an extension of an earlier reaction against approaches that paid inadequate attention to the inherent nature of the literary work as a construct, as a formal entity and aesthetic phenomenon; in this sense it sustains a critical outlook that is both defendable and eminently creditable. The renewed emphasis on textuality, on the strictly formal status of all linguistic manifestations, has had however as its concomitant the denial to structured language of its natural (or conventional) referential function and has promoted what amounts to a new orthodoxy in the area of literary criticism: it has led to what is visibly an extreme position in which the relation of literary expression to a lived world of human values and consciousness is being eroded.

The fact that African criticism has developed and is still being pursued in the shadow of Western scholarship has meant that those of us who are professionally engaged in the examination of African literature have come under intense pressure to conform to this new orthodoxy. We are required, it seems, not only to place our literature in a formalist perspective in order to establish its claim to consideration as a corpus worthy of critical attention, but also to adopt a certain idiom of contemporary critical discourse in order to validate our status as serious scholars. It is increasingly common to assume that an approach that makes a large concession to content, to the historical and sociological factors reflected within the literature, not only places the literature itself beyond the pale of any kind of esteem but is also inappropriate to a rigorous critical and scholarly undertaking.

I hardly need to say that I have found it difficult to give unequivocal assent to this view. It remains my conviction that the objective of criticism in the African context cannot be merely to apprehend literature in its nature, in its numinous inwardness, as it were—though this can in other contexts represent a valid preoccupation for the literary scholar—but to provide, as far as it is in the power of the critic to do so, an understanding of its immediate function, implicit in the character of literature both as a symbolic mode and as a means of social discourse, representing by that very fact a privileged channel of inter-subjective communication, with therefore an objective value and significance for the elaboration of a field of vision from within the recesses of the collective consciousness.

One might observe in this regard that African writers have not yet quite succumbed to the solipsism which marks much of the accepted literature of the West at the present time. I would argue that this fact enjoins upon the African critic an obligation to take account of the writers' striving towards a meaning that reaches out beyond the formal modes of signification discoverable within their works in order to engage a felt universe of life, a world involved more than ever in the tensions of a historical process whose outcome is of the greatest import for us as Africans. The manifest concern of the writers to speak to the immediate issues of social life, to narrate the tensions that traverse their world—to relate their imaginative expression to their particular universe of experience in all its existential concreteness—this seems to me to leave the African critic with hardly any choice but to give precedence to the powerful referential thrust of our literature: it is only at the risk of deviating from the determined direction of this literature that one can disregard its gesture towards a focused and particularised meaning, its expressed implication in the collective experience.

It seems to me then that African critics have their work cut out for them. They require in the specific context of this work to adopt what I would like to call a "pragmatic" approach to the object of their critical endeavour, recognizing in the procedures they bring to its scrutiny the uniqueness of the literary mode and at the same time striving to make clear the reference to the living context of life in which African literature is being created today.

Columbus, Ohio
September 1989

The African Experience in Literature and Ideology
▼▼

Introduction

▼▼

'All art is propaganda, though not all propaganda is art.' In these words – or similar words to the same effect – did Chinua Achebe once, to my hearing, state his understanding, as both writer and responsive individual, of the nature and function of art. The statement has the terseness and cogency we have come to associate with the man. It sets before us a truth about art that is often obscured by theories which fail to take account of the elementary fact that all forms of artistic expression, and most especially literature, must have a reference to human life and consciousness if they are to take on any significance.

It is perhaps natural that the statement itself should have come from one of Africa's most significant writers, for it can be said that Achebe does no more than sum up in it his conception of the role which he himself has played in the specific African context. This role has consisted in bringing fully to our consciousness the processes and forces that have determined our peculiar experience in the modern age. No one was better placed therefore to understand and to point out the directive purpose of literature in the crisis of consciousness that has attended our experience of colonialism and its agonizing aftermath.

I should like to think that the essays brought together in this volume have represented, in their own way, a form of collaboration in the African writers' enterprise, envisaged in the particular perspective defined by Achebe's statement. At all events, they have arisen out of a preoccupation that has been more than academic with our modern expression – both the imaginative and the ideological closely associated – in its immediate bearing upon, and specific illumination of, our modern historical experience.

It is perhaps not too much to say that if modern African writing has any value at the present moment, any *significance*, it is essentially as a function of the comprehensive testimony it offers of the turns and patterns of an unfolding drama of existence in which we have been and continue to be involved. That drama has its source of course in our relation to the Western world, which has crossed our historical path and modified the realities of our life as well as our entire perspective upon the world. The imaginative writing in particular stands both as a direct representation of the concrete facts of our collective experience and as a reconstruction, in the form of images, of the states of consciousness induced by that experience: the very process of symbolic projection revealing itself as a means of drawing this experience more fully and intimately within the collective self, so as to enable us to comprehend its meaning for ourselves in the immediate present and for the future. To quote Achebe again, our modern literature has served to indicate to us 'where we have been beaten by the rain'.

That much can be stated, at least, as the significant direction of modern African literature. It is evident however that such a view does not exhaust its possibilities of meaning and reference. For if it is true that the sensibility and intelligence of the writer, placed at the focal point of the collective awareness, constitute him into an ideal witness, it is also true that what distinguishes him is not only this heightened capacity for perception and response but also a special capacity for expression, for the organization of experience into significant form. The writer's expression must not only capture the flow of experience but also propose a broader vision of life that transcends the immediate situation to which his work refers. To return to Achebe's proposition and to take up its second term, the ultimate distinction between true art and mere propaganda is that the former contains within it a profound human implication.

This larger human import has sometimes been denied to African literature on account of what is considered to be its limited reference to the African environment and its too close involvement with the specific African experience – factors which are supposed to reduce, if not remove altogether, its universal appeal and interest. This charge – for it is such – carries with it the assumption, especially by Western critics, that the Western consciousness has become today so central to the world's scheme of values that only its categories and modes of apprehension can properly be thought of as 'universal'.[1] To a great extent, the whole movement of mind designated in and by our modern literature, the affirmation of which it is an expression, has derived from an imperative need to confront the practical effects of this assumption – effects we have experienced in the flesh and in the spirit. In its initial thrust, therefore, modern African literature presents itself both as a challenge to the pervasive spirit of imperialism of the West and as a mode of a creative process of self-differentiation.

But though this was a legitimate reaction, it is probably true that today our need is less to press our claim, however justified, to an original difference, than to begin to restate our common involvement with the rest of humanity. It is precisely in this perspective that our modern literature will derive its enduring interest – in the way it throws a vivid light upon an area of human life and experience which, though circumscribed in its immediate reference, has nonetheless a fundamental correspondence to other areas, in other climes and other times.

This question of the universal relevance of literary expression which is involved in the judgement of our new writing can indeed be viewed from an African perspective. There is an obvious sense in which Achebe's *Arrow of God* means more to me than, say, Balzac's *Le Père Goriot*, or Soyinka's *Death and the King's Horseman* than Racine's *Phèdre*. The African works are closer to a reality and to an experience of which I feel myself a part and therefore engage my responses in a way that is both direct and immediately real. To say this, however, is not to deny that the two French works also have a meaning for me, at a different level of my total 'structure of feeling', a meaning which has less to do with my capacity to participate directly in the worlds they evoke and the social values they embody (which I can only come to appreciate through study and in an abstract way) than with the intense quality of their imaginative engagement with the issues of the social and moral life. The force of their insights into the complexities of the human spirit gives a depth to these works through which they come to express a general human condition. Thus, if Balzac and Racine can be proposed to an African for his admiration, it is precisely because, in all great literature, value and meaning derive from the two complementary levels of the local and the universal reference. The point then is that a literary work need not be dissociated from its reference to a particular context of life and experience, of existential awareness, to have a general human relevance and application.

But to speak of 'value' and 'meaning' in this way is at the same time to raise the question of artistic achievement which can be considered inseparable from the quality of the writer's vision. This question is complicated in the case of modern African literature by the fact that our writers employ the European languages to express an African experience and so force comparison with the established figures of the Western literary tradition. Even the most sympathetic Western commentators sometimes give the impression that the African writer cannot but suffer from the comparison.[2] They may even deem it necessary at times to justify their interest in African literature by an apologetic stance which concedes the point, so that the literature is considered from the point of view of its documentary rather than literary/aesthetic interest. There is certainly an unevenness to the quality of accomplishment in the present body of African writing, as indeed there must be in any literary corpus. And it is possible that there is a less sure sense of language and of form in much African writing expressed in the European languages than in the equivalent metropolitan writing – this is perhaps only to be expected in view of the language problem, as I have tried to show in one of the essays in this volume. But it seems to me that there has been undue apprehension on this question. For in its development so far, the movement towards a modern literary expression has fully justified itself, if only because we can point already to a number of works that are valuable, and to a few writers with both a human concern and a capacity for expressing that concern that is as serious as any that can be found anywhere.

It is of course one of the critic's functions to propose the discriminations that help to establish works of value and to distinguish them from those that are not. And it is not the least of the ambiguities of the critical enterprise that there is no absolute measure of achievement in literature. The truth indeed is that, even within the same culture, the canons of literary judgement are fluid, if not vague and undefinable. The recognition of greatness in a writer is thus often a matter of conditioning (taking this term in a positive sense), relative to the historical and cultural circumstance in which his work is felt to operate.

But it is also evident that in the case of the established literatures, a consensus upon certain key figures does emerge, a convention which helps to place each individual response within a common framework of valuations. Moreover, the convention itself is buttressed by a constituted body of past works which provides a constant reference against which new creations can be judged. In other words, the critic in such a context has the advantage of an established literary tradition, often supported as well by a critical tradition. The African critic on the other hand enjoys this advantage in an ambiguous fashion. For even when the indigenous oral tradition and the Western tradition both combine to provide him a background area of responses as a basis for judgement, the fact remains that modern African literature offers the special challenge of *newness*. In a situation then in which a new literature is being constituted as an exploration of a new area of experience and expression, an important function of the critic becomes the determination of which works and which writers have value and meaning in relation to just such a situation.

It will perhaps be apparent from the essays in this volume that my approach to African literature, as indeed to our entire expression in modern times, has been commanded primarily by this last consideration. The three essays that form the first part of this volume and which are devoted to the critical problems raised by our new literature, represent a personal effort to examine the implications of this approach and to state the critical positions from which it proceeds. It may be thought that such an approach in its 'theoretical' formulation as in its application to actual works, places an undue emphasis on the 'message' of the literature rather than on the manner of expression. I will be the first to admit the emphasis: my justification being, as I have tried to argue earlier, that the recognition of achievement is not simply a question of mastery of form but of the degree and level of *seriousness* which a writer's work evinces, the art of expression being a handmaid to his vision rather than an end in itself. I hope however that it will also be clear that I have not carried this view so far as to refuse to propose value judgements as regards matters of form and technique; that I have not ignored competence in these matters in coming to my personal understanding of what makes for seriousness in each writer or work I have considered.

My preoccupation with 'meaning' in our modern expression also explains the inclusion in this volume of essays devoted to the ideological writings, which must in my view be taken along with the imaginative literature, for a full understanding of the historical development and present temper of our modern consciousness. The essays in the second part of this volume are accordingly concerned with the ideological movements that have been involved in this development, with those ideas that have had a hold on African minds and emotions in modern times. These essays are in the main expository, and the extent to which I have relied on the original research of other scholars for my basic information and analytical concepts will be obvious from the notes and references. It is not false modesty therefore but elementary prudence that obliges me to point out that as the questions discussed lie somewhat outside my field of competence, in writing about them, I have conceived my purpose primarily as that of a vulgarizer, presenting the facts and leading ideas of these movements to a non-specialist audience, and in the case of Négritude, attempting to throw a light upon it that is somewhat different from that in which the English-speaking African public is accustomed to seeing it. It is especially my hope that the essays in the second part will offer the student as well as the general public a broad and coherent picture of those developments in ideas that constitute an indispensable aspect of our modern intellectual history. In this respect, the outstanding contribution of New World black intellectuals to the formation of our contemporary consciousness must be considered sufficient justification for considering their work and activities as an integral part of modern African expression.

This observation underlines the fact that the main focus of our imaginative and ideological expression in its development so far has been upon the colonial experience. This volume reflects this preoccupation which remains an active element in the total complex of African responses even now. African concerns are however beginning to move in new directions related less specifically to the colonial phenomenon and more to the internal contradictions of post-colonial African society. The final essay in this volume – on Wole Soyinka and the Nigerian crisis – is concerned with this new orientation of African literature which is beginning to be reflected in current African criticism and which I hope to explore further in a forthcoming essay.

It remains for me to point out that these essays span a period of some fifteen years and that they were produced under very varied circumstances. I have not thought it necessary to arrange them in their order of composition or of first appearance for their reissue in this volume, preferring rather to group them by affinity of subject matter or theme. Furthermore, except for three, the essays are being reprinted here in the form in which they first appeared. Revisions have been undertaken in the case of two – 'African Literature and the Language Question' and 'French-African Narrative Prose and the Colonial Experience' – to permit a somewhat further development of certain points broached in them than was possible under the circumstances in which their earlier versions were either written or published. In the case of the third, 'Négritude and African Personality', originally written in French and addressed specifically to a francophone audience, it has been necessary to rework the material for the present English version. For the rest, I have limited myself to carrying out necessary corrections to the earlier published texts and to bringing some of my references up to date. My thanks go to the editors and publishers of the various journals and collective volumes in which these essays first appeared.

Finally, there will perhaps be found a certain amount of overlapping between some of the essays and even some self-repetition on my part. For this, I'd like to request the reader's indulgence, in the hope that the volume as a whole will present enough interest to make him overlook this unavoidable peculiarity.

Abiola Irele
Dakar, 1980

Notes and References

1. In a comment tucked away in one of the notes to her essay *On Violence*, the late Hannah Arendt reacted to black demands for the introduction of African literature and Swahili into the curriculum of American universities by dismissing them as 'non-subjects'. The comment and the attitude it illustrates make it apparent that even the best minds are sometimes limited by the scheme of values of their particular world, such that they become incapable of responding to situations that do not fit at once into its mould. It requires no great erudition but an open

intelligence to appreciate the fact that Swahili, which Hannah Arendt contemptuously calls a 'bastard' language, has a linguistic status exactly equivalent to French which, historically, developed as a pidgin form of Latin. Like French too, Swahili developed to become a medium not only of a wide intercourse of peoples stretching from the East African Coast to the Congo Basin, but also of an impressive literary culture with a respectable written tradition. The Arabs played a role here which corresponds to that of the Roman conquerors in the case of French or any of the other Latin derived tongues. It is true of course that Swahili has not, at least in recent times, been aided by the gun for its further spread.

2. The American writer James Olney, in the introduction to his book *Tell Me, Africa* (Princeton: Princeton University Press, 1973) thinks he is making a point by saying that no African writer has as yet produced work that can be placed alongside the great classics of European literature—the works of Homer, Dante, Shakespeare or Racine—as if John Steinbeck, Arthur Miller or for that matter Ezra Pound for instance, could be considered to have a comparable achievement to their credit.

Part One
Critical Positions

I. Studying African Literature
▼▼▼

To engage upon a discussion of the question of an adequate approach to the scholarly study and critical interpretation of African literature is to postulate at the outset a specific character of this literature which distinguishes it in some particular respects from other literatures and which for that reason requires such an approach. Such a distinctive character I do indeed postulate, without however wishing my position to be considered in any sense as absolute. There are certainly external factors and internal traits that, taken together in their attachment to our literature, both traditional and modern, mark it off as a specific area of literary production and of imaginative expression, and which make it imperative to undertake a kind of clearing of the ground in order to place it within a critical perspective appropriate to it. But before going over what seems to me to be the main lines of the possible approaches to African literature, and going on from there to define what I conceive to be for the moment the most appropriate – or perhaps I should rather say, that which I find most congenial to my personal dispositions – I should like to emphasize that I am not making a case for a unique essence of African literature but consider in fact that our literature needs to be related to other areas of literary expression, and has a significance for human experience beyond our continent.

Indeed, if this discussion is to have point and purpose at all, it is simply to clarify a number of issues that tend to obscure that significance. Above all, the aim of such a discussion is to see our way to a fuller grasp of the literature of Africa, both in its distinctive lines of articulation and in its essential connections to the total configuration of life and experience on our continent. The preoccupation with methodology with respect to African literature can then have an interest that goes beyond the merely technical or academic, to touch fully upon that which is central and essential in our concern – the human implications of the literature of Africa, both traditional and modern.

The problem then as it has been posed by the conveners of this conference is to see whether the traditional methods of literary analysis developed within Western culture are appropriate to African literature, whether they are adequate to account for its full range of expressive means and for the contextual background from which such means derive their significance – in other words, for its distinctive sources of strength. As a first approach to the problem, I would myself state that it is not so much a question of the misapplication of Western scholarly and critical methods to our literature that strikes me, as that of their adjustment to the particular circumstances of our literature, which have thrown up a whole range of problems that scholars and critics have been meeting from the very beginning of the serious and organized study of the material. It is to a general and necessarily limited review of these questions that I intend to devote some attention in this communication.

The very first problem that we encounter in studying African literature is that of definition. This involves the clear demarcation of the very field of investigation with which we are concerned, of the boundaries which that body of texts – either oral or written – which can be properly situated within the field of African literature, can be thought to define around itself. The term 'African' appears to correspond to a geographical notion but we know that, in practical terms, it also takes in those other areas of collective awareness that have been determined by ethnic, historical and sociological factors, all these factors, as they affect and express themselves in our literature, marking off for it a broad area of reference. Within this area of reference then, and related to certain aspects that are intrinsic to the literature, the problem of definition involves as well a consideration of aesthetic modes in their intimate correlation to the cultural and social structures which determine and define the expressive schemes of African peoples and societies.

As can be seen, with what has been tacitly taken to be 'African literature', we have already gone well beyond the convenient association of a literature with a particular language. Not only is there a general tendency to group the various oral literatures together as one single field, without too much emphasis on their particularities, and in that grouping, to seek interconnections between them, there is also the broad designation of the new written literature as 'African', so that, apart from the relationship that is already postulated between the oral and the modern literature, there is also the problem posed of drawing firm lines between the various areas of the written literature: that written in the various African languages, as distinguished from that in the European languages, that of black Africa as distinguished from North Africa, or the settler communities; and even within the narrow area of black Africa, that of the important distinctions that could be made between the emerging national literatures and the connections within them between the oral tradition, and between the written literature in the indigenous languages and the new literature expressed in the European languages.

At the bottom of this problem, there is the unspecific use of the word 'African', as applied to our literature, and this manner of using the word has arisen from the historical factor which has linked literary activity with the political fact of nationalism, thus extending the term 'African' over a wide range of literary and ideological expression. From the strict scholarly point of view, the term 'African literature' must admittedly be considered to be confusing, and this is why it has not been possible to arrive at any satisfactory definition.[1] On the other hand, it is quite possible to see that we are dealing here with a false problem which, if pursued with relentlessness, may have the result of diverting from the more practical problem of investigating the material we have at hand. Indeed, the problem itself may well be reversed, so that we go on from the practical investigation of such material to the recognition of such distinctive external and internal features as would enable us, if the need is really felt as that pressing, to arrive at a workable definition.

I say if the need is pressing, because I do not even consider it necessary to preoccupy oneself unduly with this kind of definition. The criteria for demarcating the various areas of literature in the world are nowhere as tight as one would like, and are generally based on political considerations – even the recognition of variant speech forms as languages are so determined, rather than decided on purely linguistic grounds. It is not only from the practical point of view, however that the problem of definition loses its edge, but also from a more fundamental consideration. For however gratifying it might be, for the sake of intellectual rigour, to arrive at a precise definition of African literature, the effort would still be beside the point, which is to place into focus what I consider to be the essential force of African literature – its reference to the historical and experiential. It is this which, in a real and profound way, justifies the ready attachment of the historical and politico-ideological connotation of the term 'African' to such a diversity of texts and material. Seen in this way, the problem of definition, if it does not dissolve, at least does not prevent an opening to the business of investigation and interpretation, and we can go on to consider what means of approach can be adequately applied to the serious study of that body of literature that relates to the history and experience of African peoples and societies.

Literary studies have generally been divided into two main branches:

on one hand, we have literary history which is concerned with the external circumstances and deals with questions of development and the relationship of literary movements to currents of ideas at particular periods or in particular areas; more modestly, it investigates matters such as sources and influences. On the other hand, we have literary criticism as such which can be said, *grosso modo*, to occupy itself with interpretation and evaluation.[2] There is of course no clear-cut division between the two branches, since one must take cognisance of the other, and they often so interpenetrate that it is often really a matter of emphasis which distinguishes one from the other. Any form of literary study implies however a recognition of 'the significance' of the literary phenomenon: not merely its value as an object of aesthetic contemplation but also its importance as a social and moral force.

In the case of African literature, both aspects of literary study have often gone together and even merged imperceptibly. The various collections of oral literature that we have, have come to us accompanied by editorial apparatus which both document and evaluate the primary material they are presenting. The very fact that much of this work arose originally out of the discipline of anthropology (or ethnology), accounts for the fact that the studies we have, have been concerned with the material conditions of the oral literature to a considerable degree and thus provide indispensable elements of its 'history'. For although such work has seldom involved a detailed consideration of the development of the oral tradition in the sense of a linear progression, they do give us a comprehensive image of this literature in terms of its social determinations – its relationship to social systems and values, its modes of insertion, in short, within the total culture of the traditional world. In a sense, the oral literature represents our classical tradition – i.e. that body of texts which lies behind us as a complete and enduring literature, though constantly being renewed, and which most profoundly informs the world views of our peoples, and is thus at the same time the foundation and expressive channel of a fundamental African mental universe.

In the restricted sense of a precise documentation of the growth and development of themes and features within the oral tradition, literary history is, in the circumstances, not always possible or easy – it has been attempted in some cases, notably by Trevor Cope in his study of Zulu praise poems,[3] but an idea of such a development can still be obtained if scholars turn to the comparative approach, and exploit even further the methods of anthropology, to examine even more extensively than has been done so far recurrent patterns of themes and motifs and thus arrive at an acceptable theory of diffusion within previously delimited geographical and cultural areas. Such an approach, used in conjunction with the disciplines of ethno-history (oral literature of course forms an important sector of oral history) and linguistics, should yield a picture of those interconnections between the various areas of our oral literature that could reasonably be situated within a historical perspective. Even more historical, in the narrow sense, would be the comparative study of African oral traditions that have survived in the New World, and of the existing forms on the mother continent.

It might be asked why we need to look at the traditional literature from this 'historical' perspective. The answer to that question has been partly supplied in some of my remarks above – to obtain a global view of this literature. But the most important reason for requiring to see the main lines of growth and patterns of development of our oral tradition is so that we can derive from our obtaining such an image of it, a sense of our history, a sense that proceeds from the consciousness of a living background of creative endeavour within our world, and which provides to the literary artist of today a vital source of reference.

It is certainly true that, when we turn to the new written literature, literary history in the strict sense becomes easier to carry out. The majority of the initial studies of modern African literature were in fact general surveys, which also combined documentation with evaluation, but their main interest was in tracing the development of the new written literature of Africa within a clear historical setting. We are all familiar, thanks to Lilyan Kesteloot,[4] with the circumstances which have attended the emergence of the literature of Négritude and the influences which have shaped its course. Again, thanks to Janheinz Jahn,[5] we even have a comprehensive account of the literary efforts of black men insofar as they have been situated to European history and culture. And what has emerged from these and other studies, is a history of those concerns and preoccupations that have, in relation to historical and sociological factors, featured as the poles around which have crystallized a modern African consciousness and thought – to which Robert July has devoted an impressive study.[6]

Apart from these, we are also being supplied in numerous articles and a number of books, with necessary information on the growth of the new literature in the African languages in various parts of our continent. It is interesting to note, for example, the influence of the translations of the Bible in creating standard varieties of some of our languages and thus preparing the way for the written literatures in those languages.

A more recent area of investigation is that of the appearance of 'generations' within African literature – younger writers reacting to and against the work of the older writers and endeavouring to chart new directions – these efforts themselves being responsive to new lines of preoccupations within African society. In this respect, it is obvious that to obtain a true account, it is essential to work across the language divisions within the contemporary writing, and apply not so much a comparative as a global approach to the study of modern African literature, even though, as in the case of Nigeria, some attention will need to be given to a national development, to the outlines of what begins to appear as a national school.[7]

The overall picture of the development of African literature in contemporary times is thus clear. There remain however some outstanding questions that literary history concerned with the new literature still has to investigate. One that seems to me especially important, and which is related to the problem of definition evoked earlier on, is that of the relationship of the new writing in the European languages to the European tradition. It is of course understood that the relationship exists in an organic way – there is a sense in which all this new literature is derivative, and the question that arises here is whether the fact of this derivation is a positive or a negative thing. I leave aside, in putting forward this question, the issue of the propriety of speaking of an African literature in English, French and Portuguese, inviting us rather to consider the more fundamental issue: whether in fact, our writers have, working through and adapting the conventions of literary expression taken from Europe, created an autonomous area of their own, a distinctive current that merits recognition in its own right.

The starting point of our consideration has to be an examination of the precise lines of the relationship in individual cases, of specific influences as they manifest themselves from one European writer to another, and from one trend in European writing to a line of development in African writing, the point of preoccupation here being, I hardly need to add, not simply the mechanical tracing of such influences, but of the way in which they affect the expression of our writers and integrate within their works. It is thus not enough to see the influence of Hopkins on Clark, or that of Claudel on Senghor, without, through that seeing arriving at an understanding of what such an influence contributes to the vision of the African writer.

For beyond the question of influences lies a consideration of the historical and thematic correspondence of European literature to our literature, and the way that correspondence touches upon the present status of modern African literature and is likely to affect its future destiny. Each generation of African writers has employed the prevailing idiom of its time in Europe – each, also, with its own measure of success. In short, there has always been a degree of imitation of European literature. Are we then sure that what we accept today as a virile and authentic expression in African literature will not be condemned in the next century as 'sterile imitation' of the prevailing modernism of the day, in the same way that we tend to dismiss the writers of the nineteenth and early years of the twentieth century as inferior? In a sense, the poetry of Césaire carries conviction with us certainly because it accords with a certain shift in sensibility occasioned by the surrealist revolution and employs an idiom appropriate to that revolution. The question again, to reformulate it in more direct terms, is then, how much originality can we accord to our writers?

It is of course an important interest of literary history to identify changing literary fashions and tastes, and especially to trace the evolution of criteria that have made for evaluative judgement and acceptance of certain works: to trace in short, changes in sensibility and outlook. In the case of modern African literature, such a study can hardly be separated from the general European context, since in fact the first commentators on our literature were Europeans, conditioned in their attitudes to their subject by the cultural climate in the West. I should add that we too are conditioned by that climate. The fact of course that the new writing formed part of a general awakening in Africa and expressly articulated that awakening can be held to account for its impact – apart from the appeal of newness, of course – but it seems to me clear that, along with the adoption of a contemporary idiom, the new African literature also provided, in a way in which the earlier literature did not, a certain elaboration of an African sentiment, indeed the contemporary idiom making possible the emergence of just such an original note. The close parallel between the modes of poetic thought in European literature since the latter part of the nineteenth century and in modern African poetry is of course far from fortuitous, since there were definite influences at work from the former to the latter, and it is this correspondence which could permit Jahn to compare Négritude and German expressionism.[8] At the same time, that correspondence registers something of a convergence in ways of looking at the world between European thought reacting against its traditional canons and African thought as apprehended by a new African élite. It is here that the originality and the achievement of our new writers resides – to have employed with success those conventions of expression taken from the European tradition and adapted them to their particular needs.[9]

The principal importance of literary history is to make clear the continuities and the relationships that constitute a literature, to establish the total framework within which the single work occurs. As Dr Leavis has again remarked recently, literature is not the isolated work, but a complete whole, a movement that implies a living tradition.[10] Literary history in the manner in which I have seen it here has the function of bringing clear to us literary tradition in its stretch back to the oral, and in its forward movement as inscribed within the new written expression.

But if the principal benefit of literary history is that, in its documentary role, it arrives at placing a body of texts into perspective as literature, the properly interpretative role belongs however to what we have come to designate as literary criticism. It is through the introspective method implied in criticism that we begin to envisage the inner reality of the work as that reality becomes inherent in its structure of words and meanings, and through that reality to apprehend its human significance. It is here, of course, that the whole question of adequacy of method really arises.

The whole theory of criticism, its very status even, is fraught with contradictions. But if criticism is accepted as a valid activity, secondary to the creative activity of writing itself, but a useful adjunct to it within the total culture, then one is entitled to a personal view of its purpose. In a general kind of way, that purpose consists in rendering a valid and integral account of the work, in which case the very notions of validity and integrity as applicable to a literary work – or for that matter to a whole body of literature – require clarification. I do not intend to indulge here in theorizing, but I take it that once we get beyond the text as it presents itself to us initially – in its immediate integrity as it were – then the purpose of criticism resides in providing an understanding of the work through an elucidation of its multiple aspects as expressive of a creative intention. Without going so far as superposing upon the work itself a second level of meanings – for that way lies the high road to arbitrariness[11] – it seems to me that we need to go beyond the text itself in order to restitute its total meaning – its profound significance, its import. But before going further than this general proposition in the realm of theory, let me get down at once to how I see it work out in its application to African literature, both traditional and modern.

There is a real sense in which the task of elucidation is more difficult with respect to the traditional literature than to the modern. We can point to an immediate difficulty, in order to dispose of it – that of literal interpretation of texts. There are often several versions of the same text, and the problem of interpretation is often compounded by the fact that the greater part of our oral literature is in a language that is archiac and in certain cases deliberately hermetic, in which case, textual analysis encounters formidable problems and requires a high degree of expertise. Seeing how the words in a text link up with each other to create a system of signs by which they manifest their expressiveness is one of the lessons we have learnt from I. A. Richards,[12] and to practise 'practical criticism' at all with the traditional literature, we have to be fully and intimately acquainted with the language which that literature uses.

But there is another direction where analysis encounters difficulties of a less obvious kind, and which if not properly focused, can affect critical evaluation. The point of departure of this set of difficulties is the status to be accorded to the various kinds of material that often presents itself as oral literature. One begins to understand the need for critical judgement in the sense of a faculty of discrimination, when one sees the amount of labour expended upon what are palpably minor and even marginal forms like riddles, proverbs and tongue twisters. We encounter here a problem which arises from the very oral nature of this body of texts which makes it difficult to determine clearly at what degree of speech activity we are dealing with literature, considered as imaginative expression, as distinct from the mere communicative use of language. The fact is that there is indeed in our traditional societies a pervasiveness of stylized forms of speech activity, such that the exact line of distinction between literature in our normal understanding of the term and an ordinary functional use of language is often very thin. The ubiquitous presence of the proverb in our culture attests to this phenomenon – in the most ordinary situations, language is used in such a way as to draw attention as much to itself as to its referent, such use of language constituting a cultural value. In such a situation, it is not always clear whether, to identify the literary use of language, we need to go by the formal or functional criteria, whether to rely on set patterns that are either elaborated and conventionally established and thus set apart, or on the specific context of occurrence, or whether to trust ourselves to the vague aesthetic appeal of specimens that we encounter.

The problem, it seems to me, is really one of levels, for while through the whole spectrum of speech activity in African societies, there is evidence of conscious relish in language and a heavy reliance on what Jakobson[13] has distinguished as the 'poetic function' of language which embraces poetry proper within its ambit, there is no doubt that degrees of intensity are recognized, and literature exists (and especially poetry) as elaborate constructions of words which have more a connotative than a denotative character and function. We may distinguish therefore three principal levels of speech activity in the African context, within a sort of hierarchy: the basic level of communication, whose role is purely referential; an intermediary level of verbal art, in which the poetic function is at least as important as the communicative, since it involves the conscious manipulation of words by the speaker for effect and the response of his audience as much to the presentation as to the message; and, at the top of the hierarchy, the level of literature, at which we find a consecrated body of texts that stand well outside the quotidian, denotative use of language.

Closely related to the problem of identifying the literary within the oral tradition is the question of classification. It might be thought at first that this problem arises primarily out of our use of European languages and concepts in describing African literature. But the situation is in fact more

complex than that. It is of course not true that our societies did not develop means of judgement and evaluation of the oral texts which were produced within the cultures and that our languages do not have descriptive
terms for various kinds of literature. There exists in fact a body of critical
opinion and authoritative reference for judgement upon performance and
integrity of texts (such opinion is of course implied in the very training of
the artists, and the whole process of transmission of the oral tradition).[14]
However, there is no African society that, to my knowledge, has carried
the judgement of texts and reflection upon literature to the same degree of
elaboration which we are today used to in the Western tradition (which, at
any rate, is a derivation from classical criticism). The result of this lack of
a developed critical language – of a metalanguage of literature – in our indigenous languages is that the terms they offer for distinguishing the
various genres are often elastic. In the Yoruba language for example,
though the generic term for poetry exists (*ewi*), it has been one of the main
issues of contention among Yoruba scholars to determine its subclassifi-
cations, so that different scholars use different criteria to distinguish *rara*
from *oriki* and *ijala*: subject matter, mode of chanting, structural features,
and so on.

Of course, the clear-cut divisions that traditional Western terminology
makes between genres are often not possible with African literature: even
the basic dichotomy between prose and poetry is not perceived in the oral
tradition with anything like the same degree of clarity as in the Western
tradition nor indeed is it felt that such a dichotomy has any real significance. To take again a Yoruba example, the Ifa corpus comprises a body
of texts which only a superficial view would want to classify either as prose
or poetry – the only term that in the European languages seems appropriate is the German word *Dichtung*, which refers to the intensity of the text
rather to its material disposition either in the mind or on the page. In conjunction with what I have called 'levels', we can then, in our analysis, recognize broad formal categories according to the structural features which
characterize them.

This leads me at once to the central question of formal analysis of the
oral literature.

Valéry once defined poetry as 'language within a language' ('langage
dans un langage')[15] and this definition extends to all forms of literary expression. The great French poet was clearly thinking of language here
more in its idealist sense – as a system of signs and structure of discourse
– than in its material sense (the structure of sounds and combinations of
sounds that modern linguistics deals with), yet literature has its basis in
that material structure,[16] and oral literature in an even more immediate
way, reminding us of Saussure's precept that the primary language is the

spoken one. Within the particular structure of each language, literature creates a second order of reference which draws upon the primary features of that language to compose its distinctive configuration, and to establish its peculiar mode of significance. Thus, for an understanding of its literary modes, every language requires attention to the mechanics of its various levels of articulation, brought into relation with the structure of expression that sustains the literary modes. The need for formal analysis of oral texts, arising from this order of considerations, though recognized, and practised, should begin to be viewed from a more comprehensive theoretical and methodological perspective.

The marked difference of African languages from the European has meant that the focus of internal analysis of our oral traditions has been linguistic, but there are a number of questions still unresolved with regard to the distinctive patterns of our oral literature. The questions begin to emerge from the moment we begin to collect and transcribe the texts. It is again often not clear where the line endings occur, so that the first issue to decide, even where we are sure we are dealing with 'poetry', is that of versification. It is generally accepted that the idea of metre is foreign to traditional African literature, but where we are confronted with a patterned succession of enunciations, then we must assume some kind of structure, with rules which need to be discovered. Jakobson's terms, 'verse design' and 'verse instance' seem to me to be particularly appropriate here to give us an account of the workings of our oral literature from this point of view. The larger and fundamental 'verse design' would thus give us the framework for the investigation of such features as parallelism, alliteration and tonal and rhythmic patterns, in particular texts.

The linguistic-stylistic analysis of oral texts has the primary function of giving us an insight into intrinsic qualities of the oral tradition, over and above its importance in establishing the texts and providing indices for their methodical classification. But it cannot be divorced from a consideration of the semantic values of the internal features it reveals, nor of the social functions of the forms which it classifies. Structural analysis finds a meaning only in relation to the poetic values which lie at the end of its investigations, and those poetic values themselves are values precisely by reference to social values, so that, necessarily, we are led from text to context. Take the example of sound symbolism of which our oral literature makes elaborate use, and which can only be adequately felt when we move from the purely formal analysis of them to their situation within the dramatic context of African oral literature – the enactment by the narrator of a folk tale for instance – and from this to their resonance within the minds of the immediate audience. Willie Abrahams has given a particularly striking example of the way in which sound symbolism, in the oral literature, can attain evocative power of a cosmic dimension.[17]

It is even more important to take the semantic along with the structural in the analysis of the schemes of metaphor elaborated by our traditional literature. The close correlation of poetic form to social values is nowhere more evident than in this area. We can speak of meaning here both in the immediate sense of poetic function within the context of a particular instance of oral literature, and in the larger sense of reference of particular metaphors and symbols to the expressive schemes of particular cultures. To take an example of this progression from poetic form to social values: according to Coupez and Kamanzi,[18] the image of the cow is central in Rwanda court poetry because of its preeminent economic and social value, and the affective charge with which it is endowed by the culture makes it possible to extend the praises addressed to it indirectly to the king, who is the embodiment of these various values; the image of the cow thus acquires in this highly elaborate oral poetry a polyvalence of reference and suggestion.

In other words, mode and function are perceived together in our oral literature, and it is only when we refer its forms and features back to their social meanings that they acquire life, because, as Calamé-Griaule has demonstrated,[19] it is within language that our traditional societies elaborate their relationship to the world, and literature is the primary instrument of that process of collective self-situation.

The interest of the formal approach to the study of oral literature resides in the possibility it offers of establishing a valid typology of African oral literature, derived from the internal evidence gathered from representative texts across the continent, so that through such evidence we may arrive at some conception of an African literary aesthetic which not only informs the traditional literature but also exerts an influence, either directly or indirectly, on the new writing. In some African literatures, there has been a direct development from the oral to the written within the indigenous language itself, and it is obvious in these cases that the forms handed down from the oral tradition exert a direct pressure in these cases, as regards both themes and internal features – a structural connection exists therefore between the 'old' and the 'new'. But it can also be assumed and in specific cases demonstrated that a similar connection links the oral tradition to the new writing in the European languages, either because of the conscious and deliberate reference of some of our writers to the forms of the oral literature in their writing, or through the unconscious but pervasive influence of the oral tradition upon the modes of perception and of expression of our writers. It is possible in a number of cases to point to specific traits where this connection manifests itself – in the quality of imagery and even 'verse design' of Senghor's poetry, in much of Okigbo's work; and we know that Clark's *Ozidi* is a transposition of a traditional epic into a modern dramatic medium. I have myself attempted to examine the line of continuity that links the work of Fagunwa, Tutuola and Soyinka, a line that derives from the Yoruba oral tradition.[20] In the case of Achebe, the use of the proverb is merely an indication of his larger design, to conceive the Western novel as an African form of narrative. These examples point to the direct relevance of the study of the oral tradition to a critical appraisal of the new literature, to an understanding of the specific context of expression in which it has been developing.

They also point to another issue in relation to the modern literature, that of the relative interest of the formal approach in the study of modern African literature. This leads me back, through the issue of its opposition to what has been called the 'sociological method', to the question with which I started – that of the adequacy of any single form of approach to African literature.

But I do not think I need to take any more time to discuss this question, since all along, as I have been proceeding in this review of the various problems that arise in the study of African literature, I have been at pains to strike a balance between the formal approach and the other approach that places its emphasis on the social reference of the work. I only want to conclude with a clarification of the position that I find most satisfactory for myself.

There can of course be no sensible discussion of literature that does not imply an awareness of the close and intimate reciprocity between form and content, between structures of expression and their significance in an outer world beyond the text. It is this which makes literature, the reference value of words intervening all the time to indicate some order of reality, however tenuously signified, which those words point to. This is the essential difference between literature and music: it might even be argued that the significance of literature – fiction, poetry, and drama above all – resides especially in its reference to a lived world that stretches from that of immediate sensation to that of mental vision, and whether there is any purpose in frustrating, as the current accepted writing in Europe consciously tries to do, that tendency of words to achieve a correspondence to a concrete universe of experience.[21]

Whatever the case, I do not believe that there should necessarily be an opposition between the formal, the technical approach, and the sociological approach. It is of course true that there can be a heavy emphasis one way or the other, leading to the two extremes of formalism and sociologism. It is against this latter extreme that there has been a reaction recently as regards African literature. The current complaint is that works

by African writers have been approached merely as social documents –
inevitable, of course, in the initial stage, and necessary at all events in
documenting literary history, as we have seen. The more serious charge is
that we have had too many commentaries concerned with tracing and
elucidating cultural references, and not with criticism of the works qua
literature: the charge here is against what I'd call a certain anthropolog-
ism, and one might remark that some of our writers have called for this
kind of treatment of their work – but these have not been the best and
most significant. The trend then today is towards formal analysis, having as
its declared purpose a consideration of those features of the modern
literature that make for aesthetic appeal.[22]

I have however been simplifying, because I should have added that the
influence of certain trends of criticism in Europe has not been foreign to
the reaction I've mentioned. Their purpose in Europe has of course been
quite different, and has nothing to do with establishing their literature, but
in fact with establishing criticism as a genre, if not as a scientific discipline.
This is the central concern of all the various revolutions in Western criticism in this century: of the Cambridge men (with Richards and Empson),
of the American new critics, and the Russian formalists, and today of the
movement that has crystallized around the figure of Roland Barthes in
France – to get literary study away from the impressionism and dillettant-
ism of an earlier generation, to pose literature as an object of rigorous study
and thus give to criticism the status of a science, that is, in every sense of
the word, of a *discipline*.

This is obviously an admirable purpose, and the methods they have
elaborated, the concepts they have provided, can enrich the criticism of
African literature, as I have no doubt has happened in at least one impressive case – Anozie's study of Okigbo.[23]

However, that example itself has led me to entertain serious reservations, for I observe that in the poetry of Okigbo, Dr Anozie pursues complexity and erects it into a value, whether that complexity bears upon the
human interest of Okigbo's work or not – there is no other way of explain-
ing his perfunctory discussion of Okigbo's last series of poems, *Path of
Thunder*, in which that human interest most convincingly and supremely
expresses itself. Similarly, I cannot go along with Melone's exploration of
the 'topology' of Senghor's poetry,[24] simply because I could not, while
reading him, see where he was leading to – such criticism carries the danger
of ineffectuality in its detachment from any pole of concrete reference.

It is against this kind of abstract preoccupation with presentation that a
sociological approach can provide the counter of interest and substance.
But we need to be clear about what we mean by a sociological approach.
There are at least four different ways in which we can envisage a socio-

logical approach to literature. We can have a sociology of literary production – of organization of literary artists, of the conditions of creation, of the literary public and so on; this kind of work is hardly distinguishable from literary history, with the notable difference that it is synchronic rather than diachronic in emphasis – Escarpit's *Sociologie de la littérature*,[25] gives an idea of what I mean. We can also have content analysis of literary works in a sociological perspective – in African literature, the example to refer to is the masterly study by Emmanuel Obiechina, *Culture, Tradition and Society in the West African Novel.*[26] There is the third kind of sociology of literature which attempts to correlate forms and themes with moments of social production and consciousness – Goldmann's work[27] stands out in this respect. There is a fourth possibility, which is really not 'sociological' in any methodological or technical sense, but implies a strong awareness of the social implications of literature, and which is represented by the position of Dr Leavis in England. In the actual practice of Leavis' criticism, this approach tends to substitute literary criticism for social theory, indeed, is based on a strongly articulated social theory – of an élite in touch through the best literature with a vital current of feeling and of values, and having responsibility for maintaining, in the practice of criticism, the moral health of the society – in the event, therefore, despite the impressive force of Dr Leavis' presentation of the case, highly questionable. But the basic idea is to my thinking, not: it is a position which has the eminent merit of making us take literature seriously enough to commit one's total intelligence to making explicit what in it takes the forms of nuance and symbol, in other words, of applying its insights to the actual business of living.

My position then begins, I should think, to become clear. Formal analysis is an intrinsic part of literary study, but it is there simply to lead us into the work so that we can penetrate its significance. Perhaps looking at the question in this way is to close the door to the formalists, I don't know. In any case, the question of an adequate approach to the criticism of African literature can probably never be settled to any degree of satisfaction, at least in such a way as to compel universal and total agreement on one point of view. No single approach, really, is adequate as Izevbaye has suggested,[28] and it cannot be otherwise, for we are dealing with a phenomenon which, by its nature, is irreducible to any sort of common measure. Literature can be posed as an object of study, such study envisaged as a scientific investigation of its objective features, of its contours and expressive articulations. But it cannot be an object, simply because, as the symbolic transposition of lived experience, literature involves our deepest responses to the facts of human existence and intervenes in those areas of experience where we assume consciousness of our situation with regard to others and to the world. To be meaningful, any kind of discussion of literature implies a responsiveness not only to the text, in its inherent capacity for suggestiveness through a unique structure of signs and meanings, but also to those areas of experience – of feelings, attitudes and insight – which that structure evokes to take on significance.

Our examination of the possible approaches to African literature needs then to be placed in the only context in which literary study can be meaningful in the sense in which I have defined it – in its effective relationship to the actual conditions of our collective situation, the placing of our literature in relation to the concrete choices which our society, out of which a literary development is taking place and on behalf of which our literary artists express themselves, can be seen or thought to be making. The fundamental question, then, to conclude, is not simply one of understanding African literature but of apprehending it in its complex resonances – of each individual text related, even in its uniqueness, to a common framework of consciousness and in that way integrated into a cultural whole which situates the aesthetic event within the living context of the historical.

Notes and References

1. For a fuller discussion of this question, see D. Izevbaye, 'African Literature Defined', in *Ibadan Studies in English*, Vol. 1, No. 1 (May–June, 1969), pp. 56–67.
2. I have followed here the division by René Welleck and Austin Warren in their book, *The Theory of Literature*.
3. Trevor Cope, *Izibongo–Zulu Praise Poems*, (London: Oxford University Press, 1968). See in particular pp. 50–65 of the 'Introduction'.
4. Lilyan Kesteloot, *Les Ecrivains noirs de langue française* (Brussels: Institut de Sociologie, Université Libre de Bruxelles, 1963).
5. Janheinz Jahn, *A History of Neo-African Literature* (London: Faber and Faber, 1966).
6. Robert July, *The Origins of Modern African Thought* (London: Faber and Faber, 1968), and also Claude Wauthier, *l'Afrique des Africains* (Paris: Editions du Seuil, 1964). Translated as *The Literature and Thought of Modern Africa* (London: Pall Mall Press, 1966; 2nd edition, London: Heinemann Educational Books, 1978).
7. D. Izevbaye, 'Nigeria' in Bruce King (ed.) *Literatures of the World in English* (London: Routledge and Kegan Paul, 1974), pp. 136–53.
8. Janheinz Jahn, *Muntu* (London: Faber and Faber, 1961), pp. 146–55.
9. Chinua Achebe has presented his own view on this question in the essay 'The African Writer and the English Language' included in his collection of essays entitled *Morning Yet on Creation Day* (London: Heine-

mann Educational Books, 1975), pp. 55–62. But perhaps the most fundamental examination is contained in the critical essay by J. P. Clark, 'The Legacy of Caliban', in *Black Orpheus*, Vol. 2 No. 1 (February 1968).

10. F. R. Leavis 'Mutually Necessary', in *Universities Quarterly*, Vol. 30, No. 2 (Spring 1976).

11. I have in mind here what seems to me to be the extreme position taken by Roland Barthes in his book *Critique et vérité* (Paris: Editions du Seuil, 1966), in which the critic's relations to the writer's work is accorded the same status as that of the writer to the world, which gives the same quality to their relationship to language, such that the critic's work creates a second order of literature: see pp. 63–75 for Barthes's development of this idea. See also Gérard Genette, 'Structuralisme et critique littéraire' in *Figures I* (Paris: Editions du Seuil, 1976), pp. 145–70.

12. See I. A. Richards' two celebrated works, *Practical Criticism* and *Principles of Literary Criticism*, and William Empson's application of his principles in his *Seven Types of Ambiguity*.

13. R. Jakobson, 'Linguistique et poétique', in *Essais de linguistique générale*, tr. N. Ruwet (Paris: Editions de Minuit, 1963).

14. See Ruth Finnegan, *Oral Literature in Africa* (London: Oxford University Press, 1970).

15. Valéry's definition is contained in his essay 'Situation de Baudelaire', in *Variété II*.

16. See André Jolles, *Formes simples* (Paris: Editions du Seuil, 1972), pp. 16–26.

17. W. Abraham, *The Mind of Africa* (London: Weidenfeld and Nicolson, 1962), pp. 90–2.

18. A. Coupez and Th. Kamanzi, *Littérature de cour au Rwanda* (London: Oxford University Press, 1970).

19. G. Calamé-Griaule, *Ethnologie et language* (Paris: Gallimard, 1965).

20. Abiola Irele, 'Tradition and the Yoruba writer ...', in *Odu*: New Series, No. 11 (January 1975); Chapter 10 of this volume.

21. Consider for instance the approving tone of Gérard Genette in the following remarks on Flaubert, 'Mais il a formé un jour comme par surcroît, ce projet de *ne rien dire*, ce refus de l'expression qui inaugure l'expérience littéraire moderne'. Further on, Genette writes: 'Ce retournement, ce renvoi du discours à son envers silencieux, qui est, pour nous, aujourd'hui, la littérature même, Flaubert a été, bien évidemment, le premier à l'entreprendre'. ('Silences de Flaubert' in *op. cit.*, p. 242).

22. Romanus Egudu, 'Criticism of Modern African Literature: The Question of Evaluation', presented at the Conference of African Literary Critics, University of Ife, Nigeria, 19–22 December 1975.

23. Sunday Anozie, *Christopher Okigbo: Creative Rhetoric* (London: Evans Brothers, 1972).

24. Thomas Melone, 'De la Topologie à la typologie: y a-t-il une théorie critique chez Léopold Sédar Senghor?', mimeographed paper. (I have not been able to ascertain if this paper has been published yet in any review).

25. R. Escarpit, *Sociologie de la littérature* 2ème édition (Paris: Presses

Universitaires de France, (Que sais-je?), 1960); also Michel Zeraffa, *Roman et société* (Paris: Presses Universitaires de France, 1971).

26. Emmanuel Obiechina, *Culture, Tradition and Society in the West African Novel* (Cambridge: Cambridge University Press, 1975). A far less subtle work in this category is that of G. C. M. Mutiso, *Sociopolitical Thought in African Literature* (London: Macmillan, 1974).

27. In particular *Le Dieu caché* and *Pour une Sociologie du roman*. As is well known, Goldmann's work derives from that of Lucàks.

28. D. S. Izevbaye, 'The State of Criticism in African Literature', in *African Literature Today*, No. 7 (London: Heinemann Educational Books, 1975).

2. The Criticism of Modern African Literature

▼▼

I should like to begin my discussion of the criticism of modern African literature by making a very general observation about the kind of distinction we tend to make between what we call 'traditional' African literature, and 'modern' African literature; a distinction which is probably useful in the sense that traditional African literature is something which exists in our indigenous languages and which is related to our traditional societies and cultures, while modern African literature has grown out of the rupture created within our indigenous history and way of life by the colonial experience, which is naturally expressed in the tongue of our former colonial rulers. I say this distinction is useful because in their separate characteristics, both with regard to content and to form, the two kinds of literature do show clearly marked differences and derive from two different sectors of the African experience. Furthermore, the fact that they relate to different moments and phases in the collective experience and consciousness of African peoples, gives to their present-day, side-by-side existence a certain historical and sociological significance.

The development in particular of what we now recognize as modern African literature over the past few decades, has its own specific significance, not only in a broad historical sense with regard to such issues as the transformation of African societies and also, consequently, the creation of a new mental universe in this continent, but in the more restricted, the more immediate sense of the social and cultural situation now prevailing amongst us. The peculiar position of the new literature of Africa written in the European languages involving, at least at first sight, a divorce between the substance of this literature and its linguistic medium, is in itself a reflection of what I would call the state of incoherence within our societies – the state of incoherence which our societies are passing through – of which we have several objective indications and with which our writers are becoming more and more concerned. Yet what is significant about this literature is not only that it provides in its own historical development and in its preoccupations a record of the tensions and the contradictions in present-day Africa, but also that in its directions it is providing our writers, that is the sensitive minds amongst us, with a means of exploring intensely and intimately the well-springs of our modern experience in all its range and complexity. In other words, our writers are groping implictily, through the imagination, towards the creation of a new order in Africa.

Now if I raise these large issues at the outset, these issues which appear to me to be involved in the existence of modern African literature at the moment, it is in order to stress the very vital role which creative writing is playing in modern African society, to emphasize its central position in our contemporary existence and, also, in order to indicate the importance of relating this new literary expression in Africa in a clear and meaningful way to the African situation and specifically to the African peoples themselves – to their total experience. It is in this particular respect that the problem of creating a criticism adequate to modern African literature appears to me to be extremely important and I am going, therefore, to examine some of the problems involved in the criticism of modern African literature in order to define what I would like, personally, to see emerge as its function and purpose.

Now the problems of the criticism of modern African literature arise out of the unusual situation of modern African literature itself. We have a literature written by Africans who have a distinct background as far as their experience is concerned and who are writing, or at least striving to write, within a specific cultural, social, and historical framework, but who are expressing themselves in a language that they have not deliberately chosen, a language with its own structure and literary tradition, in its nature far removed from their own frame of experience. The implications of this unusual situation appear to me to be twofold.

In the first place, from the sheer technical point of view, the artistic burden imposed on the writer which is implied by an incomplete mastery of the linguistic medium and of the literary tradition associated with it, and also the fact that our responses as readers are conditioned to a certain extent by an awareness of this specific linguistic problem. Our appreciation must therefore take in to a more than usual extent the problem of the adequacy of the writer's means of expression to his imaginative purpose.

The second problem involved in the present situation of modern African literature is the fact that it is 'new' in every sense of the word: in the obvious sense, that it is by and large a recent development and still growing; and secondly, in the more significant sense, that whatever its derivation, whether we see it as having grown essentially out of the Western tradition (to which in any case it is bound by language and some at least of its forms), or whether we prefer to look upon it as being a re-adaption in modern terms of the African imagination. Whichever way we look at it, modern African literature is at the moment a fairly indeterminate thing, something, in fact – to borrow Wole Soyinka's term – something of a 'half-child'.

A third problem I see is also a consequence of the previous two and has to do with the whole question of finding a place for a modern literature in our society; quite simply, bringing it to its African public – to its own public. Modern African literature necessarily had to be directed at a foreign audience to start with, firstly because of the language factor and secondly because the habit of reading was, and is, still new in these parts. It brought its letters of credit from abroad and it is only just finding its way home as more and more of our people become not only literate in the European languages, but also acquire the kind of literary attitudes associated with written literature and with the particular literary conventions of Western culture. The position of the critic in this whole process of giving our literature an audience on its home ground is an important one and must be seen in the broader context of the cultural evolution in our societies at the heart of which I believe literature today is situated.

The issue here, then, is to define the function of criticism in relation to what amounts to the extraordinary situation of modern African literature, to see in what sense a specific critical approach can help not only in rendering a true account of its nature and development, but also of giving it meaning and relevance within the context of the contemporary African situation. We need, I think, to remind ourselves of some elementary facts concerning the critical function and in this connection, the most satisfactory and comprehensive definition of criticism that I have come across is the following one by Irving Howe in his book *Modern Literary Criticism*:

> Secondary though it always is to the work itself, criticism offers seemingly endless possibilties for the discrimination of values, the sharing of insights, the defence of a living culture.[1]

I believe this definition offers us the three essential aspects of the critical function. In the first place, it indicates its elementary character as an activity of the intelligence and as a body of skills which enable us to determine among written works offered to us the grain from the chaff, so to speak. Criticism here is the act of making reasoned judgements upon literary works based upon fairly clear and definite criteria. In the second place, Howe's definition recognizes the fact that despite the technical requirements of critical judgements, they are, in the last resort, of a subjective character – relying on the personal responses of the critic as a reader, even though an attentive reader, to the work before him. A good part of criticism depends, therefore, on intuition which is later corrected and given an intellectual formulation. Yet the faculty which provides the critic with his insight is not for the most part an individual endowment but derives also from his total experience, from his education, from his society, from his culture and, indeed, from his age – from his own age. It is bounded, therefore, and defined by the cultural factor – the third aspect of criticism to which Irving Howe's definition refers. Literature takes place within a cultural setting, and no meaningful criticism is possible without the existence of a community of values shared by the writer and the critic which the latter can, in turn, make meaningful to the writer's larger audience. Furthermore, the stream of communication, which is established across this line of common relationships in which the critic is a kind of middleman, constitutes an important current in the cultural life of the community.

Now, with these three essential considerations as my point of departure, I should like to examine the function of criticism with specific relation to modern African literature, bearing in mind what I have called its peculiar situation and the problems I have evoked. Let us consider first the questions raised by Irving Howe's term 'the discrimination of values', or more generally speaking the question of standards. What strikes the casual observer of the literary scene in Africa today is the abundance of works that are becoming available. In proportion to the number of literate Africans, the quantity of writers and would-be writers must appear impressive. An examination of Jahn's *Bibliography* and other similar works indicates that the number of writers with a serious purpose is out of proportion to the significant part of the African population within which the literary activity in contemporary Africa presumably takes place. Put quite simply, this means that there are more writers in Africa today than there is an educated public for it.

It is also true, however, that the quality of much of this writing is of an indifferent kind. It is difficult indeed, given the concern that we all share to see a new literary movement get really under way, to take a truly 'critical' attitude, in the literal sense of the word, with regard to this proliferation of works. On the other hand, when it is also borne in mind that no body of writing requires critical attention more than a new one such as ours, in order to impose standards - if one is to put it so crudely – to ensure a healthy growth, the need for discrimination and for a certain flexibility as well, appears urgent.

Yet it appears quite clearly that it is not a simple matter to impose standards. We are faced with a problem which is directly tied up with the fact that our writers are newcomers to the language. The criticism of modern African literature tends to oscillate between two extremes. In the first place, the critical apparatus brought to bear on the works of African writers may sometimes appear to be too heavy. Our writers are analysed and commented upon with the use of concepts which in certain cases may be at a level well above what the writer himself is offering. Related to this use of an over-sophisticated critical approach is the application of such rigorous standards of evaluation that works with a certain interest and a certain value in themselves tend to be dismissed out of hand and treated without any sympathy.

At the other extreme is the kind of indiscriminate attention given to insignificant writers which has tended to create a confusion of values from which our better writers may eventually suffer. There is at present a reaction against this kind of patronizing criticism; against the uncritical acclaim of any and every African writer solely on the grounds of his origin; against the kind of blanket appraisal that is unable to make the necessary discrimination between what is valuable and what is not. There doesn't seem to me to be any point, for instance, in discussing Cyprian Ekwensi's novels with the same seriousness as Chinua Achebe's, for I don't think there can be any reasonable doubt as to the distance in purpose and achievement which separates these two writers, from a purely artistic point of view. It is this kind of condescending praise that is making some of our writers reluctant to be considered African writers, an attitude which I regard, I must say, as in itself not only objectionable, but also unreasonable.

I think what we need to consider in this matter is how far the reality of the literary situation in Africa permits a balanced criticism which makes due allowance for the restriction imposed by the linguistic problem, but which does not lose sight of the need to maintain a reasonable standard of evaluation. The terms of reference of evaluating modern African literature are being provided at the moment by the critical tradition which has grown up alongside Western literature. The problem now is to apply them without either frustrating our writers and stultifying the development of a vigorous movement among us; or, on the other hand, by excessive indulgence in encouraging second-rate work and condemning our literature for ever to a minor position. This is a dilemma which the critic has to resolve, but in my view, far from hampering an intelligent response to what our writers are trying to do, it should in fact encourage the cultivation of a more flexible and a more subtle critical awareness – which will establish the necessary relevance between critical judgement and its immediate object, approaching it and grasping it in all its peculiarities, in its specific relation within a cultural and historical perspective.

At the root of the problem of evaluation which I have just evoked, is the fact that modern African literature, being written in the European languages, has had its audience and its early critics abroad. The temptation for the European to see it either charitably as an offshoot, or uncharitably as an imitation, of his own literature, creates for us at this end complications of a quite serious nature, not least of which is the difficulty of defining the situation of modern African literature concretely, with the resultant confusion of values to which I have referred.

A fundamental issue related to this problem is the whole question of interpretation which is to my mind the central function of criticism, what Irving Howe in the definition I have quoted has termed so aptly as 'the sharing of insights'. Criticism cannot be pure scholarship and is not simply an intellectual exercise. I believe the best criticism implies an affective and intense participation in the creative act. The most worthy and enduring appreciation of the writer's work is that which partakes in the imaginative process, in which the senses are alive to the verbal signposts which the writer has planted along the path to his profound intentions. T. S. Eliot has pointed out the importance of the critical faculty within the creative process itself and thus made the point that we cannot usefully make a rigorous distinction between the two in considering the writer's work. His observation must surely, by the same token, apply to the work of the critic who needs to have in him something of the writer's intuition, a certain measure of his creative impulse in order to feel his way through the writer's work and to move at ease within the universe of the writer. The critic cannot therefore be a pure technician. Whatever form of analysis he employs cannot suffice unless he brings to his task the full measure of his own sensibilities. His technique has a meaning in relation to the writer's own means of expression but his task is to see how far they serve the writer's purpose, to determine in what way the work before him creates a satisfactory balance between the writer's imaginative and artistic faculties.

If we accept this view of criticism, then we must see the critic himself as the active and intelligent mediator between the writer's consciousness and the responses of his larger audience of readers. If we accept the unifying role of the critical intelligence, we must expect the critic himself to possess as complete an awareness as possible of the entire range of all that has gone into the literary work, and his activity as one which brings into sharp focus the various directions within the work as well as the relations outside the work itself which have determined, or at least shaped, the imaginative process which brought it into being. This means that the critic's intuition, to which I have referred earlier, must consist to a certain extent of some form of knowledge, of a common sensibility that unites him with the writer and that relates him instantly to his work.

Criticism has been called 'the vision of a vision' by the French critic Ramon Fernandez. In other words, the mirror of the creative act. In order that this mirror should give a true reflection of the work and not a deformation, there needs to be a coincidence of feeling and experience between the writer and his critic. The application of this general principle to the African situation is already obvious. It is a relatively simple matter for a critic of a European work to relate it first to a settled and accepted framework of thought and feeling and to distinguish within this framework the writer's individual scheme, but when we are considering the modern African writer it is clear that some adjustment of the critic's sights becomes necessary and this is something that very few commentators have been able or even willing to do. Because the literature as a distinctive development is recent, it is not clear within which tradition it has to be seen, or in which web of relations within a total development each work occurs.

This ambiguous position of modern African literature can be illustrated quite simply by observing, for instance, that an African novel belongs to the European tradition by its language and by its form but perhaps stands outside that tradition not only by its references, but also – in the case of some of our novelists, some of the best novelists – by the way the language and the form are handled. I have made the remark elsewhere that it is a far cry indeed from Maupassant's *Une Vie* to Oyono's *Une Vie de boy*. Thus our criticism must grow with our literature, necessarily adjusting its concepts, seeing itself essentially as the exploration of a new territory which provides familiar signposts, but which is nonetheless new, demanding respect for its integrity and its specificity.

I think that I need to make clearer here what I mean by the 'integrity and specificity' of the work with reference to modern African literature and I will endeavour to do so by looking at the question of cultural references. Despite the fact that our writers use the European language to express themselves, the most original among them do so with the conscious purpose of presenting an African experience, and the best among them reflect in their works a specific mode of the imagination which derives from their African background. Our writers are recognizably African only in the sense in which they give an African character to their works and conversely, we who are Africans, will only accept them as speaking about us and for us in so far as they take our voice and speak with our accent. The work of criticism, of interpreting modern African literature, must be brought to recognize this fact. What I have called the integrity and specificity of an African work can only be brought to light, therefore, if the work itself is situated within its African perspective and related to its African references. And I believe we need to insist upon what we mean by the African references of the work if we are to avoid the misunderstanding that I feel is at the bottom of certain reservations that are often made about African writers being more concerned with their African purpose

and too little aware of their universal purpose. We might open a paren-
thesis here. Such reservations come mainly from those critics who think
(quite wrongly, I believe) that the universal and the general can be attained
without passing through the concrete and the local and are based on the
implicit assumption that the terms 'universal' and 'western' are synonymous.

The African reference of an African work can be elucidated, I believe,
by approaching the work with an insight into, and a feeling for, those
aspects of African life which stand beyond the work itself, its extensions
into the African experience, and its foundations in the very substance of
African existence. Something like a 'sociological imagination', to borrow
Wright Mills's term but using it in a new sense, is what I think at the
moment the critic, in particular the foreign critic, needs to sustain his
intelligence. Let me at once make quite clear that I do not mean by this
only that criticism should concern itself with anthropological details. This
kind of work has its place, although I think it is useful also to bear in mind
that such knowledge derived from literary works belongs more properly
to anthropology than to literary criticism, and there is no point at all in
creating enthusiasm around the writer who throws anthropological details
to the hunters of the strange and exotic. The tracking down of anthropological details is meaningless if it does not reveal how they form part of
the imaginative life of the work and how they are integrated into its
artistic purpose. A more fruitful kind of sociological approach is that which
attempts to correlate the work to the social background to see how the
author's intention and attitude issue out of the wider social context of his
art in the first place and, more important still, to get to an understanding
of the way each writer or each group of writers captures a moment of the
historical consciousness of the society. The intimate progression of the
collective mind, its working, its shapes, its temper, these – and more – are
determinants to which a writer's mind and sensibilities are subject, to
which they are responding all the time and which, at a superficial or profound level, his work will reflect in its moods and structures.

For us in Africa, one of the most significant developments, perhaps the
most significant of our modern experience, is the transformation of our
mental landscape. Not only are our writers recording this process, the
very movement of their works is in itself a reflection of what is happening
in the deep recesses of our collective soul. It is in this connection that what
I have called a sociological imagination, forming part of the business of
interpretation, takes on its meaning with regard to modern African literature. For in the same way that our culture and societies are going through
a development which involves a complex process of change and yet continuity, so too our literature is moving through a process tending towards

the realization in symbolic terms of some form of resolution and harmony. Our modern literature is therefore an indicator of an essential aspect of our spiritual evolution; more, the principal channel through which the collective adventure of the new African is being given expression.

I began this talk by remarking upon the fact that we distinguish between traditional and modern African literature, and I would now like to qualify this by adding that this is, in fact, a distinction that we should not carry too far. It is one that is more apparent than real and which we make for the sake of convenience, for if we look at African societies in their long-range developments, if we focus rather on the essential than on the contingent, on the substance rather than on the accessories, these societies will strike us more as so many snakes shedding their old skins. I personally take the view that the African is being transformed not into something or somebody else, but into something or somebody new, and similarly I tend to look upon our literature as tending towards the transposition of an old scale of feelings and attitudes into a new key of expression.

The implication of this view for the criticism of modern African literature is clear. Unless we are prepared to take into consideration the whole imaginative tradition in Africa, we who set out to interpret the writings of new authors are going to miss the finer modulations which give to the best in modern African literature interest and value. This is not only because most of these writers have the express purpose of giving their works an African quality, or an African character, and draw consciously for their material upon their background; that is something I think which we should normally take for granted, and if this was all they were doing they would constitute no more than a regional school. It is rather in their appropriation of the European language and tradition, and the adaptation of both to an imaginative mode upon which each one imparts an individual stamp, that their Africanness is revealed. What touches me, for instance, in a novel like *Danda* by Nwankwo, is his ability in bringing to life a folk hero as a sharply individualized character. What I consider personally to be the achievement of Tutuola, for instance, despite his obvious limitations, is the extension he has given to the traditional fantasy in Yoruba folk tales, and to the mythical novel in Yoruba created by Fagunwa, purely by the poetic quality of his own individual evocations. Our appreciation of what an African writer does cannot be complete unless that African dimension is considered and consequently brought to light. Not only can our criticism be limited if we do not relate the work to its specific cultural framework, it can also be falsified.

I still cannot get over the shock I experienced upon reading D. J. Enright's review of Achebe's *Arrow of God* in the *New Statesman* when it first appeared. That a critic of his calibre should have dismissed such a work out of hand, that he should have been so irritated by what remains for me one of the supreme merits of Achebe, his use of language, and thus missed the whole point of that novel: this was something that I could simply not understand. And I give this particular example because I am sure that if Professor Enright had been more familiar with this corner of the former British Empire, with the way we live and, above all, with the way we speak, his assessment of *Arrow of God* would have been entirely different or at least modified. We do not, however, need to accept his judgement any more than he himself would be prepared to accept the judgement of say, a French or Italian critic, which might place the poetry of Byron above that of Keats.

But what appears in so flagrant a manner in this particular example seems to me to be happening all the time to a greater or lesser degree when our writers are discussed as if they had not 'two hands' as J. P. Clark has reminded us, but only one – the European. As if it were reasonable to suppose that the tradition of literary expression to which they are first exposed cannot matter for an understanding of their work in their adopted language and in the tradition that they have come to know at a second remove. As if, in fact, the whole question of the double register which determined their work, is not there. It is not only unreasonable to adopt this attitude, it makes for a lack of rigour in the intelligent discussion which is expected of the critic when he offers to interpret for us the work of an African writer. Furthermore, we all tend to forget that the dichotomy between traditional and modern, as applied to Africa, expresses itself not as an opposition of two worlds but as a unity, as an entity which is more unified than our distinctions are wont to make clear. Traditional African culture and society are in fact contemporary, and traditional literature is all around us, alive, growing, and transforming itself and still, therefore, available to our modern writers. Its impress on their works is far from negligible. It shows itself both directly in their conscious assimilation of its forms and of its conventional symbols, and indirectly in the way it influences the manner in which our writers construct their works, in the way in which they give a formal pattern to their sensibilities, and present a certain order of the imagination. It seems to me then legitimate to assume that in a fundamental and significant way, a continuity of form and reference exists between the oral literature of Africa and the modern literature written in the European languages; a continuity that J. P. Clark has endeavoured to demonstrate in the English adaptation of the Ijaw saga, *Ozidi*, in his play of the same title. Similarly, L. S. Senghor while writing in French, has consciously adapted the borrowed tongue to the feel and movement of the oral poetry of his native Senegal, and one can point to the same clear trend in the work of a substantial body of significant writers who are today already giving to modern African literature new directions and even a distinctive figure.

It is in this perspective that the 'sociological' approach, in the sense that I have given to the term, presents itself as the most apt to render a full account of modern African literature. This approach, in its fullest and widest meaning, implies that our criticism should take into account everything that has gone into the work, and specifically for our literature; everything within our society which has informed the work, as Leavis would put it.

This raises a final point which I would like to touch upon with regard to this question of interpretation. It is a point which is connected with what, in another context, Eliot has called 'the problem of belief' and which I would like to interpret in relation to our literature as 'the problem of identification'. I mean by this the extent to which a critic can respond fully to a work which not only contains references outside his own realm of experience but which, in the structures which make up its mode of existence, appeals to a kind of sensibility with which he is not familiar. For I do not believe that it is enough to track down the origins of these references. There needs, I believe, to be a measure of identification and belief in them in order to feel in one's bones, as it were, their place in the work of the writer. It is not adequate criticism, for instance, to point out the rises and falls in the tonal pattern of an African work in the European languages. The work of art is an invitation to a dialogue of sensibilities and nothing can replace the immediate response to this invitation if one is to arrive at a satisfactory apprehension of the essential coherence of the work, at an intuitive and real awareness of its profound truth. Some inner experience or some inner knowledge, either immediate or acquired, of the relations outside the work is necessary for this kind of understanding, and at the heart of the African frame of reference of a modern African work stands, I should think, the very use of language which is not the same among us as in present-day Europe. Therefore to judge the language of Wole Soyinka or J. P. Clark in their plays without regard for the tradition of speech behind them, is to miss an original dimension of their work. For if their language appears 'formal' is it not because, in fact, they have achieved what they set out to do, to capture the movement of the lives of their people in their very speech? Is this fact, too, not significant in the sense that Ijaw and Yoruba, like so many other languages of other traditional people, have not yet been made to relax their formal structures in order to adapt to the technological age, are still archaic in the purest sense of the word – that is every word, every syllable even, retaining its value as a sign, as a metaphor. And it is that sensuous delight in language which characterized earlier societies in Europe and which is so supremely reflected in Shakespeare for Elizabethan England, which our best writers are restoring to the language of their erstwhile colonial masters.

This feeling for language, which derives from their African background, is an essential part of their purpose. In our traditional literature, in traditional society, the ideal, in fact, is to make every utterance as far as possible memorable. This is what underlies the principle which governs Achebe's use of language, for instance; as he himself has said: A proverb is the palm oil with which words are eaten'.

The meaning I attach then to the application of a 'sociological imagination' in the criticism of modern African literature may perhaps now begin to emerge in something of its full light and import. The double relationship of this literature to two cultures and to two imaginative traditions, with the particular forms of human universe which lie behind each of them, calls for a special orientation of criticism in dealing with it, an orientation which is sociological by implication. It involves a process whereby the very differentiation that marks the two frames of reference of this literature imposes upon the critical function important adjustments of those principles worked out in the western tradition, to the peculiar modes of sensibility which feature in the African works, and which derive from the African background, of which the uses of language, both conditioned by and conditioning the traditional modes of feeling and apprehension, constitute a distinct social reality.

And because the very fabric of our original African consciousness, as it continues to be reflected in our various imaginative traditions, is bound to leave significant traces in the work of the truly sensitive modern African writer, the handling of the European language and of the forms associated with it to express an African awareness which constitutes the principle on which modern African literature is founded, calls for a critical understanding culled from a double standpoint, of the process by which, in the work of our best writers, a true integration of an African content with a European means of expression is being worked out. For it is out of this linguistic situation, in itself contradictory, that they are wresting their triumphs; their significance resides, apart from the human interest of their works, in the fact that from the basic dissociation of the realities they express and the language in which they express them, they create a unity. It is impossible to realize this fact fully without placing their works in this total perspective; and at the present moment, this means an increased consideration of the African wing of that perspective.

Now I am conscious that in pursuing the logic of the issues which I am raising I may be drawn little by little into an extreme position. I may in fact appear to be overstating the case for an African understanding of modern African literature but if I do so, my intention is not to take an exclusive and narrow view of the function of criticism with regard to African literature, but rather to re-state with some emphasis, in my opinion justified, the need to see this literature for what it is, to judge it on its own terms, and to comprehend it in its essence. Indeed, on this point, I would hate to be misunderstood as suggesting, by my emphasis, that the business of interpreting African literature should be made the exclusive preserve of African critics. I would like my emphasis to be seen rather where I mean it to fall: on the need for a serious and intelligent approach, which pre-supposes a minimum level of intellectual preparation, the acquisition in fact of an adequate measure of foreknowledge, and its application to the task of critical interpretation. We are all aware that this kind of prepara-tion is not available automatically to the African intellectual, in the same way that the Western critic is equipped through his education to meet literary works in his own environment, for most of us educated Africans possess a mind largely trained away from our own cultural background. The African who wishes therefore to interpret African literature needs to do his homework as strenuouly as the Western critic, in order to satisfy the demands that I have been formulating here, even though one may admit that he is, by the very nature of things, placed in a privileged posi-tion to acquire the necessary qualifications. My concern then is to make a case for a critical approach which is appropriate to its object, and this not only for reasons of intellectual method, but also for other reasons which have to do with the place of this literature in the intellectual and cultural life of contemporary Africa.

And this brings me to the third and final point I abstracted earlier out of Irving Howe's definition of criticism – its role in the defence of a living culture. The critic of literature has not only an important role to play in establishing adequate standards and in presenting an authentic and com-prehensive interpretation with regard to the works themselves, but also a responsibility towards the public which our literature is intended to represent. If the critic is to guide, he must do so with competence, and all I have said so far implies that we cannot simply assume that this competence exists, as far as modern African literature is concerned, because of its peculiar situation and nature. If we are to ask an African audience, for instance, to recognize the works of Tutuola, we must then be armed with an insight into his work which enables us to relate it to its African context and therefore to an African audience. This problem has very important consequences and I am not concerned here, simply for ideological reasons, with the question of the imposition of authors from outside which, in any case, is in itself an unsatisfactory situation. For the decolonization of African literature, which Professor Eldred Jones has spoken of, needs

certainly to be accepted and to be carried into criticism if we are to avoid
misunderstanding and even bitterness.

What worries me in particular, however, is the danger that modern
African literature, if things continue this way, may gradually begin to
occupy, from its present ambiguous position in our midst, a marginal
position in our modern culture. We want now to decide whether it will
for ever remain a tributary of Western literature, or a full literature in its
own right with a legitimate place in the modern culture of Africa. And its
only claim to this kind of legitimacy can come from its original African
quality and from its relevance to contemporary African existence, and it is
here that our critical effort assumes a wider social and cultural significance.
I should like here to quote a sentence from Eliot which has a direct bearing on my theme. 'The greatness of literature,' he says, 'cannot be determined solely by literary standards though we must remember that whether
it is literature, or not, can be determined only by literary standards.'[2] Now
this is a view with which I am in total agreement and I would like to apply
it to the situation of modern African literature.

The impact of our writers' efforts will only come across if we, as critics,
can relate their works to the whole state and condition of our people's
existence, draw out their meaning for them by demonstrating not only
their excellence, at least where the best ones are concerned, but also their
relevance and significance. Because our writers are using mostly foreign
languages, our own people do not catch their African accent which is un-
mistakably there. This problem is well dramatized by the curious position
of Fagunwa and Tutuola : the one recognized by his own people as a great
writer but unknown abroad; the other praised abroad – largely for the
wrong reasons. The lesson here, of course, is that Tutuola will in the long
run be the loser in this situation and I would consider this to be a tragedy.
The danger is that Tutuola's fate may overtake the whole of modern
African literature. For how long can his acclaim in Europe be sustained if
he hasn't got roots at home? – and I am reminded here of what happened
to so many Haitian writers who won recognition in France, and who are
today totally unknown *anywhere* in the world. I consider that literature
has no meaning detached from the feelings of the people whom it represents. It is not the work itself which in the last resort is of value, which is
sacred, but the human beings behind the work and it is out of their lives
that literature draws its significance and its truth. Every work, therefore,
must be seen as a summing-up of experience, in some profound way must
be situated at the live centre of the collective interest and the common
experience of the writer's group.

The quest for coherence in the literary work on purely technical grounds
seems to me, therefore, a dangerous procedure with regard to modern

African literature, at least for the moment. What we must look for, I think is the fine balance between art and life, their conjunction in the imaginative creation. I do not hesitate to say, therefore, that as far as the critic of African literature is concerned, he must take the view that literature has no autonomy outside of reality. The critic of African literature thus has a double responsibility: to show the literary work as a significant statement with a direct relevance to the African experience; and related to this is what I want to call the educative role of criticism in the present context of the literary situation in Africa. We have a duty not only to make our modern African literature accessible to our people in terms which they can understand, but also in the process, to promote an understanding of literature, to widen the creative (as well as responsive) capabilities of our people – the two essential elements in a fruitful literary life.

The capacity for response to literature in Africa does not need to be demonstrated. The imaginative tradition in this continent is a solid and rich one, yet we know how poor is the response of students in the schools to literary works. Their difficulty here is essentially one of language and references, and it is not reasonable to expect from them a correct response to a literature that still presents a foreign aspect. We are fortunate that our writers are beginning to provide us with something that we can now call our own and it is important that our criticism should show in fact that this literature is of us, and with us, and that it should help our students and the new literate public to surmount the barrier of language in order to penetrate the world of the modern African writer, a world that they should be able to recognize because it is theirs. In practical terms this means that we may have to develop our criticism, if only for a while, as a method of teaching adapted to the need and level of our public. We will need to write, perhaps, as simply and directly as possible, although I do not think it always necessary or possible to write down. (After all, an important aim of education, in teaching, is in fact to come down to the student in order to bring him up.) We should also think of ourselves as providing a training in literary awareness to our people, using our modern literature more or less as material, a new literary awareness specifically related to the development of the written tradition and which can be extended to other literatures thus helping to enrich and to broaden their cultural experience.

The upshot of my comments then is this. The criticism of modern African literature must take as its aim the creation of a public at home, to provide a base for it here in order to foster its healthy development. Our purpose in the last resort must be to found modern African literature veritably; to promote the full emergence of a literary life as a part of the intellectual and cultural development of modern African society; to help

literary expression find its place as a vital dimension of our existence in
this day and age.

Notes and References

1. Irving Howe, *Modern Literary Criticism* (Boston : Beacon Press, 1958),
   p. 37.
2. T. S. Eliot, *Selected Prose* (Harmondsworth : Penguin, 1953).

3. African Literature and the Language Question

▼▼▼

Literature occurs within language. In any consideration of the literary phenomenon, the centrality of the linguistic factor obliges us to a recognition of the fundamental and determining nature of the association between language, in all its forms and extensions, and literature, considered as formalized expression of the life of the imagination. Literature is not, of course, a mere category of language, and cannot simply be reduced to a system of signs but possesses its own peculiar nature and reality which go beyond the immediate fact of language as a means of communication. But even when this autonomous dimension of literature is granted, it remains true that there is an absolute sense in which it is grounded in language of one kind or the other; a sense in which literature is at the moment inconceivable without recourse to the elementary means of communication represented by language. For it is in and through language that the imaginative process takes place and manifests itself in order to be communicable to any degree and thus to take on an objective life. It is a simplification, perhaps, but one not devoid of real significance, to say that language serves as the concrete vehicle of expression of the imaginative: the relationship between literature and language becomes in this light somewhat equivalent to that between content and form.

If this general proposition is accepted, we are further obliged to a recognition of the fact that a significant part of our response to literature is determined by the way in which the literary artist establishes a satisfying degree of adequacy between the imaginative content of his creation and its linguistic medium. It is not only the range and depth of the one, nor the degree of elaboration of the other – neither of the two elements taken each in isolation – that provides the true measure of the creation, but their full correlation within a unified scheme of suggestions by which the imaginative experience is not only illuminated but communicated in its original tone and quality.

We need, I believe, to recall such elementary but fundamental considerations in order to appreciate fully the seriousness of the situation in

Africa today with regard to this question of the association between literature and language. The African situation is marked by a radical anomaly, in which the intimate collaboration between the imaginative impulse, expressing itself either as individual creation or as collective representation, and the linguistic resources through which the imagination works itself to complete realization, this collaboration seems at the moment not only to be affected by complications of various kinds but indeed on the way to losing its meaning.

There are two broad areas in which this anomaly can be observed. It is immediately evident in the divergence that characterizes the relationship between the content and references of the literature produced by Africans in the European languages and the medium in which this literature is expressed. This particular anomaly carries with it a whole host of implications and consequences, the most notable of which are, to my mind, the distortion of critical values which it entails, and the difficulty of determining its true direction – because of the distance placed between this literature and the generality of Africans by the language factor. The second area in which the general anomaly we're speaking of manifests itself concerns the position and the role of our traditional literatures. It is indeed curious to observe, in this connection, the strange reversal of the norm that seems to be taking place. For in the elaboration of our modern culture in Africa, the dominance of the European languages is leading to a devaluation of those literatures that are original to the peoples of this continent, and in which one observes the normal coincidence between imaginative thought, fully furnished with those elements that have sustained and continue to sustain the common culture, and the language which provides a connection between the individual artistic and imaginative consciousness and the collective life. To put the matter in another way, the true literatures of Africa are being relegated to marginal positions in almost every single one of our contemporary national communities;[1] and within the broad intellectual and cultural perspectives that we are beginning to see emerge across the continent, there seems no doubt that a new literature attached to the European languages is being seen and accepted as the rule and direction of creative effort.

The anomaly here resides specifically in the fact that this attachment of our modern literature and culture to the European languages is at odds with the facts of African life today, for the truth is that none of these languages can be said, outside of a few circles, to carry fully with it the reality of African experience as it exists today,[2] and the new literature that is being expressed in them, for all its value and significance, must be seen for this reason, from the African point of view, to be placed in a most ambiguous, not to say, precarious situation.

The observations I have so far made should be taken in the first instance as a statement of a problem – a problem that is real, and which has constantly engaged the attention of writers and critics, and has a way of cropping up at every discussion of African literature. It points to a general feeling of *malaise* and even to a vague and undefined sense of guilt among many of us when we are confronted with this problem. There is no doubt that our relation to the two areas of literature co-existing on the continent is marked by a kind of estrangement that forms part of our general sense of alienation – cultural as well as political and economic – as contemporary Africans. We are unable to talk meaningfully and confidently of any literature than can properly be called 'African', even in our very efforts, in this day and age, and given our historical antecedents, to define ourselves collectively as *African*. The very attachment of the literature that goes with this effort of definition to the European languages constitutes, by a strange paradox, a barrier between the processes and the fact of this literature and our African consciousness. We cannot feel that we are in full possession of this literature so long as it is elaborated in a language that does not belong to us in an immediate and original way.

It is really in this sense that one can speak of a contradiction in terms in such labels as 'African literature in English' or 'Francophone African literature', unless we are meant to accept them as merely convenient and provisional references to a literary state of affairs that is far from simple. There is thus much justice in the strictures that Obi Wali has brought up against the efforts aimed at validating these labels, without regard to the confusions which they mask.[3] It is significant too to note that Wali's remarkable article on the subject is marked (at least in my view) less by the overt tone of indignation which it exudes than by the profound sense of ambiguity which informs his attempt to establish a reasonable point of view on the language question. That sense of ambiguity proceeds from Wali's acutely felt awareness that the new literatures of Africa written in the European languages are direct by-products of the colonial experience, reminders of our continuing dependence, even in this inner area of our collective life and expression, with regard to Europe.

On the other hand, there is no indigenous literature at the moment that we can call 'African' in a wide continental sense, and in the modern perspective of our contemporary existence. What we have is a diversity of literatures expressed in the various languages native to Africa, and each one bound to the specific peoples and cultures using those languages. Moreover, the vast majority of these literatures are still in the oral stage and this constitutes a serious limitation to their diffusion and to the role they are able to play in a modern culture. This is not to disregard the prospects offered by the new means of communication such as radio and television, which offer excellent chances of reconciling our traditional literatures to the technological age. Nor is this intended to imply that orality and literacy are by the very force of their different natures mutually exclusive. The real point here is that the area of application of the literatures indigenous to Africa may remain as narrow as they are at the moment, precisely because of their oral expression: to extend and transform and still hope to retain the significance of our traditional forms, a conversion to written expression becomes imperative.

The fact, then, is that as Africans, we are surrounded by a vigorous process of creativity at all levels, without being able to mark our bearings properly within the general situation. Literature exists in a three-tier perspective in Africa: the oral traditional, the written traditional (with modern or modernizing tendencies) – these two categories expressed in the various African languages – and finally, the modern literature in the European languages, in which the reference to Africa and the recourse to certain modes of African thought and expression are made to serve as the distinguishing factors that differentiate this literature from the 'mainstream' of the European traditions to which they are related by languages and consequently by forms.

There is some sense in which we can say that these three categories have a measure of relation between them but they do not seem to me as yet to form an integrated whole, except in a few isolated and scattered instances.[4] And the main difficulty in coming to a sense of wholeness about our literary situation seems to me to derive principally from the fact of language. There is a separateness of the traditional literature of Africa and the new literature in the European languages which makes it difficult, if not impossible, to speak of a single stream of imaginative expression, in which the flow from the old tradition into the new one being elaborated can be said to be truly continuous. The most natural way of course to assure this continuity is to create new forms and new modes within the language, in such a way as to reflect not only the adaptation of the African imagination to new realities, but also of each African language as it develops under the pressure of the modern age. As far as I'm aware, there is no general development in this direction on the African continent. A number of African languages have certainly begun to develop written literatures on a large scale,[5] but they all lie in the shadow of the only literature that can be called modern – the literature in the European languages. The linguistic factor – the very conflict of the African languages and the European ones inherited from the colonizers – is without doubt certainly the most powerful inhibiting factor to the healthy development of the new African literatures in the indigenous languages.

To a great extent, the problem that we are faced with is a consequence of history, and represents at the moment part of our general dilemma of authenticity. Is there a unified reality that we can call African, and to which we can attach a body of literary creations as belonging specifically and uniquely to that reality? There can be no categorical answer to this question, even though our subjective disposition, determined by our recent historical experience, and our intimations of a common cultural reference – common traits in music, dance, art, social organization etc. – lend a significant measure of objective direction and even validation to our efforts to evolve a concrete African personality. But the contradictions introduced by history into this process are in no sphere as evident as in the literary. Without a common African language, we can only speak as yet of various literatures in African languages, if we are to speak with true meaning. The language question not only bedevils every effort at defining an African literature – not only throws up each time it is considered thorny issues related to the content and nature of this literature[6] – but also points to other problems of a sociological character in which the question of literature is implicated: problems related to education; to the social structure of our various communities as they are being shaped today; and perhaps, more fundamentally than anything else, to the issue of national integration in each of the African States.[7]

There is no need, within the scope of this chapter, to go in detail into the historical factors that have landed us in this truly agonizing situation. The general frame of these factors is well known, although some purpose can be served in clarifying a number of loose notions that are still prevalent with regard to the language question in the world community. One such notion that needs refinement is the idea commonly held that language is necessarily tied to clearly defined national groups, a notion that ignores the facts of history and even the present day reality even in Europe where this notion has contributed immensely to the relative triumph of the national idea.

But however one may qualify such beliefs, there remains the fact that language is not a mere functional tool, but that everywhere it is invested with the force of communal life. It is possible for a borrowed language to be so internalized by a community as to become totally identified with it, but this process requires a considerable time-span to be complete, and in any case, the language itself must have such a wide area of application within the community as to make the process possible.

With regard to the European languages in Africa, this is for the moment

clearly not the case.[8] The adoption of European languages by the majority
of African states as the official languages can only be regarded as a measure
of convenience, arising out of the circumstances of the colonial experience,
and not as a logical response to the truth of the African situation. It is not
here a matter of whether the present policy is in itself good or bad, but
rather of assessing, in relation to our present circumstances, and by looking
at the history of language development in other areas of the world, whether
the policy can succeed in the long run: success here being determined by
the eventual massive adherence of African populations to the adopted
languages.

No one, I think, can pretend to forecast the outcome. One can only point
to the enormous problems that the language question poses among us, and
express doubts as to the possibility of the European languages – English
and French – ever taking root in Africa firmly enough to become native to
us in some form or the other. But although I am prepared to concede that
nothing can ever be said to be final on an issue like this, due precisely to
the imponderable factors of history, the assumptions that lie behind the
doubt I've expressed here stem from the very urgency that we all feel the
language problem poses for us on this continent, and from a personal
concern with the implication of this situation for our literary culture.
The sociological issues with which the language question is bound up
today in Africa represent in fact the ultimate determining factor of the
issue whether we can ever have, properly speaking, an African literature.

The problem is an extremely complex one, and presents itself first of all
on the ideological plane. There *is* an African sentiment, an African consciousness, an idea of Africa, and I believe, a common African vision unified not only by history but by a fundamental groundwork of values and
of cultural life.[9] But there is no African nation; in other words, the felt
idea and vision have not yet found an objective political form. What we
have is a plurality of African states, multi-national, with a diversity of
customs, folkways, and especially of languages. This in itself is not an
unusual situation, for most countries of the world are in fact multi-
national. The peculiarity of the African situation resides in the extreme
and intractable character of our present arrangement which makes it difficult to adopt a coherent language policy in any of our states. With the exception of the few fortunate countries where the circumstances of history
have imposed an official language native to the country, all the African
states have been compelled to adopt a European language as the common
medium of communication and as the linguistic channel of national life.
Government and administration, justice, and education in particular are
carried out among us in languages foreign to us. The corollary is that
cultural life at anything above the level of the primary group follows this

same pattern. Leaving aside for the moment considerations of national pride involved, it is clear that this is an arrangement that must at some point in the line pose serious problems of a practical nature, more so as the rigidity with which it is adhered to is not accompanied by anything like a serious effort of reflection on this matter in official circles.[10] The essential ambiguity of the situation is thus conveniently masked by the undisciplined use of such terms as 'English-speaking Africa' and 'Francophone Africa' – terms which have a meaning only with respect to the tiny minority of the educated élites which employ them and which bear no relation whatsoever to the truth of the matter. The truth, anyhow, is that we are so far in Africa from achieving a true bilingualism in our relation with the European languages – so far from a spontaneous deployment within our communities of the European language along with our local languages – that one can speak of a real state of crisis today in this connection. Educationists in Africa are only too well aware of the seriousness of the problem posed by the dogged application of the European languages in the educational system, the tensions that it causes in the learning process, and the considerable wastage in educational material that it produces.[11] The sociological significance of the language question as it is evolving among us today is even more ominous, for language, as Pierre van den Berghe has pointed out, is fast becoming a factor of division between the new élite and the masses, and between the urban centres and the rural communities.[12] The élite can be defined all too readily in Africa as that section of the society which is in full possession of the European language, which differentiates it from the rest. The importance of education along European lines thus lends to the European language a real sociological significance. The fact is that the official languages are associated with the formal system of the State and the levers of administration, but in practically every other respect they remain foreign, divorced almost entirely from the true centres of local life and expression.

There is a kind of double system of alienation for the African implied in this situation. For the educated African, in particular, there is the continuing estrangement from the wellsprings of the traditional culture implied by an educational system that is carried out in the European language, and doubled by the impossibility of a successful assimilation of the culture of that language on anything like a meaningful scale. The educated African completely at home in his traditional culture as well as in the European culture is a very rare bird indeed. The vast majority of us move and live in a dim region of cultural and linguistic ambiguity: the fact may not be always present to our consciousness, but it is there, incontrovertible, and heavy with real sociological and psychological implications. For the uneducated African, the situation is certainly no less fraught with difficulties. There is for him the real estrangement from the modern system, his disadvantage in the economic and social system which places a premium on the possession of the European language.[13] And in the global context of national life, there is the discontinuity of cultural expression as between the 'masses' and the élite, a discontinuity that is determined along the language line. The traditional cultures continue to be expressed in the local languages, while the new culture is being elaborated in the European languages.

The implications of all this for literature in Africa are clear. The most immediate is the fact that the African writer who employs a European language must first reckon with the problem of the disparity between his African material and his medium of expression. For even if it is true that all languages are systems whose reference to reality is arbitrary, there is a 'naturalization' of particular languages to specific environments which plays an important role in the process by which they not only come to signify but to achieve a correspondence with the total configuration of the perceived and experienced reality within the environment. Indeed, since Whorf, it has become nearly a commonplace to say that the language of a people directs their perception and offers a structured framework for expression of feelings. Literature extends this feature of language considerably, through its connotative functions, so that the truest correspondence must be, one might say naturally, that between a language spoken by a group and the literary expression which proceeds from its immediate environment.

This natural correspondence is denied to the African writer who wishes to express his African world in a European language. The balance that he must achieve between the particular quality of his imagination and sensibility and the European language in which he strives to cast them, is a hard one to attain and there is no doubt that many a potential writer in Africa must have been defeated by this problem.

There is of course the success of several African writers before us, and it is remarkable. But we cannot be blinded to the problem I've raised here by this success. The truth is that, along with the real achievements, we have had perhaps more than our fair share of middling works: many a work that was hailed in the early years of the emergence of African writing reads today like an amateurish exercise. It is not to be expected of course that each time an African picks up his pen to write, he should produce a masterpiece. But apart from the fact that there is an indiscriminate lumping together of significant works with those that really belong to a different order, a general tolerance seems also to have been determined by the language problem towards an insensitive use of language in much African writing – a tolerance that is not far removed from a complacent paternalism. The African writer seems not to be expected to write well if he uses a European language: a strange inversion indeed of critical values.[14]

Even in the work of those writers whom we acknowledge as real masters, there is often apparent a lack of flexibility and a self-consciousness in their handling of language which betrays their distance from the affective centres of the European medium of expression. This may often issue in positive results, leading some of them to a creative reshaping of the European language for a fuller expression of an African feeling. This process of re-appropriating the European language to place it at the service of an African vision has even been established as a norm by the work of Achebe, and there is no doubt that it has its value. But one cannot but wonder how much of the African tone can really be felt and appreciated by a non-African audience in the works of writers like Achebe himself, Soyinka on the English-speaking side, and Senghor or Birago Diop for example, on the French-speaking side. The case of Tutuola, as is now generally recognized, is singularly problematic.[15] And that of the Okara of *The Voice* must be seen as a further complication of the problem installed at the very centre of the linguistic expression of the African imagination by Tutuola.

The difficulties that the language question poses to literary creation in Africa are even more evident in the realm of drama. In an African play written in a European language, the divorce between the environment and the language simply stares us, quite literally, in the face. Very few Africans use a European language all the time in their normal lives: the areas of experience to which the imported languages are applied are not only circumscribed but in fact particularized, and no amount of 'proverbialization' of the European language can remove the fact that the qualities sought for belong originally and are really truly at home in the African language.[16] In drama, the use of a European language has the effect of making it difficult for an audience, either African or European, to suspend its disbelief sufficiently to make for the deepest kind of response to the dramatic situation. The cleavage between an African 'content' and a European 'form' appears at every stage in African drama of European expression, underscoring unduly the artifice of drama.

The African dramatist who puts a European language in the mouths of his characters is thus at a greater disadvantage than the novelist. It is largely possible for the novelist to create a dialogue that ignores to some extent the demands of a 'realistic' presentation. Achebe's art, for instance, consists precisely in making us believe in the language of his characters, and he is able to win our conviction because we do not have to confront them physically. The dramatist, on the other hand, has to consider the fact that his characters will have a real presence before his audience, so that on the stage, the unnaturalness of their speech becomes all the more pronounced. He has to secure our participation in what they are doing and saying through a much more difficult effort of language than the novelist. I cannot think of any African dramatist who has completely succeeded in solving this problem. Martin Esslin has, in a review of the plays of Soyinka and Clark, well posed the problem of language in African drama, and his remarks are so pertinent that it is worth quoting him at some length:

> But, it might be argued, the work of the two playwrights we are here discussing, Wole Soyinka and J. P. Clark, should be largely exempt from these considerations; for, after all, they are writing in English. Far from being an advantage, in my opinion, this is a further handicap. Not that these two playwrights are in any way at a disadvantage in using the English language. On the contrary: both are real masters of all its nuances and, indeed, very considerable artists in English. Here again the problem arises from the nature of drama itself. These plays are by Africans about Africans in an African social context. And they are, largely, about Africans who, in reality, speak their own African languages. It is here that the problem lies. We are here presented with African peasants, African fishermen, African labourers expressing themselves in impeccable English. Of course in reality they speak their own languages equally impeccably and the playwrights have merely translated what they would have said in those languages into the equivalent English. Precisely! Which is to say that these original plays labour under the universal handicap of all translated drama.[17]

A further difficulty in African drama of European expression is that of diction: questions of articulation and intelligibility and other factors related to what one might call the 'phonic' aspect of dramatic productions, arise on the stage, which the 'silent' form of the novel does not present. Because of the need then for its actual realization, an African play in a European language, unless it deals with that extremely narrow range of African life that is carried on in that language, will always suffer from the divorce between the African reality and the European language.[18]

We can sum these questions up under the two headings of *competence* and *credibility*. The first concerns the relation of the African writer to the European language in its character, as regards both the resources it offers him and the limits of those resources, as well as his ability to deploy those resources adequately or respect those limits or transcend them, all the time in full control of the medium. Peter Young has summarized this problem:

> This belief in the need for writers to use English in an unusual way to reflect unique material depends for its realization on how the process is seen by the writer. *It must be decided whether experiment is a search for an adequate medium of expression for particular purposes, or an attempt at establishing a highly individual form of English for its own sake, or as a means of national identification.* For most West African

writers the question is literary first and, as their writing is the expression of the African situation, national or regional only second.[19]

The second arises from the first and relates to the degree of conviction which the writer is able to win in his use of the European language in his effort to make it accommodate to an African reality, *as if it were an African language.*

We know of course that there have been writers who have created great and enduring works in languages into which they were not born – the achievement of Conrad has been so complete in this regard that Leavis has placed his work within the 'great tradition' of the English novel. But that placing emphasizes the fact that the contribution of Conrad is to English literature and not to Polish, and the same is true of Ionesco and even of Beckett today, who are figures of French literature by the very fact of their writing in French – Beckett's work in English being, by the same token, ascribed to English literature.

These examples point to the fact that the African situation is by no means unprecedented or unique. It recalls that which obtained for the various communities who were assimilated into Hellenic or Latin culture, and whose writers were perhaps content to employ the dominant language for self-expression: the position of Senghor today in the French literary tradition is thus comparable in this respect to that of the Latin writer native of one of the Roman colonies, to that of Seneca or Catullus, for example. We know too that the reaction against the dominance of Latin from about the Renaissance onwards constitutes one of the most important aspects of the political, social and cultural history of Western Europe.[20] Again in Europe, there are more recent instances of minorities who have been obliged to employ the language of dominant groups for self-expression above the level of the elementary – the Irish in Britain and the Czechs in the old Austro-Hungarian empire are two important examples. The particular case of Kafka and of other writers and intellectuals of his race, class and time has been highlighted in this observation by Hannah Arendt who draws directly upon Kafka's own words:

> Thus they lived 'among three imposibilities ...: the impossibility of not writing' as they could get rid of their inspiration only by writing; 'the impossibility of writing in German' – Kafka considered their use of the German language as the 'overt or covert, or possibly self-torment-ing usurpation of an alien property, which has not been acquired but stolen (relatively), quickly picked up, and which remains someone else's possession even if not a single linguistic mistake can be pointed out'; and finally, 'the impossibility of writing differently', since no other language was available.[21]

It is surely significant that Jacques Rabemananjara should employ nearly the same terms to express a similar sentiment in his address to the historic Congress of Black Writers and Artists held in Rome in 1959. Remarking upon the irony of history which has brought the colonized peoples together through the agency of the European language, he observes:

> The very speech of the conqueror now makes it possible for the conquered, scattered all over the planet, to beckon to one another, from one continent to the other. The West become the signal post of Négritude!

And he adds, 'Our Congress is, in truth, a Congress of language stealers'.[22]

What these parallels show is that cultural imposition almost always provokes some kind of discomfort, and this often first manifests itself at the level of language, which is the most important single area of the collective affectivity. But there is a further point which requires to be noted as regards the present African situation and which seems to deepen the anomaly we're witnessing in African literature. This is the fact that with us, the movement of renaissance has taken an opposite direction to that of Europe as regards Latin. George Steiner has pointed out how the European vernaculars were made to take charge, through translation, of the intellectual and literary tradition elaborated within the classical languages, such that these vernaculars were enriched, and they developed literatures in which the specific native genius could flourish in proper collaboration with the cosmopolitan spirit of the classical heritage.[23] With us, when we consider the modern literature in the European languages, it is the reverse process that is taking place: our writers are carrying over into the European languages a whole stock of symbols derived from the African environment; it is difficult to judge whether, as has often been claimed, these European languages are in fact being truly enriched in the process. If we are to go by the example of Yeats, who abandoned his early efforts to differentiate his poetry through a recourse to Irish mythology, we may well doubt whether the effort of our writers will turn out to have any significance to it.[24]

We need to remember that for the European writers of minority groups, the language of the dominant group was often a first language, at the very least a dialect or register of a speech which they shared in close intimacy with the majority, so that they were able to participate directly and on an equal footing with the original owners of the language in a common culture. These writers only incidentally achieved a particularization of their accents within a common literary expression. To them, that expression and the world it relates to were as immediate as they were to the writer from the majority.

The situation of the African writer is thus quite different. His problem lies in the fact that, however intimate his relationship to the European language, there is always the pressure upon him, in addition to the normal demands of artistic creation, to bridge that distance between the African world and the European language. The point at issue here is not whether an African can successfully write in English or French – we have enough evidence that that particular issue is resolved – but whether in the present circumstances, the work that he produces can have a meaning for his African audience.

This observation raises the grave question of the divorce between African writing in the European languages and the African public, leading to what I've alluded to earlier as the distortion of critical values. The vast bulk of this writing is not accessible to the African public – and this concerns not simply the illiterate sections but also the growing body of educated Africans. The serious study of African literature – the insertion of this literature in a stream of cultural development determined by the educational and institutional framework of the whole national community – is hampered by the language problem. It is difficult to expect a proper individual response, on which ultimately the wished for general development will have to rely, where the student is confronted with a text in a language which he masters very improperly. The delicacy of Armah's prose and the intensity of his symbolism, to take a single example, will always remain at a distance from the sensibility of all but the few Africans who have had a chance to acquire the close and continued familiarity with the English language necessary to appreciate those qualities. And where a writer relies on deliberate echoes and direct allusions to the Western tradition in order to fill out and extend the scheme of suggestions of his individual work – as with the poets, especially – the African reader cannot hope to enter with a significant part of his heart and mind into such a scheme without a fair measure of familiarity with the Western tradition which legitimizes, through the very bond of language, the African writer's procedure. Such a familiarity is a difficult thing to realize, in our present circumstances, on anything like a general scale. At the present moment, therefore, our writers are finding that their audience is located elsewhere than where their original vision has its roots.

The dilemma involved for the African writer himself, of having his works received by an outside audience with what he senses as only an imperfect grasp and understanding as well as only a partial and indirect interest in the concerns to which he is himself committed, can only be complicated by the absence of an adequate crop of African critics possessing the same 'double self' as the writer himself.[25]

The divorce of African literature in the European languages from the African public underscores the sociological significance of these languages in Africa – this literature presents itself, even more than works at a comparative level in the Western context, as out and out élitist. Not only is it suspended in the rarified intellectual atmosphere created by the European language, it has very little possibility of drawing upon a popular tradition of literary expression to revitalize itself, as much European writing has done.

What is at stake, ultimately, is the role that literature can be expected to play in the cultural process in a situation where some of the best creative minds are operating in a medium that is essentially foreign to the vast majority of their countrymen. If literature is to have any role to play at all in our collective life at the present time, that role cannot be obvious or effective as long as our modern expression remains attached to the European languages.

The complexity of the problem becomes all the more evident when we turn from a negative analysis which is the only possible manner of posing the problem to the search for a solution. The trouble here is that there is none at hand, unless we are prepared to abandon a good number of notions and perspectives. The first that would have to go is the very idea of Africa itself as a unified world, and of African literature as the expression of a whole continent with its specific identity. In other words, the problem would be much simplified, at least at one level, if we were to stick to the primary language level of the various peoples in Africa: we would thus have a Yoruba literature, an Akan literature, a Kikuyu literature, a Zulu literature and so on and so forth. The trouble with that is of course the fact that most of us who have received an education do not as a rule define ourselves, at least consciously, at that level. There is the political implication too that goes with that view of things. And however artificial our boundaries may be thought to be, it is incontestable that a certain amount of national integration is taking place, a certain common organization of life and values, within these boundaries. The African states already have a certain measure of objective reality to them.

And yet it is not possible to speak of national literatures in Africa, except in one or two cases. There are no national languages, there are only 'official' languages, and until these languages – English and French in particular – become fully ours, both in a quantitative and a qualitative sense, the literatures produced in them by our own writers cannot be fully possessed by our people.

Does the solution then consist in a pure and simple abandonment of the European languages by our writers? In a situation in which our national lives are still channelled through these languages, in which specifically, the development of sensibility and intelligence still passes through the medium of these languages, so that the potential writer is more likely to be drawn to these languages in which he is educated, this solution seems for the moment impossible.

One solution that has sometimes been canvassed is the adoption of pidgins, where they exist, as the nearest equivalent to a national idiom. In particular, the case of Krio in Sierra Leone is often made on the ground that it is not only a national idiom – an assertion of doubtful value, and which appears to be self-evident only to the dwellers in Freetown isolated in more ways than the linguistic from the rest of the population – but also, and especially, a developed language which has married an African form and spirit to an English-derived lexicon. But this solution is patently un- workable. For one thing, Krio and the other 'pidgins' that we have today have not reached the stage of development which can make them sustain as fully developed a literary expression as either 'standard' English or the indigenous languages.[26] The writer's range of expression can only be re- stricted if that solution were adopted. Perhaps the most important ob- jection, however, is that very few educated Africans possess pidgin suffi- ciently firmly to employ it in their works as anything more forceful than as the occasional concession to its existence among us as a poor relation of the 'real' English.

These are desperate suggestions, but perhaps the most desperate of them all is that made by Soyinka that a single African language, Swahili, be adopted for sub-Saharan Africa, and that all future writing should be done in that language.[27] The result of adopting such a measure would be that in the meantime, literary life will be suspended, except for those writers competent in that language, until such time as the decreted langu- age has been mastered. Furthermore, there is no likelihood of a consensus on the language to be chosen among the members of the OAU (on which Soyinka makes his suggestion depend), and without such a consensus, the whole idea becomes from the start impracticable.

The desperate nature of these suggestions derives from the conflict that we are all experiencing on the language question between our desire to emancipate Africa from the hold of the European languages, and the firm- ness of that hold in certain significant areas of our contemporary life. Where literature is concerned, the whole range of the anomaly I've been looking at here deepens that sense of conflict between fact and desire, precisely because it is in this one area of our deeper life that we feel, in its most intense manifestation, the alienation and cultural ambiguity created by the colonial past. But in addition to this subjective factor, there are also the practical problems that I have touched on in this discussion.

But the apparently intractable nature of the problem arises as well from another conflict – between the historical fact, and the autonomy of art. It is not by choice that our writers are using the European languages, but as a matter of necessity. For all of them, the language in which they write is the only language in which they can write at all, in which they can express themselves with any degree of adequacy. Both Achebe and Senghor have written justifications of their use of English and French respectively, and J. P. Clark has tried to argue that the African writer using English is simply availing himself of a legacy.[28] They are all the more persuasive in that they are, all three of them, masters of the language in which they write. But their arguments hide the fact that for them, using the European language is not a matter of deliberate choice, but of necessity. Senghor, enamoured of the French language as he is, concedes this point where he declares:

> I repeat, we did not choose. It was our situation as a colonized people which imposed the language of the colonizers upon us.[29]

The implication is that if he had been able to choose – if he had been as well educated in Wolof or Serer as in French – he would probably have written in either of the former two than in the latter. Certainly, if the choice had been open to Achebe, he would have written in Igbo rather than in English, and all he has said about the English language being able to carry the burden of his African experience must be taken, in the final analysis, as a rationalization.[30]

The fact remains however that the new literature of Africa in the European languages has a significant existence for us and does represent a considerable achievement. All I have said so far must not therefore be taken to imply a condemnation of this work: on the contrary, I do not see why we should repudiate the achievement of our writers simply on the ground that it is channelled through foreign languages. The historical circumstances, as we've seen, not only imposed these languages on our writers, but compelled them to an assertion which was historically necessary and legitimate. There was no other language in which this could be done, given the circumstances, and it is important to consider the positive aspect of this expression. Ulli Beier has neatly put his finger on the paradox involved historically in this process:

> The West African poet writing in a European language finds himself in a difficult position. He is almost bound to be a nationalist and more often than not he is actively engaged in the fight for self-government. His poetry is naturally concerned partly with a criticism and rejection of European values – and yet he has to use a European language to express the same rejection.[31]

The very tension at the heart of this process also comes to manifest itself, as Sartre has remarked, in the very handling of the European language by the black poet. His revolt thus takes the form of an assault – as in the case of Aimé Césaire in particular – upon the connotations and attachments of meaning and value that go with the European language and which are often negative in respect of his race.[32] The Promethean relationship of the black writer to the language of the colonizer defined by Rabemananjara thus comes to imply for him a greater alertness to the quality of the language, a livelier response than would perhaps otherwise have been the case to its various possibilities of suggestion and modes of symbolic resonance.

But even beyond the exigencies of a peculiar historical experience, there is a more general perspective within which to consider as a positive thing the fact that our writers have this access to the European languages, especially English and French. We must recognize that these two languages now serve as transmitters of a new kind of cosmopolitanism developing in our time and have become as such 'extraterritorial',[33] to borrow Steiner's expression. In this situation – which cuts across linguistic factors to define a common area of ideas, of feeling and of vision for the artist in our troubled century – it could be an advantage for a writer to be able to use directly one of the privileged languages of contemporary international life. Our common involvement in the problems of our world means that the African writer has as much of a stake in shaping it as any other. His command of a language that has a widespread use cannot therefore but place his work, if his command of that language is assured and his human responses mature, at the very centre of a necessary communion rite of cultures, of minds, of sensibilities. The situation of the African writer would merely appear then as one with that of any other writer from any of the numerous 'minor' language groups of the world; at any rate no worse than that of any writer – a Nabokov, a Ionesco or a Beckett – choosing to write in a language acquired in addition to his native tongue. In the general perspective of this line of argument, the literary aspect of the language question in Africa would then appear as merely an aspect of a global situation which a linguist has described thus:

> In many parts of the world, a basic need is precisely that of expressing one's culture linguistically through means other than one's own.[34]

The point then that needs to be steadily held on to is that the literary artist will produce his best work in the medium that he most confidently controls.

There are therefore important considerations on the other side of the argument, and it is apparent that no simple solution offers itself at the moment, for the facts of our situation make for something in the nature of an agonizing contradiction. Nonetheless, there seems to me to be a possibility of taking the edge out of the difficulty, and to some extent at least of resolving the dilemma.

We must start from the assumption that our languages in Africa will, on the whole, continue to show the strength that they manifest today – the resilience and adaptability to new realities that they share with other languages of the world. There may indeed be some languages that will die out, but the vast majority can be expected to survive and thrive. This assumption makes it necessary to suppose that our present attachment to the European languages may well continue to be a source of problems unless we take a number of measures to arrange for a more harmonious future. For if we need the European languages at the moment to operate conveniently in the modern world, we need not sacrifice our cultural future to meet this immediate requirement.

The example of the Soviet Union seems to me to suggest the way out. As is commonly known, the position of Russian as the official language of the State has not hampered the development of the various languages of the other nationalities that make up the union. Indeed, the official policy of promoting these languages has given many of them a new lease of life. The active and constant effort of translating the major works in the non-Russian languages has made for the development of what must be recognized today as Soviet literature, distinct from the Russian, even if the tradition of the latter continues to serve as a reference for the former.

In a similar way, it is possible for us to retain the common European language in each of our national communities, while working strenuously at the same time for the full development of our various indigenous languages in the modern context. Full development here means not only the devotion of research to them, but their integration into the educational system as well. There can be nothing more natural than for one generation to pass on its inherited stock of symbols, images and thought to another through the common language, but this is the natural order of things that colonialism has disrupted among us. Where literature is concerned, we would be giving to the potential writer not merely the natural language of his own people, but the symbols that go with it. For there is no clearer road to the inner recesses of our traditional culture, of our fundamental mental universe, than through our oral, traditional literature. It is clearly absurd that our educational systems should continue to ignore this important area of our cultural expression, to draw our young minds away from this basic structure of the collective consciousness of the overwhelming majority of their countrymen. There is clearly an urgent need to open up our languages and the literatures they have sustained in their full scope to the coming generations. That way lies also the only possibility of renewal of our indigenous inheritance of literature.

This approach seems to me to represent the only kind of solution that we can hope to achieve in our present situation. It ought to create a situation in which our literary culture will find a mode of elaboration that is many-sided, within a cycle of mutual responses to the various resources available to us. Where the writer is concerned, he will at least be offered a real choice in the matter of language, so that, in the event of his opting for the European language, he will be able to bring to his expression in that language the vitality of an imaginative consciousness nurtured within the climate of his original culture and the language which is its natural vehicle. We may even envisage here the ideal profile of the African writer of the future, that of a man able to give form to his inner life in both an African and a European register of expression: an ideal to which the career of Rabearivelo yesterday and of Mazisi Kunene today, afford hopeful pointers.

In formulating this view, my concern is to keep open the possible avenues that history may take us as a people into: we may very well find that our reliance on the European languages will increase, not decrease, with time. Alternatively we may have to turn for our international life to some other language (quite possibly a Far Eastern one). But as long as we retain a sense of the value of our own culture – and much of our fight for political independence has been predicated on just such a consciousness – we must keep the future wide open for our languages in which is lodged our fundamental authenticity.

For all its value and significance at the present time, modern literature in the European languages may very well turn out in the future to occupy a marginal position for us. A new surge of literary creativity may very well lie ahead of us, in which our languages will then be playing their natural role – serving as the vehicle of our modern experience at every level in which that experience manifests itself.

Notes and References

1. The seriousness of the situation can be judged from the attitude of an African literary scholar, expressed in the following remark: 'The bulk of early African literature belongs to the oral category. It is conceivable that progress in electronics will bring another age of oral literature. But for the time being, as long as Marshall McLuhan has not been able to gnaw a mouthful in John Gutenberg's reign over us, we will have to relegate African oral literature to the same liminal confines it occupies in Russian, German, French, British and Irish literature'. (Simon Mpondo, 'Provisional Notes on Literature and Criticism in Africa', in *Présence Africaine*, No. 78, 2éme trimestre, 1971, p. 125). The only comment I'd like to make on the remark is that it ignores not only the

present vitality of the oral literature in the African context, but also
the role it has been able to play in recent times in renewing critical
perspectives on literature in Europe, notably in the work of the Russian
formalists; one has only to cite the names of Propp and Jakobson to
make this point.

2. Consider the following observation by John Spencer, a professional
   linguist, on the place of English in the lives of West Africans: 'English
   is primarily the language of the westernized areas of their lives, an institutional rather than a domestic tongue': West Africa and the English
   Language' in John Spencer (ed.), *The English Language in West Africa*
   (London: Longman, 1971), p. 4. The analysis of Ayo Bambgose, a
   native linguist, on the precise relation between English and the vernaculars in Nigeria (pp. 35–48 of the same volume), confirms Spencer's
   observation, which, it must be said, applies equally to the so-called
   francophone areas of West Africa in relation to French.

   The conclusions of the professional linguists, if not the everyday
   experience of Africans, must therefore cast doubt upon Ali Mazrui's
   confident assertion as follows: 'English is already becoming the first
   language in the functional sense of dominating the lives of many
   Africans': 'Who are the Anglo-Saxons?', Introduction to *The Political
   Sociology of the English Language*, (The Hague: Mouton, 1975), p. 10.
   It becomes clear from the rest of Mazrui's discussion that his observation applies chiefly to the élite, and that the rest of the African population is not worth being taken into consideration on the language
   question.

3. Obi Wali, 'The Dead-end of African Literature', in *Transition*,
   Kampala, No. 11, September 1963, pp. 13–15.

4. The case of Yoruba literature as it is presently developing, in its relation both to the traditional oral forms and to the new literature in
   English by Yoruba authors, as well as to the syncretic art forms such as
   the so-called folk operas, provides an interesting illustration of the point
   being made.

5. Cf. Albert Gérard, *Four African Literatures – Xhosa, Sotho, Zulu,
   Amharic*, (Los Angeles: University of California Press, 1972).

6. Cf. D. S. Izevbaye, 'African Literature Defined', in *Ibadan Studies in
   English*, Vol. 1, No. 1, May–June 1969, pp. 56–67.

7. Cf. R. B. Le Page, *The National Language Question*, (London: Oxford
   University Press, 1964). Le Page focuses his analysis on the language
   problem as it arises in the 'new' nations primarily of South-East Asia,
   but nearly all the points he makes are applicable to Africa.

8. I take a stand here against Randolph Quirk who, in his preface to the
   volume edited by John Spencer already cited, has this to say: 'But the
   position of the English language in West Africa, as a medium of utili-
   tarian communication and of aesthetic expression alike, as the instrument of national unity, of African faith in a corporate, unified future,
   and of contact with the world at large, *is decidedly central to all the
   developments, both political and economic, in which Africa's hopes
   reside.*' (Spencer, op. cit., italics mine). The least that can be said is that
   a statement like this is much too sweeping to be of much value. Besides
   the fact, moreover, that it ignores the strong claims of French and Arabic

in certain areas of Africa to the role being canvassed for English, the Nigerian situation, at least, has evolved in the decade since this statement was made towards a less assured sense of involvement with the English language. And all over Africa today, the interest that is developing in the promotion of the indigenous languages is being in fact fostered by quite practical reasons of the order suggested by Quirk.

9. These are the same factors, of course, that have determined the emergence of ideological concepts such as Négritude and African personality; for all their subjective character, it seems fair to say that these concepts do have a certain relation to an objective truth of African life and forms of cultural expression.

10. Take for instance the following testimony by a Nigerian magistrate of the absurdity of the present policy as it affects the administration of justice: 'I have often felt myself a hypocrite when I sit in court and the interpreter interprets the Yoruba evidence of witnesses to me in Yoruba when I myself speak Yoruba. From experience one finds that the court clerks (with a Class Six or a Class Four pass) are illiterate in Yoruba. Their Yoruba is so inadequate that, for the most part, they make wrong interpretations': A. O. Adeyemi, 'A Day in the Criminal Court', in T. O. Elias (ed.) *The Nigerian Magistrate and the Offender*, (Benin City: Ethiope Publishing Corporation, 1972), p. 27.

11. Cf. Ayo Banjo, 'The English Language and the Nigerian Environment', in *Journal of the Nigerian English Studies Association*, Ibadan, Vol. 4, No. 1, May 1970, pp. 45–51.

12. Pierre van den Berghe, 'Les Langues européennes et les mandarins noirs', in *Présence Africaine*, Paris, No. 68, 4è trimestre, 1968.

13. This is the situation that Sembène Ousmane has so memorably caught in his novel *Le Mandat* and the film made out of it. Published in English as *The Money Order* (London: Heinemann Educational Books, 1972).

14. In his article, 'The Problem of Language in African Creative Writing', in *African Literature Today* No. 3, in *Omnibus Vols. 1–4* (London: Heinemann Educational Books, 1972) B. I. Chukwukere examines this question by contrasting Achebe's creative use of English with the failure of Ekwensi in this regard. Similarly, Peter Young has analysed the faulty use of English registers in the novels of Onuora Nzekwu. ('The Language of West African Literature in English' in Spencer, op. cit., pp. 173 passim.) For further views on the question, see Isidore Okpewho, 'African Fiction Language Revisited', *Journal of African Studies*, Los Angeles, UCLA, Vol. 5, No. 4, 1978, pp. 414–426, and Juliet Okonkwo, 'African Literature and its Language of Expression', in *Africa Quarterly*, Vol. XV, No. IV, pp. 1–11.

15. Cf. Harold Collins, *Amos Tutuola* (New York: Twayne Publishers, 1969), pp. 110–16 and articles in Bernth Lindfors (ed.) *Critical Perspectives on Amos Tutuola* (Washington DC: Three Continents Press 1978; London: Heinemann Educational Books, 1980).

16. I have in mind here the plays of Ola Rotimi in particular which seem to me to provide a striking illustration of this point. But for a more sympathetic view of Rotimi's language, see Akanji Nasiru, 'Ola Rotimi's Search for a Technique' in Kolawole Ogungbesan, (ed.), *New West*

African Literature (London: Heinemann Educational Books, 1979), pp. 21–30.

17. Martin Esslin, 'Two Nigerian Playwrights' in Ulli Beier (ed.), *Introduction to African Literature* (London: Longman, 1967), p. 256.

18. A different kind of difficulty arises when the actors do deliver the text in an impeccable European style, as happened in a production I once saw of Cheik Ndao's *L'Exil d'Alboury* by the Senegalese National Theatre Company, in which the scenic background and non-verbal effects in their African character contrasted sharply with the formalized style, reminiscent of the *Comédie Française*, adopted by the actors in their diction and movements.

19. Peter Young, op. cit., p. 172; emphasis mine.

20. The remarks of St Augustine concerning his dislike of the Greek language and of its literature suggest that a certain ambivalence may well have existed in the minds of individuals assimilated to classical European culture even in his own time – see *Confessions*, Book II, ch. 14 in the Penguin translation by R. S. Pine Coffin. The most celebrated movement of reaction against the dominance of the classical languages remains of course that of the French poets known as the 'Pléiade', whose manifesto was Du Bellay's *Défense et illustration de la langue française*, which has often been evoked by the Négritude writers as a reference for their reaction against French culture – though, ironically, that reaction did not seriously call into question the position of the French language in its formulation.

21. Hannah Arendt, 'Introduction' to Walter Benjamin, *Illuminations*, (London: Fontana Books, 1973), p. 32.

22. Jacques Rabemananjara, 'Les Fondements de notre unité tirés de l'époque coloniale', *Deuxième Congrès des Ecrivains et Artistes noirs, Présence Africaine*, Nos. 24–5, February 1960, pp. 68 & 70.

23. George Steiner, 'Introduction' to *Poem into Poem* (Harmondsworth: Penguin, 1970), p. 27.

24. The point and emphasis of my remark here concern Yeats' deliberate abandonment of a conscious reference to Irish mythology in his later poetry, though I'm aware that critics have continued to discern an Irish quality in all his work–for example F. R. Leavis in his *New Bearings in English Poetry*, and especially A. G. Stock in her authoritative study, *W. B. Yeats: His Poetry and Thought*.

25. Cf. Chinua Achebe, 'Colonialist Criticism' in *Morning Yet on Creation Day* (London: Heinemann Educational Books, 1975), pp. 3–18.

26. Eldred Jones, who looks with favour upon the attempts to employ Krio as a literary language in Sierra Leone, has had to admit that 'the use of Krio as a literary medium has never really got under way ...' ('Krio: An English-based Language of Sierra Leone', in Spencer, op. cit., p. 91). However, Swahili, originally a pidgin (like any of the Romance languages) has developed over the years a significant body of literature, having established itself as a language indigenous to those parts of Africa where it is spoken. Our English-derived pidgins in West Africa have attained no such status for the moment, despite their widespread use along the coast, so that their literary role is confined to comic episodes, as in the Nigerian TV series, *The Village Headmaster*.

27. Wole Soyinka first made the suggestion in an unpublished paper presented at a UNESCO conference held in Dar-es-Salaam in July 1971, and entitled 'The Choice and Use of Language – the Only Answer'. He reiterated the call in his paper at the FESTAC colloquium, 'The Black Scholar', in 1977.

28. J. P. Clark, 'The Legacy of Caliban' in *The Example of Shakespeare* (London: Longman, 1970), pp. 1–38.

29. L. S. Senghor, quoted by Irving Leonard Markovitz, *Léopold Sédar Senghor and the Politics of Négritude* (New York: Atheneum Press and London: Heinemann Educational Books, 1969), p. 62.

30. Achebe has more recently qualified his earlier position on this question in the preface to his collection of essays: 'The fatalistic logic of the unassailable position of English in our literature leaves me more cold now than it did when I first spoke about it ... And yet I am unable to see a significantly different or more emotionally satisfying resolution of that problem.' (*Morning Yet on Creation Day*, op. cit.)

31. Ulli Beier, 'The Conflict of Cultures in West African Poetry', in *Black Orpheus*, Ibadan, No. 12, 1957.

32. Jean-Paul Sartre, 'Orphée noir', *Situations III*.

33. George Steiner, *Extraterritorial* (London: Faber & Faber, 1972).

34. J. B. Pride, *The Social Meaning of Language* (London: Oxford University Press, 1971), p. 23.

Part Two
Négritude and Nationalism

4. What is Négritude?

▼▼

The term 'Négritude' has acquired, in the way it has been used by different writers, a multiplicity of meanings covering so wide a range that it is often difficult to form a precise idea of its particular reference at any one time or in any one usage. The difficulty stems from the fact that, as a movement and as a concept, Négritude found its origin and received a development in a historical and sociological context whose implications for those whom it affected were indeed wide-ranging, and which ultimately provoked in them a multitude of responses that were often contradictory, though always significant. In its immediate reference, Négritude refers to the literary and ideological movement of French-speaking black intellectuals, which took form as a distinctive and significant aspect of the comprehensive reaction of the black man to the colonial situation, a situation that was felt and perceived by black people in Africa and in the New World as a state of global subjection to the political, social and moral domination of the West.

The term has thus been used in a broad and general sense to denote the black world in its historical being, in opposition to the West, and in this way resumes the total consciousness of belonging to the black race,[1] as well as an awareness of the objective historical and sociological implications of that fact. It is perhaps not without significance that Aimé Césaire, who originally coined the term and was the first to use it in his long poem, *Cahier d'un retour au pays natal*[2] should have given the kind of general definition which not only indicates the scope of the black consciousness embraced by the term in its relation to history, but also its extension beyond this contingent factor:

Négritude is the simple recognition of the fact of being black, and the acceptance of this fact, of our destiny as black people, of our history, and our culture.[3]

In this broad perspective, Négritude can be taken to correspond to a certain form of Pan-Negro feeling and awareness, and as a movement, to represent the equivalent on the French-speaking side of what has come to be known as Pan-Africanism.[4] It thus forms a distinctive current of a larger movement of black nationalism, inasmuch as the French-speaking black intellectuals involved in the movement faced special problems in their relationship to French colonial rule, which gave a particular dimension and quality to their reaction. The French-speaking black writers and intellectuals tended therefore to develop a distinctive style and language which, by giving a specific coloration to a general sentiment, and a distinctive orientation to a common preoccupation, came to mark off their reaction to the colonial situation from the form this reaction took among their English-speaking counterparts.

It is with respect to this formal expression of the black nationalist consciousness – or to be more precise, of black cultural nationalism – that a second and closer sense of the term Négritude can be defined. It can be taken here to describe the writings of the French-speaking black intellectuals in their affirmation of a black personality, and to designate the complex of ideas associated with their effort to define a new set of references for the collective experience and awareness of black people. In this sense, Négritude has come to mean the ideology which was either implicit in the production of the literary school associated with the French-speaking black intellectuals or came expressly to be formulated for it.

The body of imaginative and ideological writings produced by the French-speaking black intellectuals represents an extensive exploration of the black condition in both its historical setting and in its direction towards an ultimate significance. The constancy and intensity of this exploration have come to establish in the literature of Négritude a number of characteristic themes and a particularity of tone which give it a certain distinction. In this literature, the preoccupation with the black experience which has provided a common ground base for the imaginative expression of black writers develops into a passionate exaltation of the black race, associated with a romantic myth of Africa.

The immediate polemical significance of this revaluation of Africa merges itself into a quest for new values, for a new spiritual orientation, such that, in the most expressive parts of the literature, the cultivation of Africa formulates itself as an intense imaginative celebration of primal values. It is clear that beyond their immediate preoccupation with the historical experience of the black man as expressed in the leading themes that have emerged in their writings, the French-speaking black writers have been concerned in a fundamental way with seeing through the facts of history as it affected the black man, to the essential relation between the race and African civilization as a more positive determination of its destiny. A distinctive vision of Africa and the black man, and of his relation to the world, thus stands at the very heart of the literature of Négritude and informs it in a fundamental way, provides what can be said to constitute the 'mental structure'[5] that underlies the imaginative expression of the French-speaking black writers, and which emerges with a sharp clarity in the ideological writings. The rehabilitation of Africa which stands out as the central project of Négritude thus represents a movement towards the recovery of a certain sense of spiritual integrity by the black man, as the definition of a black collective identity, as well as of a new world view, derived from a new feeling for the African heritage of values and of experience.

In this respect, the writings of Senghor afford the most coherent expression of Négritude considered as a body of ideas relative to the identity and the destiny of the black man, and to his experience of the world. Indeed, in a very narrow sense, Négritude can be considered to be the philosophy of one man, Senghor, whose efforts have been outstanding in the extension of what started out as the ideological stand of a historical class into a comprehensive world-view.

In considering Senghor's theory of Négritude, it might be useful to begin by setting it against the view of Jean-Paul Sartre, whose contribution to the formulation of the concept can be said to have been determinant in its establishment.

It is common knowledge that Sartre was the first, in his now celebrated essay 'Orphée noir', to offer an extended exposition of the concept.[6] However he was much less concerned with defining Négritude than with identifying and clarifying the collective sentiment which ran through the poetry of the black writers whom he was introducing, and with exploring its historical possibilities. The fact is that, for Sartre, Négritude appeared as a historical phenomenon – a contingent stage in a total historical process. It is simply an articulated moment in the movement of the black consciousness breaking through the bounds of its historical and sociological determination towards the recovery of its original, existential freedom. This is why he describes Négritude as 'the weak stage of a dialectical progression', a stage which is to be transcended in the synthesis defined by him as 'the realization of the human society without racism'.[7]

Senghor's conception of Négritude lacks this relative dimension. For him, Négritude is an inner state of the black man, and lies outside the historical process. It is first and foremost a distinctive mode of being and of existence, particular to the black man, which can be deduced from his way of life – and which constitutes his *identity*, in the original sense of the word.

The opposition of Sartre's viewpoint to that of Senghor serves to emphasize the fact that Senghor's formulation of Négritude stems from an absolute vision of the Negro race. It remains true however that there is a sense in which this vision is historical, that is, determined by circumstances. The external factor which defines the black man in the modern world is the colonial situation – domination by the white man, with all the moral and psychological implications that this fact entailed. It is not likely that the acute awareness of race manifested by Senghor could have developed outside of this historical fact, for in its most immediate aspect, this awareness is born of a revolt against the practical implications of the colonial relationship. The point of departure of Senghor's Négritude is the fact that for him, black peoples all over the world form a community of experience, due to their peculiar relationship with the western world. Thus, Senghor's Négritude defines itself, in its immediate aspects, as a preoccupation with the fact of racial belonging, and as an effort to clarify its particular significance. It is this aspect that he refers to as the 'subjective Négritude' – the assumption of one's blackness as the external mark of an original and fundamental identity.

The racial component of modern colonialism establishes an objective dichotomy which marks off the white colonizer from his non-white subject. In the case of the black man, this historical fact is underlined by the biological reality of race in such a striking way that it has lent itself easily to its symbolic projections in colonialist ideology. The opposition of races appears to be the overriding character of the colonial relationship. It engendered in most colonized peoples the immediate association of the political with the racial – thus the colonized population appears also as a community of blood. This same kind of association enters into Senghor's race consciousness. What is more, there are indications in his writings that he tends towards a racial explanation of history, towards the view that the particular disposition of each race explains its collective expression in history.[8] The underlying assumption of this explanation is that each race is endowed with a distinctive nature and embodies, in its civilization, a particular spirit. Each race has its genius, and is apt for a particular kind of expression conforming with its genius. And Senghor postulates just such a nature, such a genius, for the Negro race. The whole edifice of Senghor's Négritude rests on this foundation: the idea of a collective soul of the black race constituting the unifying concept of 'the collective personality of black peoples' which Senghor makes synonymous with Négritude.[9]

It is not without interest to observe at this point the parallel between this conception and the racial doctrines propounded in Europe, presenting the Negro as an inherently inferior being to the white man, and which provided the ultimate ideological *rationale* for Western imperialism. As an ideological movement, Négritude is one of the answers to such doctrines, and presents itself, in this light, indeed as a counter-myth. But it is important to note that for Senghor, the answer does not consist in a systematic rejection of Western racist theories, but rather in a modification of the terms in which they are set out, and in a redefinition of the very notion of race. Thus Senghor's conception of the black man contains important elements taken over from these theories, but in his system, they are given a new perspective. Thus while accepting the objective reality of race as indicative of a specific, inner identity and aptitude, Senghor rejects the idea that the black man is inferior in his human quality to the white man. But perhaps the really significant departure that he makes from the traditional racialist view in the West initiated notably by Gobineau is his rejection of the idea that the races are so constituted as to be mutually exclusive of one another. As he says, 'Race is a reality – I do not mean racial purity. There is difference, but not inferiority or antagonism.'[10]

It is also important to note that although Senghor's notion of race implies an acceptance of the biological evidence by the physical differentiation of members of the human family, this notion seems to have more a cultural than biological component. There is a constant association in his thought between race and culture, between the physical constitution of a people and their outlook on the world which, for Senghor, is the result of evolution within an environment over a considerable period. He once defined culture, in one of his early essays, as 'the racial reaction of Man upon his milieu, tending towards an intellectual and moral balance between Man and his milieu'.[11] The spirit of a people would then appear to be the special quality of the intellectual and moral outlook evolved by the group in response to the solicitations – if not to the rigorous pressures – of the milieu. In his work, *Les Fondements de l'Africanité* Senghor has provided the most thorough illustration of this point of view. The first part of the work is devoted to an examination of the evolution of man on the African continent and the consequent emergence of a spirit of African civilization as he sees it. The essay throws a sharp light upon Senghor's conception of race, and in particular of the Negro race. The black man is for him the end product of a long process of adaptation to the African environment, a process that has not only fashioned him into a branch of the human family, but also determined his inner disposition and his total world view.[12]

The primary factor then, in Senghor's conception of the Negro, appears in this view to be the association of the race with Africa. This association defines for all black peoples a common cultural denominator which is at the basis of their various and often disparate forms of expression. The fact of blackness, or Négritude, consists essentially in the participation, in an immediate way or at a second remove, in a fundamental African spirit of civilization.

In this spiritual conception of the Negro race, the position of the Afro-American acquires a particular – and I daresay, strategic – significance. African cultural survivals in the New World have frequently been adduced as evidence of the persistence of an African nature in the New World Negro, and this argument has served black nationalists on both sides of the Atlantic as the emotional lever of their reaction against the West, and even more, as one of the principal ideological planks of the Pan-Negro movement.[13] It is hardly surprising therefore that Senghor's vision of the race should embrace the Afro-American. The significance of Africanisms in the New World resides, in his view, not so much in the particular socio-logical articulations which they present, but in their global configurations. Negro sub-cultures in America are held by him to be derivations from a basic African culture, they represent varied extensions and differentiated manifestations of an original spirit of African culture, which, as he says, 'emigrated to America, but remained intact in its style, if not in its ergo-logical elements.'[14] From Africa, the Negro has inherited those mental traits which, more than the biological factor, establish an original bond between him and the African. Senghor has made in this respect an explicit observation: 'What strikes me about the Negroes in America is the per-manence not of the physical but of the psychic characteristics of the Negro-African, despite race-mixing, despite the new environment'.[15]

To sum up then on this point, Senghor's conception is founded upon a total, if not exclusive, vision of the black race. Although this vision is in-spired by the historical situation of black peoples, and involves a recog-nition of the biological factor as conferring an external unity to the race, the determining principle of the collective personality of black peoples is their spiritual association with African culture. Beyond the common his-torical experience and beneath the biological factor, what gives an essen-tial unity to black peoples in Senghor's conception is their participation in a common cultural and spiritual essence. The ultimate foundation of black identity, then, is the African heritage. This heritage constitutes what Senghor has called 'objective Négritude', as evidenced by the definition he has most consistently proposed – 'the sum total of the cultural values of Africa.' Senghor's Négritude is a unified concept of African culture, seen as a global entity, and as opposed to other cultures associated with other

races. It is a concept that postulates the underlying unity of the various
forms of cultural expression in black Africa, and which explains the objective difference that separates the black African from the European or
the Asian, despite their common humanity.

Senghor's aim in his exposition is to explain what constitutes the
difference as far as the black African is concerned, and to demonstrate the
originality of his culture and by implication of Negro subcultures in the
New World: the originality and the *validity* of their fundamental spirit.
The core of Senghor's theory of Négritude therefore takes the form of a
systematic exposition of the values of traditional Africa as they are embodied in the thought systems and social institutions of African societies,
and especially as they inform the mentality of the African.

The double motivation of Senghor's intellectual efforts has a direct bearing upon his whole method and approach in his exposition of Négritude,
which is aimed not only at demonstrating the human value and significance
of traditional African values, but indeed at establishing their appropriate-
ness to the experience and the situation of the modern African, and ultimately of contemporary man. Senghor's advocacy of Négritude does not
imply therefore a simple return to outmoded customs and institutions –
the point needs to be stressed, I think – but rather to an original spirit
which gave meaning to the life of the individual in traditional African
society.

The fact then is that Senghor's theory of Négritude is not so much a
descriptive analysis of African culture as a synthetic vision. Rather than
an empirical, sociological investigation of African institutions, his method
consists in a personal interpretation of African values, and in a statement,
in philosophical terms, of their informing 'spirit'. This is the point, I believe, of his paper read to the First Congress of Negro Writers and Artists
held in Paris in 1956, which bears the highly instructive title: 'L' esprit
de la civilisation ou les lois de la culture negro-africaine'.[16] Senghor makes
a distinction, as we have seen, between *culture*, which is a people's attitude
to the world, a 'collective consciousness', and *civilization*, which is the
structuring of collective life in accordance with this consciousness – its
objective correlative, to borrow Eliot's term. More recently, Senghor has
put the matter in explicit terms, when he defined 'culture' as the *psychic*
constitution which in each people explains its 'civilization', or in other
words, 'a certain manner *of feeling and thinking, of expressing itself and
of action.*' This definition is in keeping with what we have observed to be
Senghor's conception of race, particularly as he adds, in characteristic
fashion: 'And this "certain manner", this *character* . . . is the symbiosis of
the influences of geography and of history, of race and ethnic belonging'.[17]
In this view, to understand a 'civilization' which is the social and objective

embodiment of a culture, to comprehend it in its essence, one needs to go beyond the one to the other, to seek out the organizing principle of the former in the latter.

This is the perspective in which Senghor situates his formulation of Négritude, which presents itself as the conceptual exposition of a distinctive African mode of consciousness and the elaboration of a specific African vision of the universe. His method is meant to go beyond an account of African values and to move rather towards a fuller explication of their profound essence. This means, in other words, that his theory of Négritude is largely a speculative exploration of the African social and spiritual universe in an endeavour to discover and bring to light the fundamental world-view that underlies the collective consciousness of the African. This brings us to a consideration of what is certainly the very foundation of Senghor's theory of Négritude – his effort to provide an explication of the original psychology of the African as the constitutive element and determining factor in his consciousness and mode of apprehension.

Senghor has singled out, as the dominant trait of this consciousness, its emotive disposition. He presents the African as being, in his physical constitution, a being of emotion, or as he puts it, 'one of the worms created on the Third Day . . . a pure sensory being'.[18] The African's response to the external world in Senghor's conception is an upsurge of the sensibility, at the level of the nervous system, an intense, engulfing experience in which the whole organic being of the self is involved. Senghor establishes an association between the material and the psychic, an association that he holds to be particularly acute and intimate in the make-up of the African. 'Our psychology is the expression of our physiology, even though the former, in turn, conditions the latter and transcends it,'[19] he has remarked, and he explains the extreme sensibility of the African by the action of the hot and humid climate of his tropical milieu upon his nervous system which has resulted in a 'Negro temperament'.[20] He thus postulates a total coincidence of the African's nervous reactions with his psychic operations to explain his affective mode of apprehension. The psycho-physiological constitution of the African determines his immediate response to external reality, his total absorption of the object into the innermost recesses of his subjectivity: 'By the very fact of his physiology,' writes Senghor, 'the Negro has reactions which are more *lived*, in the sense that they are more direct and concrete expressions of the sensation and of the stimulus, and so of the object itself, with all its original qualities and power.'[21] It is this disposition, stemming from his physiological equipment, that one observes in the African's highly developed sense of rhythm – in Senghor's words, 'organic sense of rhythm'. However, notwithstanding the profound association between his constitution and his emotivity, the African's response to reality is not a mere instinctive reaction, but is an expression of an intention. Senghor explains the process as follows: 'But the movement of excitement, provoked by the object, is not a mechanical movement nor indeed a physiological movement. *It is the subject who is moved.* He reacts to the object, but with his own particular orientation and rhythm: his own subjective style, which he imposes upon the object.'[22] In other words, the emotive response of the African is an act of cognition, in which the subject and the object enter into an organic and dynamic relationship, and in which intense perception through the senses culminates in the conscious apprehension of reality. Thus, as Senghor says, 'the African's spirituality is rooted in his sensuous nature: in his physiology'.[23] His mode of apprehension involves a warm, living dialectic of consciousness and reality. Emotion then is the accession to a higher state of reality.[24]

As can be seen, Senghor derives from his exposition of the distinctive psychology of the Negro-African, what one might call a theory of knowledge implicit in the African's attitude to the world, a black epistemology. The African's apprehension amounts to 'living the object' in the depth of his soul, penetrating through sensuous perception to its essence: 'Knowledge then is not the superficial creation of discursive reason, cast over reality, but discovery through emotion: less discovery than re-discovery. Knowledge coincides, here, with the *being* of the object in its discontinuous and indeterminate reality'.[25] And it is this sensuous grasp of reality that Senghor refers to as 'intuition'.

It is not surprising that Senghor's theory of the African's method of knowledge and his aesthetic theory should be intimately related, and even coincide. It is certainly not a matter of chance that his philosophy of Négritude is a spiritualist one, and that the terms he uses are far from being the precise, positive and sharply defined ones that one would expect in an analytical exposition: for even in his theorizing, Senghor remains the poet. The significant factor here is that, in his theory, Senghor associates knowledge with the imaginative faculty. The African's attitude to the world precludes objective intellection, so that his mind works less by abstraction than by intuitive understanding. Thus, as Senghor says, he is 'sensitive to the spiritual and not the intellectual qualities of ideas'[26] – hence the privileged role of image and symbol in the expressive schemes of African civilization. Senghor has provided a striking illustration of what he means by this observation:

The African is moved not so much by the outward appearance of the object as by its profound reality, less by the *sign* than by its *sense*. What moves him in a dancing mask, through the medium of the image and the rhythm, is a new vision of the 'god'. What moves him in water is not that it flows, is liquid and blue, but that it washes and purifies. The physical appearance, however intensely perceived in all its particulars by the neuro-sensory organs, indeed, through the very intensity of such perception, is no more than the sign of the object's real significance.[27]

Artistic expression thus becomes the prime mediator of the African consciousness. It is singularly in artistic creation that he participates most fully with the world of creation and it is through the emotion engendered by the symbolic content of artistic form that he seizes upon the ultimate significance of reality. Thus artistic expression has for him a metaphysical import. This is the point of Senghor's essay, 'L'esthétique négro-africaine' in which he describes the place of rhythm (taken as a paradigm of African artistic feeling) in the world-view of African civilization in these terms:

> Rhythm is the architecture of being, the internal dynamics which gives it form, the system of waves which it sends out towards *Others*. It expresses itself through the most material, the most sensuous means: lines, surfaces, colours, volumes in architecture, sculpture and painting; accents in poetry and music, movements in dance. But in doing so, it guides all this concrete reality towards the light of the spirit. For the Negro-African, it is in the same measure that rhythm is embodied in the senses that it illuminates the spirit.[28]

Moreover artistic expression and religious feeling are inseparably linked, in so far as art is conceived primarily as an epiphany of the sacred, of the cosmic energy with which the visible world is permeated. Art is the imaginative restitution of the fundamental network of relationships which exist between the various manifestations of this cosmic energy. This is the foundation of the African's mystical participation in the universe. Senghor has written:

> The Black man had succeeded in perceiving the harmonious order of nature. Then, thanks to his sense and to his intuitive intelligence, to his hands and to his techniques, he had integrated himself into it. To perceive the harmonious order of Nature, that is to grasp the correspondences which bind one to the other, the cosmic forces which underlie the universe, but at the same time, those which bind nature to man: the exterior, physical universe to the moral, interior universe. *It is the expression of these correspondences that constitutes the analogical image: the symbol.*[29]

The essential idea in Senghor's aesthetic theory is that the African arrives at a profound knowledge of the world by feeling the material world to the cosmic mind of which it is an emanation, to the transcendental reality underlying it – what Senghor calls, in a modification of Breton's term, 'la sous-réalité'. The role of emotion in the theory of Négritude culminates in Senghor's enunciation of a hypothetic Negro-African *cogito*, which he

explicitly opposes to the traditional enunciation handed down to the West
by Descartes. Senghor's text runs thus:

> 'I think, therefore I am', wrote Descartes, the European *par excellence*.
> 'I feel, I dance the other' the Negro-African would say. He does not
> need, like Descartes, a 'tool-word' as my old master Ferdinand Brunot
> used to term it, a conjunction, in order to realize his *being*, but an *object
> complement*. He does not need to think but to live the other by dancing
> him.[30]

But Senghor maintains that the African's experience is a reflective and
conscious act and therefore merits the name of reason: the creative reason
of imaginative intuition. It is different in kind from the logical intelligence
of the European, because it does not follow the canons of thought which
regulate the latter. The distinction between Europe and Africa is drawn
by Senghor in terms of the cultural form that, traditionally, mental operations have taken in their respective civilizations, and of their opposed
directions, hence his well-known formula: 'Classical European reason is
analytical and makes use of the object. African reason is intuitive and
participates in the object.'[31]

It is in the light of this spiritualist conception of the African mode of
consciousness that Senghor interprets the cosmologies and social institutions of traditional Africa. The spirit of African civilization is resumed in a
Negro-African ontology, which identifies *being* with life, with 'vital
force'.[32] This vitalist philosophy which Senghor attributes to Africa explains the traditional forms of religious experience and expression on the
continent. By his emotive and mystical disposition, and by the very fact
of his intimate insertion into an organic milieu, the African is naturally a
religious being, in whom the sense of the sacred is acutely alive.

He communes directly with nature and with the elements, and through
these, with the absolute fountain-head of vital force, God himself. African
animism and totemism, and their elaboration in myth, represent the ob-
jectified forms of emotive participation in the cosmos. This is how Senghor
has more lately put the matter: 'There are three realities in presence:
man, visible nature – animals, plants, minerals – and the invisible cosmic
forces expressed by the sentient forms of nature. "African" mysticism is
thus the impulse towards union with the cosmic forces, and beyond, with
the force of forces, *God* ... The privileged mode, the most adequate mode
of this union is myth.'[33]

African society is in turn structured on the basis of this mystical world
view. Society is a complex network of individualized incarnations of vital
force, and social participation is at bottom a complex of relationships between these. The family, which is the focal unit of society, is primarily a
religious, mystical union, and extends into the clan, 'the sum of all persons,

living and dead, who acknowledge a common ancestor'.[34] The larger
society as such is constituted by a polycentric (as opposed to serial) network of families and clans; African society is thus, essentially, not so much
a community of persons, as 'a communion of souls'. All social relationships and activities, down to economic life, are informed in greater or
lesser measure by this religious vision. 'Among Africans,' writes Senghor,
'man is bound to the object of collective ownership by the legal bonds of
custom and tradition; over and above all by a mystical bond.'[35]

The line that runs through Senghor's exposition of African values to his
doctrine of African socialism passes through this interpretation of the
traditional system of social organization in Africa. The theory of Négritude
that forms the basis of the doctrine can be resumed at this point as a comprehensive interpretation of a distinctive African approach to the universe,
and of the way of life founded upon it.

Our examination of Senghor's theory of Négritude cannot be complete
without some mention of his doctrine of African socialism which is its
social expression and which is intended to give it practical significance.
The doctrine of African socialism itself is conceived by Senghor as an updating of the traditional African world view, a translation of Négritude
into the modern conditions of the technological age on one hand, and on
the other, of the nation-state, the modern unit of political association. It
is not however so much a practical programme of action as a mental projection into the future, the necessary preliminary reflection upon the conditions of meaningful collective action.

The example of European socialism inspires Senghor to elaborate a
parallel system of social philosophy which is African in its references.
Marxism in particular offers a convenient jumping-off ground from which
to review African realities in the effort to rethink them and to determine
the role of the values of the past in the modern world.

There is a certain paradox in the fact that Senghor's application of the
Marxist method to African realities engenders in him the dissatisfaction
that he has described in these terms:

> What embarrassed us in Marxism was, along with its atheism, a certain
> disdain for spiritual values: this discursive reason pushed to its outer-
> most limits, turned into a materialism without warmth, into a blind
> determinism.[36]

Despite this dissatisfaction, Senghor's *critique* of Marxism does not
imply a total rejection, for he recognizes that it provides a dynamic vision
of man in his relationship to nature, and as a consequence, a liberating
view of social relationships in which the primary concern is the fulfilment

of human virtualities. He believes however that Marxism is a theory that needs to be completed in the light cf new developments since it was propounded, especially in the sciences, and modified to suit the African situation.

In reality, however, Senghor's African socialism marks a break with Marxist theory, turning rather to the philosophy of Pierre Teilhard de Chardin for its inspirational groundwork. The exact connection between socialism and Teilhard de Chardin's philosophy is not easy to grasp, but its fascination for Senghor can be explained on three closely related counts. First, it offers a prospective ideal almost as impressive as Marxism, with the added advantage of being grounded in an appealing scientific theory. Secondly, Teilhard de Chardin's theory of convergence – the progressive development of a higher form of consciousness from all forms of life and experience – offers scope for the participation of African values in a universal civilization. Thirdly, Teilhard de Chardin restores in his vision of man, the spiritual dimension which Senghor considered lacking in Marxist philosophy. His reconciliation of science with religion, which was felt as a liberating influence by Catholic intellectuals, may also have appealed to Senghor, who is himself a Catholic. But he experienced this influence less as a Catholic than as the theoretician of Négritude, the advocate of a spiritualist outlook on the world, as is shown by this comment he makes of Teilhard de Chardin's ideas: 'Beyond material well-being, the spiritual maximum-being – the flowering of the soul, of the intelligence and of the heart – is confirmed as the ultimate goal of human activity.'[37] The specific contribution of Teilhard de Chardin's philosophy to Senghor's African socialism is more explicitly indicated in another passage: 'Teilhard's *socialization*, our socialism is nothing but the technical and spiritual organization of human society by the intelligence and the heart.'[38] In other words, African socialism is an ideal in which the spiritual values of traditional Africa are integrated into the process of modernization through new forms of social and political organization and technological progress: a synthesis of Négritude and Western socialism.

However, Senghor's African socialism does not offer more than the idea of social and political action. His socialism does not have the concrete quality of parallel ideas evolved in English-speaking Africa. It lacks the pragmatic edge of Nkrumah's pronouncements or the urgent conviction of Nyerere's manifestoes. Nonetheless, taken as an extension of his theory of Négritude and in the historical context in which Senghor's work and thinking are situated, it is not without a certain relevance and significance.

In order to appreciate this significance, it is necessary to view Senghor's theory of Négritude not only against the background of historical factors, which gave it birth, but also to see it in its character as a mental projection. The terms in which Senghor formulates his theory of Négritude resound with distinct echoes of the work of a whole group of writers, thinkers and scholars in the West who can be situated within a single perspective – that of the anti-intellectual current in European thought. The specific derivation of some of his key concepts is easily identifiable – his notion of 'vital force' for example, can be attributed to Father Placide Tempels' now classic study of Bantu philosophy,[39] while that of 'participation', as well as his distinction between the traditional forms of the collective mentality in Europe and Africa respectively, owes much to the work of Lucien Lévy-Bruhl.[40] Both Lévy-Bruhl and Tempels derive in turn from Bergson: the former explored in his work the anthropological implications of Bergson's reflections, whereas the latter applied his categories, particularly the concept of the 'life surge' (*élan vital*) specifically to the Bantu. It is not only in this remote way that Bergson figures in Senghor's Négritude but as a direct influence. To Bergson, Senghor owes the concept of 'intuition' on which revolves his explication of the African mind and consciousness. Bergson abolished with this concept the positivist dichotomy of subject-object, and proposed a new conception of authentic knowledge as immediacy of experience, the organic involvement of the subject with the object of his experience. It is largely the epistemology of Bergson that Senghor has adopted in his formulation of Négritude.[41]

Besides, Bergson's philosophy is itself the systematic conceptual articulation of what one might call the 'Romantic vision'. In the intellectual writings of Rousseau and Coleridge, this vision had been intimated, and forms the ideological framework of the Romantic movement itself. Art, this movement contends, gives a special insight into reality, and the imagination is a faculty that properly exercised can lead to truth, a deeper truth indeed than that revealed by science. It is this faculty that Wordsworth exalts in this passage from the *Prelude*:

> The imagination which, in truth,
> Is but another name for absolute power,
> And clearest insight, amplitude of mind,
> And reason in her most exalted mood.

In France, the Romantic movement produced the later Hugo, and especially Baudelaire, whose theory of correspondence foreshadows certain aspects of Bergson's metaphysics, and whose influence on Senghor is readily suggested by its application in Senghor's own explication of African forms of religious experience.

These references point up a highly significant fact – the denial within the European intellectual tradition itself of the universal and absolute

value of the classical philosophy, the reaction against what came to be increasingly felt as the narrow framework of experience that it offered. These
movements and doctrines represented an effort to establish a conception of
life fuller and perhaps more fundamental than would be embraced within
the rationalist world-view, hence the quest for larger horizons beyond
Western civilization which took poets, artists and even thinkers first to the
East, and then to 'primitive' culture – it was for this reason that Jules
Monnerot called the surrealists 'modern primitives'.[42]

The immediate importance of this anti-intellectual and romantic development is that it not only secured an opening within the Western intellectual tradition for a serious consideration of doctrines which took as
their frame of reference the non-rational, but also provided a conceptual
framework as well for their formulation. Two equally valid paths to knowledge are thus recognized: the logical and the imaginative, whose language is metaphor, or in the expression of Susanne Langer, 'presentational
symbolism'.[43] The so-called philosophies of life, based on a dynamic and
spiritualist conception of experience, proceed from this recognition.

Senghor's theory of Négritude bears a close affinity to this current in
European thought and in particular shares with them a number of characteristics which Karl Mannheim has analysed as distinctive of 'conservative
thought' in Europe.[44] It is a reaction against the rationalist view of the
world and its practical implications in terms of a certain form of organization of social reality associated with bourgeois capitalism – the trauma
of the colonial experience represents in this light a historical parallel to
the spiritual disarray of the old order in Europe in the face of the ascendancy of the bourgeois ideology and way of life. In much the same way
therefore that the romantic and conservative ideology sought to provide
a justification for the old order, Négritude also presents itself as an effort
at re-affirming the values of a society and of a historical group threatened
by the incursion of a new order. The reaction to bourgeois rationalism represented by Négritude acquires however a particular dimension in the
very fact that the implied conflict between two world views is engaged in
respect of two opposed cultures and races. The recourse to traditionalism
in Négritude is in itself the defence of a culture that had a distinct and
separate existence, the affirmation of a positive difference and of a plural-
ism that, in its profound motivation, serves as a shield against the aggres-
sive ethnocentrism that necessarily went with the imperialist venture of
Europe in Africa. Thus apart from the fact that the invocation of African
tradition serves as a means of providing moral and psychological refuge
for a westernized élite, it expresses perhaps something more than mere
nostalgic attachment to the values of an old way of life, it registers as well
a sense of discovery of a new perspective on life and experience, and the

exploratory movement towards the constitution of a mode of thought that is at once modern and African in its references, a reconciliation and synthesis of the traditional European approach and the African mode of apprehension.

At all events there is hardly any doubt that without the developments in the European intellectual context referred to above, and without the greater measure of tolerance towards non-western cultures that western scholarship and thinking had begun to foster, especially anthropology, Senghor would probably not have been in a position to formulate his theory of Négritude with the same degree of assurance that one observes in his writings. What is more, Senghor has affirmed that Europe itself is beginning to abandon its dominant intellectual standpoint even within those disciplines that have been traditionally its principal foundations, the natural sciences. And it is highly significant to note that his most general statement of the relative merits of logical intelligence and the imaginative intuition occurs in a discussion of one of the most general and characteristic of African forms of imaginative expression, the folktale:

> Discursive reason merely stops at the surface of things, it does not penetrate their hidden resorts, which escape the lucid consciousness. Intuitive reason is alone capable of an understanding that goes beyond appearances, of taking in total reality.[45]

What Senghor claims then, for the spirit of African civilization as interpreted by him, is that it is not only valid in its own right, but indeed, that it is more in consonance with the profound aspirations of man. If Senghor's Négritude can be considered as primarily a comprehensive interpretation of African values in their traditional setting, it also represents an effort to derive a modern philosophy with a relevance for the contemporary African from the traditional background and indeed, a distinctive world-view with a meaning for all mankind. Thus within its total range, Senghor's thought moves from an individual appreciation of the African heritage to what amounts to a personal African-derived system of ideas. Thus his exposition of the African world view is presented as the basis of a new Humanism, as an ideal offered for a new understanding of man and the universe.

It seems undeniable that the Négritude movement, especially in its literary expression through the works of poets and novelists such as Césaire, Damas, Birago Diop, Cheikh Hamidou Kane and Senghor himself, provided a sense of meaning to the development of African nationalism, and ultimately of a broader black consciousness. But besides the fact that it articulated deep-seated needs and projected a certain attitude of a new positive orientation to history on the part of the black man, Négritude as an ideology also provided a channel of self-reflection for the black man in the effort of its adherents to define a fundamental Africanism as a reference for black expression in modern times. It is in this respect that it appears to have thrown up a number of problems which continue to be the source of a deep controversy in African and black intellectual circles.

The criticisms of Négritude began early in its career – the opening shot was fired in 1952 with the publication of the essay 'La Négritude: réalité ou mystification' by Albert Franklin.[46] This essay was in fact a review of Sartre's 'Orphée noir' but anticipates most of the objections that have been brought up against Négritude in its further development by Senghor. In considering these objections, as they continue to be made up to the present time, it seems clear that while the historical necessity of a black reaction of the kind represented by Négritude is accepted, the terms in which the concept has been elaborated especially by Senghor give rise to uneasiness.

The objections to Négritude fall into two broad categories, according to whether they relate to the theoretical formulation of the concept, or to its practical implications. On the theoretical plane, the very foundation of Senghor's theory of Négritude, the definition of a basic psychology of the African, has been called into question. The correspondence of certain aspects of Senghor's ideas of the basic African personality with Western racist theories and with the 'primitive mentality' of Lévy-Bruhl seems to have cast a suspect light in the eye of most critics upon the value of Senghor's theory, and seems to them to leave intact in any case the racial hierarchy established by the colonial ideology.[47] The validity of Senghor's postulation of an emotive disposition of the African is denied in particular, on the grounds of its facile and unscientific attribution of a racial basis to mental processes, and the suggestion that it seems to carry of an inherent incapacity of the African to employ and to penetrate discursive forms of intellectual operations. This particular objection is linked to another criticism of Senghor's theory which relates to the character of African culture and society as they emerge in his writings. Senghor's emphasis on the dominant religious outlook of the African, and his idea of a mystical constitution of African society, have been rejected as both unscientific and too general to be valid. Senghor's conception is seen as being the mere projection of a poetic attitude on African realities, and where such a projection seems even to bear a relation to the facts on the ground, the conception is attacked as a static and incomplete view of Africa. It is pointed out that what appears to be a particular trait of African society is no more than a feature of all traditional societies in which the level of technical development is still too low to allow for a sufficient detachment from the state of nature, and for a rational mastery of the natural environment which excludes a recourse to the mystical and the supernatural.[48]

Further, the very idea of a unified African culture on which the theory of Négritude relies for much of its force, has come under attack. The varied character of the different cultures and societies on the continent is stressed in this objection, so that the cultural concept that underlies Senghor's theory is shown to be at variance with the sociological realities which the theory attempts to reflect. Perhaps the most serious objection to Négritude arises also from this particular criticism – its abstract and absolute conception of a black essence related to a certain spirit immanent in African culture, with the suggestion of a constancy of such an essence impervious to the historical process. Stanislas Adotevi has summarized this objection in the following observation:

> Négritude pre-supposes a rigid essence of the black man unaffected by time. To this permanence is added a specificity which neither sociological factors, historical evolution nor the realities of geography bear out. It makes of the black people the same everywhere and through all time.[49]

However it is particularly with respect to its practical implications that the theory of Négritude has come under the severest attack; indeed, the theoretical objections seem primarily to be commanded by the practical and political significance which Senghor's direct involvement with African affairs has given to his theory. The most persistent criticism in this connection concerns what appears to be a practical divergence between the revolutionary stance adopted by Négritude as an original project, and the politics pursued by its most outstanding theoretician. From this angle of vision, even the formulation of Senghor's theory is seen as a strategy of compromise with the colonial master,[50] and the post-independence development as a mask for a policy of accommodation to a neo-colonial situation. This has led to an impatience with the whole movement on the part of the younger generation of black intellectuals, an attitude to which the young Caribbean dramatist, Boukman, has given voice in these terms, 'It is no service to African culture to cling like an oyster to notions overtaken by history. The concept of Négritude which was revolutionary in the forties and fifties is today only fit for the museum of literature'.[51]

From the practical viewpoint, the most important reproach levelled against Négritude concerns what is taken to be its lack of content, especially as regards its extension into the concept of African socialism. The criticism that Négritude itself proceeds from an insufficient understanding of the dynamic nature of African sociological realities finds its corollary in this objection on the practical plane. Because it postulates a narrow and rigid framework of social expression in traditional African culture, it is also felt to offer little possibility of meaningful social action in the

present.[52] The recourse to traditionalism, to the values of the past as a
global reference, gives Négritude the character of a conservativism which
is felt to be at variance with the exigencies of the moment. And the
spiritualist terms in which even the theory of African socialism is cast in
Senghor's writings give his ideas an air of unreality that seem to bear no
relation to the practical issues of socio-economic and technological development. Négritude and its derivative, African socialism, thus appear to be
not only inadequate as forms of response to the demands of the times, but
indeed as a form of escape from immediate tasks and ultimately as an
ideological veil cast by the new ruling élite upon its interests.

The objections to Négritude summarized here, bring a sharp critical
focus to bear upon the theoretical and practical limitations of Senghor's
theory, and have contributed to the general distrust with which the concept seems today to be regarded in black intellectual circles. There is no
doubt that some of these objections are valid, and it would be difficult to
sustain a convincing defence of the theory on the individual points on
which they are based. It seems to me, however, that these objections do
not take sufficient account of the historical context in which Négritude as
a movement was born and the particular circumstances in which the concept was evolved into a system by Senghor, and thus miss its essential
significance as the effort of a particular historical group to project themselves beyond their immediate experience and situation. In other words,
what really counts here is the need felt by the deprived group for a sustain-
ing vision of the collective self and of its destiny. This need has perhaps
never been felt so acutely as it was by the colonized peoples of modern
times, and especially by black people, devalued by colonial domination
and demoralized by the racial ideology with which it was buttressed. The
historical connections of Négritude with the various movements involved
in black nationalism since the nineteenth century in particular show that
it forms part of an on-going process of self-reflection by the black man,
and indeed, it can be considered in many ways as the extreme point so far
reached in that process. It represents the ultimate limit of the ethnocentrism fostered in the black people by their historical relationship with
the white race. For the African in particular, the comprehensive scope of
Senghor's theory corresponds precisely to what Robert July has defined
as the significance of modern African thought when he describes it as 'a
thorough-going examination of man and society in West Africa.'[53]

The extension of Négritude into a social philosophy further emphasizes
this significance of self-reflection by the black man in its historical context.
The quest for identity, which is the motive power of cultural nationalism
on the part of the Westernized African, impels him to work out an alternative frame of reference for thought and action to that offered by Western

civilization, one that bears a direct relation to his original cultural background. The political factor of nationalist feeling dictates the immediate reaction that initiates the process, but what is involved is, ultimately, the creation of a meaningful perspective of collective life and action for the African people in the modern world.

Senghor's Négritude is an important effort in this direction. The theory may not be a practical programme. More, it may appear as purely a thing of the mind, without any basis in the empirical, sociological realities of Africa: an idealist vision. These are criticisms that can be justifiably levelled against Senghor. But these are also criticisms that can be made against any theory at all, any system of ideas. What the polemics that have raged around Négritude indicate, apart from certain misunderstandings, indeed the irony of the whole controversy around Négritude, is that it represents and is perceived to be a significant aspect of the intellectual adventure of the black man, more specifically, a significant stage in the development of modern African consciousness.

There is thus a sense in which this controversy has been important, insofar as it reflects a profound engagement of African minds upon the fundamental question of the African being in history, a question with which Négritude is profoundly concerned, and which gives it not only a historical significance but also a continuing relevance. And it is this enduring relevance of Négritude that has been brought out in this comment by the Ghanaian scholar, P. A. V. Ansah, which can serve as an appropriate conclusion to this discussion:

> At a time when Africans are trying to experiment with new ideas and institutions, adapt them to their needs in the light of their traditional value systems, there is the need for a sustained belief in oneself, and this belief can be generated and kept alive by an ideology. This has been, and still is, the function of Négritude.[54]

Notes and References

1. For a presentation of the full range of meanings evoked by the term 'Négritude', see Janheinz Jahn, *History of Neo-African Literature* (London: Faber and Faber, 1968), and also Albert Memmi, 'Négritude et Judéité', in *L'Homme dominé* (Paris: Gallimard, 1969).
2. Translated into English under the title *Return to My Native Land* (Harmondsworth: Penguin, 1969).
3. Quoted by Lilyan Kesteloot in 'La Négritude et son expression littéraire', in *Négritude africaine, négritude caraibe* (Paris: 1973).
4. Cf. Philippe Decraene, *Le Panafricanisme* (Paris: Press Universitaires de France, 1959), and Colin Legum, *Pan-Africanism* (London: Pall Mall Press, 1962).

5. The expression is used by Karl Mannheim in his essay 'Conservative Thought', in Paul Kecskemeti (ed.) *Essays on Sociology & Social Psychology* (London: Oxford University Press, 1953).
6. Jean-Paul Sartre, 'Orphée noir', preface to L. S. Senghor, *Anthologie de la nouvelle poésie nègre et malgache de langue française* (Paris: Presses Universitaires de France, 1948; 2nd ed., 1970). Sartre's essay is reproduced in his *Situations III* (Paris: Gallimard, 1949); English translation by Samuel Allen under the title *Black Orpheus* (Paris: Présence Africaine, 1963), from which the quotations here are taken.
7. *Black Orpheus*, p. 60.
8. Consider for example some of the passages in the essay, 'Le Problème culturel en AOF', in *Liberté I: négritude et humanisme* (Paris: Editions du Seuil, 1964), pp. 12 ff.
9. *Liberté I*, p. 7.
10. Ibid., p. 13.
11. Ibid., p. 12. The conservative nationalism of the French writer Maurice Barrès was founded explicitly upon this idea, and it is worth pointing out that Barrès exercised an important influence upon Senghor in his formative years.
12. *Les Fondements de l'africanité* (Paris: Présence Africaine, 1967), pp 13–43.
13. See R. Bastide, *Les Amériques noires* (Paris: Payot Bibliothèque Scientifique, 1967).
14. *Liberté I*, p. 23.
15. Ibid., p. 254.
16. This paper corresponds, in its material content, with Senghor's article 'L'Esthétique négro-africaine', in *Diogène* (Paris: October 1956), and reproduced in *Liberté I*, pp. 202–18.
17. *Fondements*, p. 47; the italics are in the original.
18. 'Psychologie du négro-africain', *Diogène*, No. 37 (Paris: 1962); English quotation from John Reed and Clive Wake, *L. S. Senghor: Prose and Poetry* (London: Heinemann Educational Books, 1976), p. 30.
19. *Liberté I*, p. 257.
20. Ibid., p. 255.
21. *Diogène*, No. 37, p. 5.
22. *Fondements*, p. 54; italics in the original.
23. *Diogène*, No. 37, p. 7.
24. *Prose and Poetry*, p. 35.
25. *Diogène*, No. 37, p. 11
26. *Liberté I*, p. 23.
27. *Prose and Poetry*, pp. 34–5.
28. *Liberté I*, pp. 212–15.
29. *Fondements*, p. 64; italics in the original.
30. *Diogène*, No. 37, p. 7.
31. *Prose and Poetry*, p. 34.
32. *Liberté I*, p. 264. For an extensive discussion of this aspect of Senghor's theory, see Sylvia Washington Ba, *The Concept of Négritude in the Poetry of Léopold Sédar Senghor* (Princeton: Princeton University Press, 1973), pp. 44–73.

33. *Fondements*, p. 69.
34. *Prose and Poetry*, p. 43.
35. *Liberté I*, p. 30.
36. *Pierre Teilhard de Chardin et la politique africaine* (Paris: Cahiers Pierre Teilhard de Chardin No. 3, 1962), p. 22.
37. *On African Socialism* (London: Pall Mall Press and New York: Praeger, 1965), p. 154.
38. Ibid., p. 146.
39. Placide Tempels, *Bantu Philosophy* (Paris: Présence Africaine, 1959).
40. See, in particular, Lucien Lévy-Bruhl, *La Mentalité primitive.*
41. Senghor has often acknowledged the influence of Bergson's, *Essai sur les donnèes immédiates de la conscience*, upon his thinking.
42. See Monnerot, *La Poésie moderne et le sacré* (Paris: Gallimard, 1945), pp. 106–19, and Ferdinand Alquié, *Philosophie du surréalisme* (Paris: Bibiothèque de philosophie scientifique, 1955).
43. Susanne Langer, *Philosophy in a New Key* (New York: New American Library, 1951), Chapter 4.
44. K. Mannheim, *op. cit.*, pp. 74–164.
45. 'D' Amadou Koumba à Birago Diop', in *Liberté I*, p. 246.
46. Albert Franklin, 'La Négritude: réalité ou mystification', in *Les Etudiants noirs parlent* (Paris: Présence Africaine, 1952), pp. 287–303.
47. Sees. Okechukwu Mezu, *Léopold Sédar Senghor et la défense et illustradition de la civilisation noire* (Paris: Librairie Marcel Didier, 1968), pp. 173–6.
48. Stanislas Adotevi, *Négritude et négrologues* (Paris: Union Générale d'Editions, 1972).
49. Ibid, p. 45.
50. Irving Leonard Markovitz, *Léopold Sédar Senghor and the Politics of Negritude* (New York: Atheneum Press; London: Heinemann Educational Books, 1969).
51. Daniel Boukman, 'A propos du Festival des arts nègres à Dakar', in *Partisans* (Paris: 1966), p. 120.
52. Frantz Fanon, *The Wretched of the Earth* (Harmondsworth: Penguin, 1967), pp. 167–99.
53. Robert July, *The Origins of Modern African Thought* (London: Faber & Faber, 1968), p. 18.
54. P. A. V. Ansah, 'Aspects of Négritude', in *Universitas* (University of Ghana, Vol. I. No. 4, June 1972), p. 77.

5. Négritude and African Personality

▼▼

Perhaps the most significant aspect of African development in modern times has been the emergence of a distinctive consciousness, on our part, of our collective identity as a function of our relationship to the rest of the world. This consciousness, historically, derives from our experience of the encounter with Europe, and in an even more immediate way, represents the profound subjective response to the peculiar pressures of the colonial situation – that is, the global political, socio-economic and moral state of dependence imposed upon us by European domination.

But although thus circumscribed in its immediate origin, the sense of an African identity and the impulse towards its explicit affirmation which gave force to nationalist expression in Africa has over the years seen a continuous progression in its elaboration which has extended its area of reference beyond the colonial situation. Today, this awareness has been prolonged into an intellectual and ideological exploration of those avenues of endeavour which might give a meaning to the collective experience, into a quest for a positive orientation of African ideas and action in the contemporary world. One might say then that there is abroad among us, governing our feelings and consequently our expression, a certain idea of Africa, a certain ideal vision of ourselves founded upon our awareness of our specific constitution as a race and as a people, of our fundamental attachment to a distinctive culture and spiritual background. The consciousness of our singularity as Africans thus forms the live core of the intellectual idea we hold of Africa and by implication of our destiny.

It is my aim in this paper to examine within a broad historical and sociological perspective the development of this idea with specific reference to the two related concepts, 'Négritude' and 'African personality'. My intention here is not only to point up the relationship between them, but to stress as well their contribution to ideological development in Africa, and their continuing relevance to African preoccupations – indeed, to those of the entire black race – at the present time.

It might perhaps be best to start this examination by recalling the origin of the two concepts. In this respect, let us take the older term, 'African personality', first used by the great nineteenth century ideological leader, Edward Wilmot Blyden, in a speech which he gave at Freetown in 1893.[1] The term was used by him to mean a distinctive physical and moral disposition of the African, and even specifically, the foundation in an African civilization of the collective personality of black men throughout the world. The term thus had a wide racial connotation for Blyden, for the notion which it covered was nothing less than a Pan-Negro *ethos*.[2]

But what is significant about Blyden's use of the term is that the notion to which it refers was not new even in his own time. The fact is that a sense of African belonging has always been (and remains till today) a functional aspect of black experience and consciousness in America.[3] The early communities of Africans transported across the Atlantic had already begun to perceive the mother continent as an entity, due to their detachment under the pressure of slavery from their immediate primary bonds, on one hand, and on the other, their differentiation in terms of race and social status from their oppressors. Thus Africa emerged in their minds as a unified image of their racial and spiritual antecedents, as is borne out by the qualifying adjective 'African' which was regularly attached to the early Negro churches. The term 'African' in this context thus referred to the black race, not only in its separate differentiated existence in America, but also in its original bonds with the ancestral continent.

It is this extended meaning of the word which appears in the term 'African personality' as used by Blyden in the 1893 address, and which was taken up later by Sylvester Williams when in 1900 he convened at London the first 'Pan-African' Congress at which W. E. B. Du Bois was present. The subsequent fortune of the latter term is now well known, but one might stress here that, in view of the specific background of experience and of sentiment denoted by the reference to Africa by both Blyden and Sylvester Williams, it is no accident that the two expressions came ultimately through the agency of Nkrumah (as we shall presently see) to stand in an intimate relationship to each other. The concept of 'African personality' thus became the inspirational notion and the justifying principle, psychological as well as cultural, for the political action in favour of African emancipation represented by Pan-Africanism.

The very origin of the term 'African personality' thus has a historical significance in as much as Blyden did no more than apply it to a feeling which had already begun to shape the collective awareness of black people in the Diaspora, and from which a vision of Africa had begun to emerge. As will shortly be seen, Blyden spent a lifetime in formulating this vision in a general theory of Africanism which in its essential elements is a striking anticipation of Négritude.

The concept of Négritude also has its source in the Diaspora, derives indeed from the same complex of historical and sociological factors, in the particular configuration which they had assumed in the first quarter of the century. The progressive development of the Négritude movement among French-speaking black intellectuals from sources and influences in black American movements is, I believe, already well known, and we do not need to go over this here.[4] What needs to be stressed in this connection is the fact that Négritude is a version, a distinctive current, of the same cultural nationalism expressed in different ways among black people and at various times in their reaction against white domination. Négritude is, in a word, the francophone equivalent of the term 'African personality' in its original meaning as used by Blyden and in its association with the Pan-Africanism of Sylvester Williams and W. E. B. Du Bois. The explicit reference to the race which the term Négritude carries thus resumes, by emphasis, the central notion denoted by Blyden's term. The two concepts thus stand in a reciprocal relationship as being, each in its own way, a formulation of a vision of the race founded upon an idea of Africa.

President Senghor is thus right, in my view, when he refers to Négritude as a synonym for 'African personality'. The justification for establishing such a correspondence can be found not only in the derivation of Négritude as a concept and as a movement from the same fundamental source of sociological determinants, and the same pool of attitudes and ideas summed up in the term 'African personality' – that is, in the theory of Africanism elaborated among English-speaking black intellectuals, for which Blyden's term can be used as a convenient general label – but in fact in the specific articulations of these attitudes and ideas on each side of the language wall, despite differences in styles of expression and emphasis. It is to this basic similitude in the structuring of the African idea that I shall now turn my attention. It seems to me that in considering the development of social and political thought which has developed around the central symbol of Africa in its full historical perspective, a certain consistency, a remarkable continuity can be observed which is not without significance for us.

The point of departure of the differentiated awareness expressed in the concepts of 'Négritude' and 'African personality' is the African encounter with Europe. It is generally admitted that the effects of the European adventure in Africa date back to slavery which not only depopulated our continent but also began the process of disruption within African societies and cultures with which we are still today confronted. African reaction to Europe also dates back to slavery, not only in the form of physical resistance in Africa and in America, but also in the intellectual and cultural response to the effects of European penetration. The most important result of slavery, perhaps, in the long term perspective adopted here, is the devaluation of the black man in terms of his human worth which it entailed, and which began to be elaborated in the west into a powerful racism as a means of justifying and rationalizing the terrible commerce to which our ancestors were submitted.

African reaction thus took the form right from the beginning of a contestation of the entire system, and what is more important, of a defence of the humanity of the black man and even early on, of a kind of *apologia* of Africa. This initial dichotomy which has been maintained till this day, albeit with a shift of emphasis from the first to the second term, was dictated by the situation with which the early writers were confronted. There was not only the objective humiliation of the race – its subjugation and exploitation in the crudest possible manner – but also, more serious, the ideological devaluation of the black man, the massive attack against his intimate subjectivity.

Thus, already, in the eighteenth century, the little group of Africans in Europe and in America who had escaped slavery and had succeeded in acquiring a western education and with it, the values of western civilization, were able to judge and to condemn slavery by reference to these values, in the same way that white abolitionists fought against the institution by pointing up its contradiction with authentic Christian and humanist tenets. But what is not less important in considering the work of these early writers is the fact that they were the first 'neo-Africans' situated, from the intellectual and spiritual point of view, at the meeting point between Africa and Europe. From this position, at once privileged and difficult, they were able to measure the historical impact of Europe on their race and at the same time put into perspective, against their European experience, the elements of life and values that made up their African antecedents.

Thus in the writings of men like Equiano, alias Gustavus Vassa, Ignatius Sancho and others, we find for the first time that deep grain of the sentiment of historical and spiritual conflict between Europe and Africa which has always formed part of the process of the assimilation of European culture by the African in the colonial context. This phenomenon does not at this period acquire the intensity that came to be associated with later writing, particularly of the Négritude movement; nonetheless, we do find the definite expression of a feeling of duality, for example in *Equiano's Travels*,[5] of a sense of otherness with respect to Europe, which was to gather force into the psychological drama of later literature. When it is considered that Equiano's origin was in present day Eastern Nigeria and possibly Igbo, and that the essential thrust of his work was to present a retrospective view of his African background in such a way as to justify it and affirm its human value in the face of European denial, it may be thought that there is a profound sense in which this work is a significant forerunner of Chinua Achebe's *Things Fall Apart*, written some two centuries later.

Moreover, this literature of the eighteenth century began to move towards a more rounded view of the human situation embracing European as well as African values, towards an effort to relate them within a single frame of reference. The eighteenth century African writers were in a sense freshly acculturated individuals, who had an acute consciousness of themselves as points of contact between two civilizations, and who were conscious of the movement of the mind implied by their integration into western civilization. They were thus the first generation of Africans to feel that dissociation of the mind of the westernized African from its ancestral universe, the cleavage out of which the African idea was to emerge.

The slave period was followed by the penetration of Africa by Europeans, and by the continuous expansion all through the nineteenth century of European imperialism, whose high point was the partition of Africa at the Berlin Conference of 1884. The sociological significance of these developments was the establishment of new political and socio-economic structures on the continent along lines dictated by European interest, and the progressive dominance, as a result, of European ideas and values. This situation implied in turn, not only the forcible and often confused transformation of African societies and cultures, but also the dramatic eruption of Europe within the African consciousness. In sociological terms, the process of acculturation began in earnest in Africa with the colonial arrangement.

It would of course be an exaggeration to say that western influences operated anything like a radical transformation of African society such as would have affected its fundamental character. What is however undeniable is the fact that the ascendancy of western civilization in the context of colonization did effect a distinct orientation of African minds away from the indigenous culture, and that the prestige of the conqueror turned his way of life and system of values into the reference-culture for the African.

Within the global process of acculturation, which was as a result affecting African society in its entirety, was situated a more intensified absorption into the western way of life of a new category of Africans which began to emerge from the colonial situation. This category comprised at first black men who had been repatriated from America to found the colonies of Monrovia and Freetown as well as indigenes converted to the Christian religion. They sometimes received a high level of western education, and acquired with it new modes of thought and judgement as well as of social behaviour – in a word, a new culture.

From these individuals was constituted a new class, an African *bourgeoisie*, which having adopted the European way of life was gradually to replace the traditional ruling class – at least within colonial society – as the dominant centre of social and political development and, from the cultural point of view, as the reference-group. The historical importance of this group in the modernization process in West Africa has now been sufficiently brought to light; so too has the correlation between their intellectual and ideological preoccupations and their economic interests and social aspirations.[6] What perhaps has not been sufficiently stressed in the socio-psychological situation of this African bourgeoisie in nineteenth century Africa, the profound stresses which are at the roots of their thinking.

These westernized Africans of the early years of the nineteenth century were especially sensitive to the racial theories which during their time reached a climax of paroxysm. They saw themselves as men on trial, and their feeling of insecurity was heightened by the fact that they formed a fragile minority in relation to the tremendous mass of other Africans around them who continued to live largely within the social intitutions and by the cultural norms of traditional Africa. It would not be too distant from the truth to observe that more than any other factor, this sense of ambiguity attaching to their situation as Africans living a foreign culture on African soil, the incongruous disparity between their way of life and the imposing reality of their immediate environment, led the most sensitive among these men to an interrogation of their situation.

The content of the writing of the period indicates quite clearly that they were afflicted with a profound *malaise* arising out of their situation 'as marginal men'. Their sense of total dependence on the west, and the singular disparity between their borrowed culture and the African reality which surrounded them, could not but provoke within them a moral and spiritual discomfort which neither the material benefits of western civilization nor the undisputed prestige which they enjoyed in colonial society could altogether palliate. They knew themselves to be men without any stable cultural links and consequently without a firm sense of identity, and tormented by an apprehension about themselves that was existential in its full import. And it is this feeling of deep spiritual restlessness that inspires the following remark by one of them which sums up the mood of self-questioning from which, in greater or lesser measure, these writings proceed:

our fault cannot be innate and incurable, if it be true that the natives

of the interior – our blood relatives – who have not known the joys of
'civilization' show off to so greater an advantage than us.[7]

The study of African intellectual life of this period done by Robert July
and from which the quotation is taken shows that the ideological expression of these men presents itself as much as an effort at self-analysis
and at filling the gap which the most sensitive individuals among the
African bourgeoisie felt within them as, perhaps even less than, the expression of the social and political aspirations of a group conscious of itself
as a distinct socio-economic force. A good part of the writing of this
period was devoted to the refutation of racial theories which raged in
Europe at this time: the work of Africanus Horton who was a scientist by
training and profession is of particular interest in this regard.[8] But beyond
this factor and the criticism of Europe which it implied, the important
element in the writing of this period for the further development of African
thought was the increasing attention to the reality of Africa to which these
early intellectuals were led. They were compelled to a reflection upon the
dual relationship of the westernized African to the two conflicting cultures of Africa and Europe. The general trend of this effort was towards
the intellectual working out of a new balance between the two, through a
conscious adaptation of European values to the African scene. In this
respect, the names of men like William Grant, Alexander Crummel,
Samuel Ajaiyi Crowther and Africanus Horton, among others, will remain
in the annals of the intellectual history of Africa as landmarks in the movement towards the emergence of a modern African consciousness.

Their importance for our subject resides however principally in their
contribution to the creation and maintenance of a climate of serious intellectual discussion within which the African idea sprouted, as it were,
and was nurtured, until it took definite form with the work of Edward
Blyden and in his concept 'African personality'. Before Blyden's career
had fully got into its stride, therefore, there was already an intellectual
recognition of Africa as a possible reference for thought and action, and
indeed awareness. Thus Alexander Crummel speaks of the 'African
essence' of all black men, without however elaborating on this idea. This
recognition may be judged today hesitant and perhaps of no real consequence in the lives of the men who came to it, but it was sufficient to
lay the foundation for a system of thought upon which subsequent African
reflection was to be grounded.

If then, the ideological leaders of early nineteenth century Africa did
not call into question the validity of European civilization *per se*, they
began to contest its adequation to African conditions and to dispute its
universal relevance. Within more or less a single generation, the Creole
bourgeoisie in Africa – at least the reflecting part of it – had begun to move

from a position of unconditional acceptance of European civilization to one
that was more qualified, ambivalent and even sometimes critical. It was of
course clearly out of the question for them to effect an authentic return to
an original African way of life. What their attachment to European culture
(to which they were conditioned by their education and their social position) needed, in order to be less oppressive in their peculiar situation, was
a new awareness and a new mental openness to the reality of Africa – a *via
media* which would resolve the contradictions inherent in their social and
cultural condition and bridge the psychological gulf created by their particular experience. It was this solution that Blyden was to propose.

Edward Wilmot Blyden has been called by Robert July in the study already cited 'the first African personality', and this title should be taken, I
believe, in at least two senses. There is, first, the obvious sense that Blyden
was the first African writer and intellectual to enjoy a truly international
reputation. He owed this to his great intellectual endowments and his exceptional gift of expression. His writings attest to a trenchant mind, sustained by a remarkable erudition which found expression in a masterly
handling of ideas and the transparent lucidity of his style. He was a cosmopolitan in the full sense of the word: open to all the great currents of ideas
in the world of his time, and at the same time, an original thinker who
internalized completely what he received from outside in order to make
it an integral part of his own intellectual substance.

Secondly, Blyden was the foremost African nationalist, the most ardent
of the nineteenth century, with a passion for Africa that became intensified with the years as, all through the century and under his very eyes as it
were, the occupation of Africa progressed in an irresistible engulfment of
practically the entire continent. As has been noted, we owe the term
'African personality' to him, and he was the first to present a total vision
of Africa which gathered up the preoccupations of his predecessors within
a powerfully articulated system of ideas. This integration of the intellectual
efforts of previous writers operated by Blyden was such as not only to express the spirit of his time but also to anticipate that of future generations
of African intellectuals. As my late friend and colleague Dr Kola Adelaja
has demonstrated in his Sorbonne thesis,[9] Blyden's work gave birth to
political thought in Africa, and the influence of his writings and of his
manifold activities in a lifetime devoted to the African cause contributed
in a measure far from negligible to the mental emancipation of English-
speaking Africans from which sprang the will to pursue the objective goal
of political emancipation.

The fact is that Blyden arrived on the African scene at a crucial moment
in African as well as European history. Imperialist expansion in Africa

was a direct function of industrial expansion in Europe. Technological progress in Europe intensified the self-confidence of the white man (as amply witnessed by the philosophy of Auguste Comte), and this attitude was translated into a cultural and racial arrogance of the European towards non-western people, into an external aggressiveness exacerbated by the large scale social transformations taking place within the European world itself. This was also the period of the most intense nationalist awakening in Europe, the culmination of the movement of ideas set in motion in an earlier age by men like Herder and to which the French revolution and the Napoleonic wars were later to give a powerful historical impetus. In the mid-nineteenth century itself, the nationalist principle was perhaps most fully embodied in the personality of the Italian, Mazzini, with whose writings and activities Blyden was certainly familiar.

All these developments had important repercussions upon Blyden's thought and helped to shape in one way or the other his theory of Africanism, which was defined along a line of progression beginning with racial sentiment and culminating in a social ideology, with a personal interpretation of Africa as its middle term. For the originality of Blyden resided in the simple fact that he conceived Africa as an autonomous entity, one might even say, as a category *sui generis*. Blyden posed Africa, and this for the first time, as the immediate reference for the black man. It was no longer a question of acclimatizing European ideas and values to African conditions, but rather of starting from a recognition of the African personality and the validity, on its own terms, of the culture and way of life which underlay and moulded that personality.

It is perhaps difficult for us today to appreciate fully the intellectual and moral boldness involved in Blyden's position, but this quality of his thinking and career emerges readily from a consideration of the historical and ideological context of his time, and of the way in which his ideas transcended the hesitant awareness of the African reality of his predecessors and contemporaries to arrive at a full affirmation of African uniqueness. In the face of the overwhelming pressures of European prejudice and its demoralizing effect on the westernized African of his age, Blyden understood that what was required was a new and firm attachment to Africa deriving from a vision of a valid African civilization. In place of the confused mass of strange and savage manners which the European saw and which the westernized African had also been led to see, Blyden proposed an image of a coherent system of institutions and customs, animated by moral and spiritual principles of the highest order. The thesis of African, and by extension black inferiority, which formed the main plank in the justifying ideology of European conquest and domination, could only be challenged by a new understanding of the African continent: of its peoples

and societies, and in a more general way, of the variety of social and cultural processes by which men everywhere organized their collective lives in
response of the peculiar solicitations of their respective milieux. This
general principle applied to Africa, which in the course of its history had
evolved its own mode of response in harmony with the environment of its
peoples, and which thus formed an integrated whole. The implications of
this view of things for Blyden's conception of Africa and the black race
are spelt out in these terms:

> The mistake which Europeans often make in considering questions of
> Negro improvement and the future of Africa, is in supposing that the
> Negro is the European in embyro – in the undeveloped stage – and that
> when, by and by, he shall enjoy the advantages of civilization and cul-
> ture, he will become like the European; in other words, that the Negro
> is on the same line of progress, in the same groove, with the European,
> but infinitely in the rear ... This view proceeds upon the assumption
> that the two races are called to the same work and are alike in potential-
> ity and ultimate development, the Negro only needing the element of
> time, under certain circumstances, to become the European. But to our
> mind, it is not a question between the two races of inferiority or
> superiority on the one side, nor absolute or essential inferiority on the
> other side. It is a question of difference of endowment and difference of
> destiny. No amount of training or culture will make the Negro a Euro-
> pean; on the other hand, no lack of training or deficiency of culture will
> make the European a Negro. The two races are not moving in the same
> groove, with an immeasurable distance between them, but on parallel
> lines. They will never meet in the plane of their activities so as to coin-
> cide in capacity or performance. They are not identical, as some think,
> but unequal; they are distinct but equal ...[10]

Africa, then, had its culture, an original civilization, age-old and fully
alive, and which accounted for the modes of life and personality of its
peoples. Blyden established an immediate correlation between the natural
environment and the collective personality extending to that between race
and culture. Moreover, as we have seen, the term 'African' had a racial
meaning among New World blacks, so that for Blyden, who was born and
grew up in the Diaspora, the word also expressed a racial notion. More
specifically, race for him corresponded to the concept of *nationality* in the
nineteenth-century European acceptation of the term, that is, an ethnic
and spiritual community.

> Among the conclusions to which study and research are conducting
> philosophers, none is clearer than this – that each of the races of man-
> kind has a specific character, and a specific work. The science of
> Sociology is the science of Race.[11]

The biological factor was the outward sign of a cultural and spiritual differentiation, of the specific inner constitution of each human group; each

nation had its genius, its particular and distinctive attributes, a unique manner of feeling and acting which impressed a seal on its cultural works. For Blyden, Africa was a 'nation' in this sense and its civilization was thus an expression of the profound collective personality of all her children, far and near.

There was an important sense of course in which Blyden's position was a tactical one – with, first, an ideological purpose aimed at combatting European prejudice, and secondly, with an immediate practical significance related to the local context of his thinking and activities. In the first respect, it appears today as the earliest instance of an unequivocal polemical stance in defence of African peoples and cultures in the face of European denigration. In the second, it was a means for him of creating among the westernized Creole class of the coast a better understanding of, and even an identification with, the African populations of the interior; to effect a *rapprochement* between the two groups whose relations had been characterized by a state of tension.[12] But even when this 'tactical' aspect of Blyden's thinking has been allowed for, there remains the undeniable fact that he came to a real intellectual and emotional sympathy with the indigenous cultures in West Africa through a deep and personal knowledge of them and an acquaintance with their history. His remarkable openness of mind, which was a condition of his erudition, led him to see these societies in a broader perspective than that afforded by an attachment to the western model. In other words, Blyden saw African societies and cultures from a functionalist and pluralist point of view which enabled him to appreciate their coherence and essential quality as human institutions.

But if Blyden's immediate preoccupation was with getting recognition for the value of African civilization, he also advanced the idea, which was original in his time, of the complementary character of the human races, each one a necessary element in the vast design of providence. He therefore did not deny that Africa needed contact with the outside world for its development and enrichment, as much with the Western as with the Islamic world, for whose religion and civilization, though a Christian minister, he had conceived a special sympathy and even admiration, as is well borne out by various essays in the volume, *Christianity, Islam and the Negro Race*. The harmonious way in which the Islamic civilization had been integrated with the indigenous cultures in the savannah region of West Africa, and the historical ties between this region and rest of the Islamic world, afforded for Blyden the testimony of the positive nature of contact between different races and civilizations. However, this particular conviction involved for him very specifically a critical view of European civilization. For while he admired the achievements of European civilization, he also considered as detrimental to the essentially communal spirit of African civilization what he regarded as Europe's elevation of the values of materialism and individualism into principles of human life and behaviour: a view of the opposition between Africa and Europe that has become classic if not commonplace since Blyden's time. At all events, Blyden sought therefore to reconcile what he clearly recognized as the need for Africa to modernize itself through technical progress with an equally urgent requirement for her to retain those humane principles of life and values upon which the traditional societies were grounded. His social ideology thus proposed the retrieval of the values of traditional African culture and their integration into a modern industrial order. In this sense, Blyden must be considered the first theoretician of what came later to be known as 'African socialism', set out in much the same terms as it was to be formulated by African leaders in the post-independence period.

For Blyden was not content with pointing out the specific character of the African personality, he wished to demonstrate as well its concrete and objective manifestations, its correlation with African social institutions. In his little book, *African Life and Customs*, he discussed the communal organization of social life in Africa as an expression of the principle of the extended family, and laid emphasis on the African's mystical conception of society as proceeding from a strong religious disposition. Indeed, for Blyden, this religious disposition was the distinctive trait of the African personality. He saw the African as a man integrated with the natural world, in communion with the elements and through these with the divine essence of the universe. He summarized the spirituality of the African in these terms of warm celebration: 'His real work is to speak to the earth and let it teach him – to dress the garden and watch over it.'[13] This comprehensive spiritual sense of the world was then to be the contribution to human life and awareness of the African continent, which Blyden described as 'the spiritual granary of the world'.

Blyden achieved a sense of identification with Africa that was not only complete but also tinged with romanticism. It is significant in this respect that he went beyond the intellectuals of the Creole community – into whose ranks he came from the outside, as it were. Much of his thinking was conditioned by his acute racial sentiment which was linked to a passion for the ancestral continent. But it is also important to consider that his origins in the Diaspora favoured a unified view of Africa, a global vision of the possible destiny of the continent and of the race associated with it. In essence, therefore, Blyden's Africanism was inspirational in character.

Blyden's perspective was threefold. In the first instance, his intention was to bring out and define a black identity, the 'African personality', to bring the black man to a knowledge of his veritable nature. Secondly, he thought to elaborate for this personality a new mode of expression in modern times, by giving to the black man the full consciousness of his potentialities, new avenues of action which would find in the African a meaningful appropriation to his nature, a coincidence with his true being. Finally, he strove to create a framework of ideas derived from his intelligence of African values that would hold a meaning for the rest of the world.

In all, then, Blyden's work tended to no other purpose than to bringing the black man, African and New World, to a sense of self-recognition and a self-knowledge. It went beyond a simple cultural nationalism, presenting itself rather as a comprehensive investigation of the African condition as a necessary part of reflection upon the human situation in general.

What I have already said about Blyden's Africanism should be enough, I believe, to indicate that we are dealing with no less than Négritude, conceptualized as a general principle of African being and formulated as a philosophy of African existence and destiny. What strikes one in this respect is the correspondence between the thinking of Blyden in the nineteenth century and that of Senghor in our own day, a coincidence across time of almost every single item in their respective systems. We cannot speak here of a fortuitous meeting of the two systems, nor even of a simple resemblance, but indeed of a fundamental identity between the concept of 'African personality' in its formulation by Blyden and that of Senghor's Négritude.

This anticipation of Senghor by Blyden by some fifty years seems to me to be highly significant in two respects. First, it illustrates in a remarkable way the continuity of ideological preoccupations and expression in the intellectual development of Africa to which I have drawn attention. What is particularly interesting here is the fact that for both men, similar in many respects and highly 'acculturated', there is this return to the fundamental sources of the black heritage in African civilization which stands as the objective and normative reference for social and cultural theory. Beyond the subjective and even pathetic reaction against Europe, there is this common will to find a sanction for thinking in the vibrant reality of African life, upon which is projected a vision of African development in the modern world. It is important in this connection to remark upon the striking parallel between the social ideology of Blyden, based on his understanding of the communal character of African life and institutions, and the social ideas of Senghor derived from his general theory of Négritude, and conceived as an operational framework of ideas for the modern reconstruction of African societies.[14] When it is borne in mind that Senghor was unacquainted with the writings of Blyden,[15] the identity of thought and ideas between the two men becomes all the more impressive.

This leads me to the second observation on the link between the two concepts associated with their names. For if Blyden cannot be thought of as merely a precursor of Négritude – since his theory is too complete to admit of such a view – neither can Senghor be seen as a simple continuator of the theory of 'African personality'. Senghor brings to the same ideas developed by Blyden the full weight of a contemporary intelligence, in such a way that his theory prolongs that of Blyden in the direction of a perfection and refinement of its terms. Senghor has had the advantage of elaborating his theory of Négritude after the great revolution of spirit and sensibility which has marked our age – that of Marx and Bergson, that operated by the European artists and poets of the early years of this century, and not least, by modern anthropology. This has given a wider conceptual framework to Négritude, so that where Blyden succeeded in posing the African being, Senghor has tended rather to found it as an epistemology.

The twenty-one years between the two World Wars represent the most fertile period in the ideological development of black people. In the United States, the dramatic upsurge of black consciousness centred largely around an African sentiment as its integrating element. For writers and intellectuals like Du Bois and the men of the Harlem Renaissance, Africa became a strongly valorized symbol and the obsessive centre of a quest for identity. With Garvey, this African sentiment assumed a massive dimension, and found a dynamic significance. The Négritude movement is a direct outgrowth of these developments in America, passing through the mediation of the Haitian Renaissance before flowering into a full-blown, independent movement by itself.

Between the various black movements of the inter-war years, the relationship of sentiments and ideas was incarnated by Du Bois. His political activities were inspired by a cultural nationalism which rested on a conception of Africa as the spiritual nation of all black men, as indeed with Garvey, and it is through this channel that he exercised so vast an influence on black intellectuals the world over. The historical importance of the Manchester Conference at which Nkrumah played a leading role and which marked a turning point in the development of the Pan-African movement, has been so fully documented as to have become today a commonplace.[16] In addition however to the influence exercised upon the thinking and career of Nkrumah by Garvey and Du Bois, it is necessary to consider that – equally determinant – which he owed to the intellectual and political atmosphere which prevailed in his own territory of origin, the former Gold Coast, during the early years of this century and well into the fifties.

It used to be thought that nationalism in the African territories under British colonial rule was a purely social and political phenomenon, in which neither a strong cultural nor racial awareness played a significant part. This view moreover carries with it the suggestion that English-speaking African nationalists were so absorbed in direct action that they had little time for the kind of intellectual reflection in which their francophone counterparts were wont to indulge. It has now become clear that such was not the case, and that political nationalism was accompanied in these territories by a strongly articulated movement of cultural revival as an essential justifying principle of the movement for self-rule.

In effect, after the death of Blyden in 1912, the process he had begun of a comprehensive reassessment of African civilization was maintained and even extended in the activities of a new intellectual élite among the Fanti bourgeoisie in Cape Coast: for centuries bridgehead of European penetration in this area, and now the centre of an intellectual and cultural movement of considerable importance. The new Fanti bourgeoisie issued directly out of the local population and by the end of the nineteenth century had become sufficiently aware of its socio-economic importance as to begin to develop strong political interests, and thus to come into conflict with the colonizing power. The roots of Ghanaian nationalism can be traced to this situation and to the writings and activities of the Fanti intellectuals of the early years of this century.[17] Moreover, their ties with traditional society were closer than was the case with the Creoles; they had therefore a more direct experience and understanding of indigenous institutions and were thus in a better position to challenge the ideological devaluation of African civilization. Despite this important difference, however, their movement must be considered a direct continuation of the earlier current among the Creole intellectuals in Liberia and Sierra Leone, with whose work in any case they were familiar, notably as regards Blyden. It is thus with reason that the Ghanaian scholar, F. K. Drah, considers them together when he observes:

> Without exaggeration, these ... were the late nineteenth century and early twentieth century British West African counterparts – in several ways – of the eighteenth century philosophes.[18]

From the point of view of his contribution to the intellectual and cultural history of modern Ghana and indeed of Africa, perhaps the most important member of this group was John Mensah-Sarbah, whose work *Fanti Customary Laws* was to initiate a tradition of scholarly documentation, by educated Africans, of indigenous institutions which has endured and has remained indeed a landmark in African studies. His other work, *Fanti National Constitution*, is the first expression of the nascent nationalism of the period and was later to prove of considerable significance in the future development of nationalist thought in the Gold Coast.[19] His early death in 1910, however, gave the leadership of the emerging movement to Joseph Caseley-Hayford, the man who for some twenty years was to dominate political and intellectual life in English-speaking West Africa.

Caseley-Hayford was the intellectual heir of Blyden, and embodied the spirit of cultural nationalism in West Africa in the years between the two World Wars. With him, the concern with the revaluation of African culture went with a militant anti-imperialism. The influence of Blyden probably enlarged his outlook beyond the Gold Coast, so that he came to conceive the idea of a political association of the colonial territories for a more cohesive resistance to European imperialism. To this end, he formed the National Congress of British West Africa, which was the first African initiative towards the realization of the idea of African unity. The name of the association well reflects the practical limitations imposed on the idea by the conditions of the period, but it is important to note that the Congress was meant as a spearhead and rallying point for a broader movement of black solidarity throughout the world.[20]

As embodied then by Caseley-Hayford, what this movement had in particular was the immediate commitment of its intellectuals to political advance for the West African colonies through constitutional and judicial means as well as through other forms of social action. With Caseley-Hayford in particular, ideas were a means of action, and his inspirational idea was the modernization of African society which could only be carried out through the agency of an African élite, in touch with both the Western culture and the traditional way of life: the comprehensive purpose therefore determined political action for the accession of the new élite to power. But although his intellectual preoccupations had this pragmatic end, they were in no way limited by the fact. The very requirement for African development implied a new consciousness of the traditional structures and the heritage of the past. Thus it was that in his *magnum opus*, with the evocative title *Ethiopia Unbound*,[21] he projected a vision of Africa and of the black race whose impulse derives essentially from Blyden and which was as much a spiritual and idealistic conception of African destiny as it was a social and political programme. The very association of these attributes in the work leads Caseley-Hayford to convey the same idea as in Blyden of Africa's mission to regenerate the world.

The significant point then about the movement among Gold Coast intellectuals in the twentieth century is the fact that political and nationalist interests led necessarily, in the circumstances, to a cultural awakening and to a new and positive reassessment of their African antecedents. It is true that they were not given to general ideas and abstract speculations concerning an African nature immanent in the personality of the race. Their orientation was more empirical, towards the monographic investigation of aspects of indigenous life and institutions, an approach that had already appeared with the work of Sarbah, and which was often linked in a practical way with the immediate exigencies of a running battle with the colonial administration.[22] This sociological preoccupation with the realities of African life determined an interest in the oral tradition, in the true nature of the African past, and gave a powerful impetus to African self-awareness and self-confidence.[23]

To the inter-war years also belong the two books by Nnamdi Azikiwe, *Liberia in World Politics* and *Renascent Africa* – the latter of which can be considered as the reflective basis of his later nationalist activity and which derives in a direct line of progression from the movements reviewed here[24] – as well as the far from neutral anthropological work by Jomo Kenyatta, *Facing Mount Kenya*. At the same time therefore that English-speaking African intellectuals were fashioning a new image of Africa and reflecting upon their condition with respect to the historical and cultural connection with Europe, similar ideas were being developed among French-speaking intellectuals, in the peculiar style they had inherited from their Cartesian conditioning with the French tradition, but directed towards a passionate reassessment of their ancestral heritage and towards a new mode of existence for the African and the black man in the modern world.

The significance of these developments, then, is the fact that – right through the black world – ideological activity took on a generalized character, under the pressure of a common situation, and was marked by a convergence of thinking, of activities, of influences and especially of attitudes, upon a single and dominating African idea.

When therefore in the years after the Second World War, Kwame Nkrumah began to use the term 'African personality' as a slogan for his political campaign for emancipation, he did so in the full knowledge of its wide racial connotation. At that period, it meant for him what it had meant for Blyden – the collective personality of black people. We must remember in this respect that Nkrumah was a Pan-Negro militant, a disciple of Garvey and Du Bois, before becoming an African nationalist. If at this time he did not spend time on developing a full theory of Africanism, this was because his special orientation was towards a definite political and economic programme, a sociological rather than cultural concern. But this did not preclude in his thinking a recognition of the inspirational value of the African heritage, and indeed a cultural nationalism which linked his vision to that of Senghor and the founders of Négritude. This fact is reflected in his attachment to the term 'African personality' which, indeed, he made popular through insistent use.

It was however through him that the two concepts came to be separated. The independence of Ghana in 1957 gave a new direction to the action of Kwame Nkrumah. In effect, without losing interest in Pan-Negro affairs, he began at this time to give increasing attention to continental unity. Africa thus appeared to him as a *continent*, that is, a geo-political area, rather than as the spiritual nation of black people. The very term 'African personality' began at the same time to lose its racial meaning and to acquire a new reference which was more political than cultural. The new acceptance of the term detached it somewhat from its earlier correspondence to the term 'Négritude', although by 1961, Senghor had launched a new word – *africanité* – to which it could be related. What this shift of meanings expresses was the growing perception on the part of Nkrumah (and Senghor), of the Arab presence in Africa, and the desire to bring it into relation with the Negro element.

There are important political reasons for this change. First, the rise of Nasser's Egypt and the African vocation which she sought to assume in addition to the Arab vocation, drew attention to the fact that Africa was in fact composed of two parts, one black and the other white, Arab: an awareness that was further intensified by the Algerian war of independence. Then the preoccupation with continental unity, with the stark emergence in 1960 of several independent African states, tended also to de-emphasize the racial and cultural factor in favour of the political. These two factors combined to give to the term 'African personality' the meaning which we now attach to it, that is, a kind of collective dynamic of all the peoples of the continent.

But in addition, African independence drew our attention as Africans away from the broader issues of the historical relationship of the race with Europe within the colonial situation towards new problems of an internal character, to the socio-economic problems of development. These factors dictated a new orientation for African ideology towards concrete questions and immediate options, affirming ideas as elaborations of the 'strategy and tactics' of national development (if one can borrow the title here of Awolowo's book)[25] – in other words, African thought began to develop clearly as ideologies of African reconstruction. This explains the spate of theorizing on 'African socialism' during the 60s, which seems today to have seen a significant lull but which nonetheless remains at the centre of our ideological and cultural preoccupations.

This is neither the place nor the time to review these theories, but I

consider it important to emphasize the remarkable correspondence between them, even in the very terms in which they are couched, on both
sides of the language wall. As is well known, the principal idea on which
all these theories are based is that of African communalism. We have already remarked the role of this idea in the social philosophy of Blyden,
and it serves as a link today between the social ideology of Senghor on one
hand, and on the other, Kwame Nkrumah and Julius Nyerere. The most
succinct statement of the idea has been furnished by Nyerere who writes:
'The foundation, and the objective, of African socialism, is the extended
family'. It is this concept that is translated by the Swahili word *Ujamaa*.[26]

One hardly needs to go further in the comparison of Nyerere's theoriza-
tion of the idea of African socialism, and its derivation by Senghor from
his general theory of Négritude. For despite the differences in the approach of the two men, and in their practical application of theory, it is
from a common Africanism that both have drawn the elements of their
thinking.

Similarly, the conception of socialism put forward by Nkrumah has
affinities with that of Senghor. In his book *Consciencism* published in
1964,[27] Nkrumah sought to establish the general principles of a new
African ideology, which has for its point of departure a minimal Africanism expressed in these terms:

> The traditional image of Africa implies an attitude towards man which
> in its social manifestations can only be qualified as socialist. This is so
> because in Africa, man is considered above all as a spiritual being, en-
> dowed with a certain dignity, integrity and intrinsic value.[28]

Here we have a statement of African communalism that is in fact
identical with anything you will find in Senghor, when all the trimmings
of the latter's personal style have been lifted to reveal the core of his
thinking.

Further, for Nkrumah, as for Nyerere and Senghor, socialism in Africa
can only mean the integration of the values of the traditional humanism
into modern life. Thus he writes:

> Socialism is a form of social organization which, guided by the prin-
> ciples of communalism, adopts means and measures rendered necessary
> by demographic and technological development.[29]

I recall a review of the French translation of this work which appeared
in *Le Monde*, and in which the Africanist Philippe Decraene described
'Consciencism' as a synthesis of Négritude and Marxism. Indeed, one is
tempted on examining the book closely to remark that what is significant
about it is less its Marxist orthodoxy – in fact, the work presents an overtly
'revisionist' thesis – as its Négritude: that is, its reference to traditional

Africa as a reference and sanction. What Nkrumah attempted here is nothing less than a reconciliation of the dialectics of Marx with the spirit of traditional Africa, the forging of a link between a cosmology that was essentially spiritual and idealist in character and a materialist explanation of the universe. Whether the attempt is convincing or not is another matter. But we may note here that it is specifically with reference to the values of Africa that he rejects capitalism and accepts socialism as more consonant with the nature of Africa: 'Capitalism', he concludes, 'would be a betrayal of the personality and of the conscience of Africa.'[30]

I have taken pains here to put Nkrumah's work in parallel with Senghor because Nkrumah was a well-known opponent of Négritude. But the quotations I've given of his works are enough to indicate that his ideas were not very different from those of Senghor, and that, at all events, at the time he was writing this book he had a definite conception of the specific nature and spirit of African civilization. In this respect, he inherited along with his Pan-Negro outlook, the cultural vision of his immediate intellectual predecessors in the former Gold Coast. He was preoccupied with what he called 'the need for a re-interpretation and a new assessment of the factors which make up our past', as much as with the purely political aspects of African emancipation. His cultural nationalism was an essential element of the political, and as with Blyden and Caseley-Hayford, it had an inspirational purpose and value, as is evident from his words at the official opening of the University of Ghana's Institute of African Studies:

> By the work of this Institute, we must reassess and assert the glories and achievements of our African past and inspire our generation and succeeding generations with a vision for a better future.[31]

Nkrumah's conception of African culture and history is not developed into a full-blown theory of Africanism, but this was mainly, I think, because for one thing he took the 'African personality' as a given point of departure; primarily, his intention was to go beyond the framework of its affirmation – of its 'defence and illustration' – in order to conceptualize a new relationship of this personality with the modern world. In this sense, Nkrumah sought to transcend Négritude; it was no longer a question of defining the African personality but of inserting it within the historical process. This orientation is expressed in the philosophy of 'consciencism', whose aim, according to Nkrumah, 'is to contain at once the African experience of the Moslem and Euro-Christian presence, and that of traditional society, and through a kind of gestation, to use them for the harmonious development of this society.'[32]

Even here, the theory of 'consciencism' remains within the same perspective as Négritude in its formulation by Senghor, for in the definition Nkrumah gives of it, it is not difficult to recognize the three poles of the present preoccupation in Senghor's thinking – the Negro-African heritage, Arab-Berber presence, and the influence of western civilization, all three currents integrated within a new synthesis directed toward the civilization of the Universal.[33]

It seems to me quite clear then that, when all is said and done, we Africans have since the beginning been thinking the same thoughts and putting them in the same words, whatever colonial flag has been waved over our heads: and here, I include our brothers in America whose condition has not been significantly different from ours on this side of the Atlantic, and whose contribution to our emancipation has been by any measure quite considerable, and indeed in the intellectual sphere determinant. Thus when we take a comprehensive look at ideological development among black people, what strikes one is the remarkable correspondence between its various areas of expression, and beyond this, the organic identity of thought. This factor excludes the possibility of seeing a fundamental disparity between the concepts of 'Négritude' and 'African personality'.

The fact remains that English-speaking Africans have often shown a surprising insensitiveness to the significance of Négritude, and to its specific and direct relevance to the African situation. At best, there is a grudging recognition that it was an appropriate reaction to the peculiar situation of French colonial rule and assimilation. This is the light in which Professor Mphahlele, for example, saw Négritude when he wrote these words:

> It is significant that it is not the African in British-settled territories –
> a product of 'indirect rule' and one that has been left in his cultural
> habitat – who readily reaches out for his traditional past. It is rather the
> assimilated African, who has absorbed French culture, who is now
> passionately wanting to recapture his past. In his poetry, he extols his
> ancestors, ancestral marks, African wood carvings and bronze art, and
> he tries to recover the moorings of his oral literature; he clearly feels he
> has come to a dead end in European culture, and is still not really ac-
> cepted as an organic part of French society, for all the assimilation he
> has been through.[34]

An attentive examination of African writing will show quite readily that this division is a very simple one indeed. One can point in fact to the same elements as those placed in relief in the above quotation in the English-speaking literature. For while it is true that Francophone writing has been marked by a self-dramatization that is largely absent (and I add the qualification 'largely' deliberately) in English-speaking African writing, it is incontestable that the traits singled out by Mphahlele and by which he attempts to distinguish the literature of Négritude from that of English-speaking Africa are in fact very much in evidence in the latter.

Indeed, in all the early poetry that came out of English-speaking Africa, there is hardly any difference in the themes and the state of mind which they reflect between it and Négritude poetry with which it is contemporaneous. In the work of this first generation of English-speaking African poets who have been called 'pioneer poets' – Gladys Caseley-Hayford, R. G. Armattoe, Michael Dei-Anang and Denis Osadebay – there is the same element of racial feeling and the same compulsion to the glorification of the African past and things African; a romanticism that issued out of the cultural and psychological stresses of a common colonial experience.[35] There is moreover a certain element of self-dramatization implied by a sense of loss and spiritual disorientation, as in these lines by the Sierra Leonian Abioseh Nicol:

> Easter morning.
> Where are my ancestral spirits now?
> I have forgotten for many harvests
> To moisten the warm earth
> With poured libations.[36]

And in a similar way as the Négritude poet, the English-speaking African poet sought too to overcome his state of cultural ambiguity by the creation of a sense of identification with an ideal spirit of African life, a poetic personality that was fostered through a conscious sense of organic bond with nature. Thus Gabriel Okara proclaims:

> My laughter is the fire
> of the eye of the sky, the fire
> of the earth, the fire of the air
> the fire of the seas and the
> rivers fishes animals trees
> and it thawed your inside,
> thawed your voice, thawed your
> ears, thawed your eyes and
> thawed your tongue.
>
> So a meek wonder held
> your shadow and you whispered
> 'Why so?'
> And I answered:
> 'Because my fathers and I
> are owned by the living
> warmth of the earth
> through our naked feet.'[37]

In their very movement and reference, Okara's lines recall Senghor's 'Prière aux Masques', and with such evidence, it is difficult to sustain the argument of a complete disparity between themes and attitudes on both sides of African poetry. The parallels which exist between the poetic concerns and cultural feelings of the Négritude poets and those of their English-speaking counterparts is to be found not only in the work of the early generation of poets, but even more generally in the literary expression of Africans as it proceeds from the colonial experience. In the novel, as in poetry and drama, there is the same concern to place this experience and the social, cultural and psychological stresses that went with it in the perspective of a history that includes the determining factors of the African background as a significant dimension. In the poetry especially, there is the same concern to interiorize and make meaningful a new experience of traditional values. With the poetry of the generation of English-speaking African poets who succeeded the 'pioneers' – J. P. Clark, Kofi Awoonor, Christopher Okigbo and especially Wole Soyinka, to name only these – the traditionalism of the Négritude poets becomes more complex and more fully integrated into a broader consciousness of human experience, but the quest for 'moorings', for a rediscovery of a new spirit of life and existence that derives from the African background, remains central to the meaning of all their expression. This movement towards a re-initiation is well conveyed in the invocation which opens Okigbo's final collection of poems:

> Before you, mother Idoto
> naked I stand
> before your watery presence
> a prodigal
> leaning on an oil beam
> lost in your legend.
>
> Under your power wait I
> on barefoot
> watchman of the watchword
> at Heavensgate
> out of the depths my cry
> give ear and hearken . . .[38]

In view of this affinity between the literary expression of English-speaking and French-speaking writers, there is a certain irony to the fact that the slogan frequently used to dismiss Négritude was first uttered by Wole Soyinka, whose writing seems in all modern African literature to be most profoundly penetrated with the conscious traditionalism associated with Négritude.

The position of Soyinka with regard to Négritude is thus an interesting one. But his criticism of Négritude is quite understandable, even though it rests to a certain extent upon a misunderstanding. I do not think one can dismiss the literature of Négritude as sheer primitivism, as a romantic animism with no enduring moral value or quality of truth as Soyinka tends to do. The poetry of Senghor and Césaire, the tales of Birago Diop, the novels of Camara Laye and Cheikh Hamidou Kane, examined closely, reveal an area of sensibility that is nothing if not significant – they express the same attachment to human existence, with the same especial vigour of communicative art, that we expect of any true literature.

In a limited sense, however, one can understand Wole Soyinka's impatience with Négritude. In the first place, it appears too closely bound up with the white-black dialectic, by reason of its initial motivation, and like Fanon the whole point with Soyinka is to break out of this relationship, out of the colonial framework which gives an apologetic character to any African idea. Secondly, Soyinka's artistic conception is turned towards a moral vision which implies for the writer, prescribes for him even, an immediate engagement with reality. The artist is for him a reformer whose mission is to draw out a meaning from his intelligence of essential values. The past is, in this view, only significant as a bearer of lessons from which the artist proceeds to what he calls 'the re-appraisal of the whole human phenomenon'.

Clearly this is a salutory view which balances the romantic image of Africa presented in the early work of the Négritude writers. Soyinka displays a realism which consists in taking the imperfections of the past as an inherent aspect of every human situation, and in an invitation to a critical interrogation of our present in order to acquire a finer and truer sense of our becoming. Soyinka restores a necessary dimension to the African idea missing in Négritude. In the thirties and all through the colonial period, such realism was clearly impossible, for it was on the innocence of Africa that it was important to insist. The new generation of African writers and intellectuals have now been freed from the restraints of the colonial situation, and are expressing the reality of Africa in a new vein that contrasts sharply with that of their predecessors. This is but a normal development.

It is important however to point out that Soyinka's position by no means implies a complete denial of the past, but rather a new integration which situates the past and the traditional culture within a moral perspective. More, he has founded his myth of the artist precisely on the vital responses established between the modern writer and the ancestral creativeness, which he has striven to actualize in the symbolism and the quality of feeling that prevails in all his writing. There is thus a real sense in which it can be said that there is no better fulfilment of the idea of Négritude in modern literature than in the work of Soyinka himself.

Ideological development in Africa, either in the form of Négritude or under its English designation, 'African personality', has been largely a strategy with which to confront the contingencies of history. It had the primary objective of awakening the African consciousness so as to render us apt for action. It is in this sense that Aimé Césaire considered himself an 'inventor of souls'.

But if African thought has been largely a transposition to the intellectual plane of the responses to the colonial situation, it is also inscribed within a broader perspective which brings out the implications of the encounter with Europe in the very fact that we, as Africans, have become conscious of ourselves as a distinct category of men, with a responsibility to other men, it is true, but with a commitment to our particular destiny as a people. It is to this articulate sense of identity, to this organizing principle of collective consciousness that one may apply different terms, which reflect a certain diversity in emphasis, but which all refer to the same African idea. There is thus a fundamental unity of African thought underlying the various forms of ideological expression in Africa. This unity resides in the effort to bring the African mind to a new coincidence with its true foundation in a new African universe, to define as it were a founding myth as the basis of our action and collective existence in modern times. Herein lies what constitutes, in my opinion, the continuing relevance of concepts such as Négritude and African personality. This myth has been necessary for us black men in view of our painful history, an experience which we can certainly not afford to forget. It links us too with our Afro-American brothers whose vitality in America is a powerful vindication of ourselves, and indeed, who merit our constant consideration, not in an exclusive racial concern, but as what an African historian has called 'part of the discovery of Africa's place in universal history'.[39]

It is thus not a matter of casting romantic glances back at the past which can no longer be fully operative for us, nor of a narcissistic enfoldment in the self, but rather of an openness to the future – of its implications for ourselves and for the rest of the world. It is a question of our regaining the historical initiative of which we were deprived as a people, and with it an originality of thought and of action, with a meaning for ourselves in the first place and ultimately for the world with which we are today ineluctably involved in a common adventure.

Notes and References

1. 'Study and Race', reproduced in Hollis R. Lynch (ed.) *Black Spokesman: Selected Published Writings of Edward Wilmot Blyden* (London: Frank Cass, 1971).

2. Cf. Hollis Lynch, *Edward Wilmot Blyden, Pan-Negro Patriot 1832–1912* (London: Oxford University Press, 1968).

3. Garvey's 'Back to Africa' movement is today the best known expression of this phenomenon, but it was only a phase, albeit a spectacular one, in a long tradition of 'Emigrationism' among black Americans in the US. For a discussion of an important earlier phrase, see Richard Blackett, 'Martin Delaney and Robert Campbell: Black Americans in Search of an African Colony', in *The Journal of Negro History*, Vol. LXII, No. I, January 1977, pp. 1–25. For an account of the significance of Africa in contemporary black movements, see John Runcie, 'The Black Culture Movement and the Black Community', in *Journal of American Studies*, Cambridge, Vol. 10, No. 2, August 1976, pp. 185–214.

4. See in particular Lilyan Kesteloot, *Les Ecrivains noirs de langue française* (Brussels: Institut de Sociologie, Université libre de Bruxelles, 1963).

5. Originally published in London in 1789 under the title *The Interesting Narrative of the Life of Olaudah Equiano or Gustavus Vassa the African, written by himself* and reprinted with introduction and notes by Paul Edwards (London: Dowson's of Pall Mall, 1967); the present title is that of Paul Edwards' abridged edition published in the same year by Heinemann Educational Books as No. 10 in their African Writers Series. For a full account of the literature by black men during the eighteenth century in Europe, see Janheinz Jahn, *A History of Neo-African Literature* (London: Faber & Faber, 1968), ch. 3, and Robert July *The Origins of Modern African Thought* (London: Faber & Faber, 1968), ch. 2.

6. See Christopher Fyfe, *A History of Sierra Leone* (London: Oxford University Press, 1962), and Robert July, op. cit.

7. William Grant, quoted by Robert July, op. cit., p. 138.

8. Horton's principal work in this connection is *West African Countries and Peoples* (London: 1868; new edition Edinburgh: Edinburgh University Press, 1967). A selection of his writings is available in Abioseh Nicol (ed.) *Africanus Horton* (London: Longman, 1969). For an account of Horton's life and work, see Christopher Fyfe, *Africanus Horton, 1835–1883: West African Scientist and Patriot* (London: Oxford University Press, 1972).

9. Kola Adelaja, *Edward Wilmot Blyden et la naissance de la pensée politique africaine*, unpublished doctoral thesis, University of Paris, 1968.

10. 'Africa and the Africans' in *Christianity, Islam and the Negro Race* (London: 1887, new edition Edinburgh: Edinburgh University Press, 1962), pp. 276–77. The italics are in the original.

11. 'The Origins and Purpose of African Colonization', ibid., p. 94.

12. The local politics of Liberia and Sierra Leone in which Blyden was involved is fully described and related to his thought in the studies by Lynch, Fyfe and July already cited.

13. *African Life and Customs* (London, 1908), p. 51. The essay entitled 'Ethiopia Stretching out her Hands unto God: or, Africa's Service to the

World' is an extended statement of this idea. See *Christianity, Islam and the Negro Race*, pp. 113–29.

14. L. S. Senghor, *Nation et voies africaines du socialisme* (Paris: Présence Africaine, 1961), and *On African Socialism* (New York: Praeger, 1964), a translation into English by Mercer Cook of various writings by Senghor on the subject.

15. This statement was true in 1971 when the original version of this paper was written. Senghor subsequently made acquaintance with Blyden's work and contributed an appreciative prefatory essay to the edition of Blyden's correspondence prepared by Hollis Lynch under the title, *Selected Letters of Edward Wilmot Blyden* (New York: KTO Press, 1978).

16. See in particular V. Bakpetu Thompson, *Africa and Unity: the Evolution of Pan Africanism* (London: Longman, 1974).

17. See David Kimble, *A Political History of Ghana* (London: Oxford University Press, 1963), and Robert July, op. cit.

18. F. K. Drah, 'Introduction' to the reprint edition of J. W. de Graft Johnson, *Towards Nationhood in West Africa* (London: Frank Cass, 1971), p. vii. For a representative selection of the writings of these black intellectuals, see Lalage Bown, *Three Centuries of African Prose* (London: Heinemann Educational Books, 1973).

19. John Mensah-Sarbah, *Fanti Customary Laws* (London, 1897), reprinted with new introduction by Hollis Lynch (London: Frank Cass, 1968); *Fanti National Constitution* (London, 1906). For a particularly interesting assessment of Mensah-Sarbah's life and career, see S. Tenkorang, 'John Mensah-Sarbah 1864–1910', *Journal of the Historical Society of Ghana*, Vol. XIV, No. 1, pp. 65–78.

20. Caseley-Hayford's ideas on this question are set out in his *United West Africa* (London, 1919). For a more extensive discussion, see Martin Kilson, 'The National Congress of British West Africa' in Rotberg and Mazrui (eds.) *Protest and Power in Black Africa* (New York: Oxford University Press, 1970), pp. 571–88.

21. *Ethiopia Unbound: Studies in Race Emancipation* (London, 1911); reprinted with a new introduction by F. N. Ugonna, (London: Frank Cass, 1969). Dr Ugonna is also the author of a study of Caseley-Hayford: 'The Influence of African Nationalism on African Literature, 1900–1960, with Special Reference to Caseley-Hayford's *Ethiopia Unbound*', unpublished M. A. Thesis, University of Ibadan, 1971.

22. The principal organization through which this confrontation was carried out was the Aborigines Rights Protection Society, which grouped intellectuals devoted to the study of indigenous institutions with the specific aim of defending them against the policies of the colonial administration. Caseley-Hayford started his career within this society before breaking away to found the NCBWA. For an account of the political and socio-economic context of the activities of the ARPS, see F. K. Drah op. cit., and M. Bjorn Edsman, *Lawyers in Gold Coast Politics 1900–1945* (Uppsala: Acta Universitatis Upsaliensis, 1979), especially chapter II, pp. 54–81.

23. When it is recalled that it was J. B. Danquah, scholar, politician and

author of the *Akan Concept of God* who first mooted the idea of 'Ghana' as a possible designation for the territory of the former Gold Coast, it will be realized how much the present state owes to the intellectual efforts of men of this generation.

24. For a discussion of these two works in the context of Azikiwe's life and career, see K. A. B. Jones, *Quartey, A Life of Azikiwe* (Harmondsworth: Penguin Books, 1965).

25. Obafemi Awolowo, *The Strategy and Tactics of a People's Republic of Nigeria* (London and Ibadan: Macmillan, 1971).

26. Julius Nyerere, *Ujamaa: Essays on Socialism* (London: Oxford University Press, 1968), p. 17.

27. Kwame Nkrumah, *Consciencism* (London: Heinemann Educational Books, 1965), reprinted 1974 (Panaf Books). My quotations are taken from the first edition.

28. Op. cit., p. 107.

29. Ibid., p. 114.

30. Ibid., p. 115.

31. 'The African Genius', speech at the opening of the Institute of African Studies, University of Ghana, Legon, p. 3.

32. *Consciencism*, p. 109.

33. L. S. Senghor, *Négritude, francité et arabité* (Beirut: Dar el Kitab Allubnani, 1969). See also 'Négritude et arabisme' in *Présence Africaine*, No. 61, 1er trimestre, 1967, pp. 94–102.

34. Ezekiel Mphahlele, *The African Image* (London: Faber & Faber, 1961), pp. 25–6.

35. The same point is made at greater length by P. A. V. Ansah in his article 'Black Awareness in African Poetry in English', *Legon Journal of the Humanities*, University of Ghana, Vol. I, 1974, pp. 35–53.

36. Abioseh Nicol 'Easter Morning' in Donatus Nwoga (ed.) *West African Verse* (London: Longman, 1967), p. 26.

37. Gabriel Okara, 'You Laughed and Laughed and Laughed', in *The Fisherman's Invocation* (London: Heinemann Educational Books, 1979), p. 25.

38. Christopher Okigbo, 'The Passage' in *Labyrinths* (London: Heinemann Educational Books, 1971), p. 3.

39. Andrew Porter, in Broshenka and Crowder (eds.) *Africa in the Wider World* (Oxford: Pergamon Press, 1967), p. III.

6. Pan-Africanism and African Nationalism

▼▼

The modern history of Africa is hardly conceivable without an attentive consideration of the role played in its development by the idea of African Unity. But although this idea owes its force to the direct contribution of the Pan-African movement to African Nationalism, it remains, despite the substantial political success of the latter, to be realized in the form of concrete political and economic institutions serving as effective channels of African thought and action at the continental and international levels. Its importance at the present moment resides less in its objective reality than in its subjective, ideological significance – in the progressive hold which it has taken of African minds to such an extent that it has assumed a dominant place in African political consciousness and expression.

So firm and so profound a coincidence between an idea and the collective sentiment could no doubt be credited to the influence of individual thinkers and leaders, who by the force of their intellectual efforts and of their personalities have been able to succeed in winning massive adherence to their ideas. At the same time, it seems pertinent to emphasize at this time that African nationalism and the Pan-African movement have a common source in the historical and sociological context of the colonial situation. An intimate correlation existed between the idea of nationalism in Africa, and the idea of African unity which found, in the early period of the anti-colonial movement, so distinct an expression that the two were in fact practically identified. Thus Thomas Hodgkin was able to apply the term 'nationalist' in a broad sense 'to describe any organization or group that explicitly asserts the rights and aspirations of a given African society (from the level of the language group to that of "Pan Africa") in opposition to European authority, whatever its institutional form and objectives' (*Nationalism in Tropical Africa*, p. 23). In fact, Pan-Africanism did not only represent a logical extension of the various localized manifestations of African nationalism, it appeared indeed as its global expression and the concept of African unity as its most complete ideological formulation.

This is the perspective in which Vincent Bakpetu Thompson has situ-

ated his study of Pan-Africanism, by pursuing in the evolution of the
movement the line of progression leading from the various movements for
African emancipation to their culmination in the Pan-African ideal. His
historical account of the Pan-African movement takes the form of a wide-
ranging discussion that constantly involves, besides the specific relationship of Pan-Africanism to nationalist consciousness in Africa, the whole
question of African aspirations in the modern world. The quest for continental unity thus appears as the fundamental reference for African
political activity, and the basic ideological principle on which African
history is revolving in the contemporary era.

It is in this respect that the study focuses attention, especially in its account of the founding of the OAU in 1963 and the vicissitudes the organization has known in its short existence, upon the implication for the Pan-
African idea of the attainment of independence by the majority of African
countries. What emerges from this discussion is the ironical turn taken in
the present post-colonial period by the historical relationship between
Pan-Africanism as a concept and as a movement, and African nationalism
as a political reality. The irony resides in the fact that today, the idea of
African unity as conceived in the Pan-African movement, and as propounded by such nationalist leaders as Nkrumah and Azikiwe, stands in
direct contradiction to the objective historical consequences of African
nationalism, which in its development has shaped the present political
reality of Africa. For the emergence of territorial units having as their
overall model the European nation-state, and equipped with such political
and legal institutions as would enable them to function as such, represents
the measure of success of nationalist agitation in Africa. At the same time,
the very political success of nationalism has created the conditions for a
limited national as against a broader continental, or even regional, feeling
and loyalty.

This situation is further complicated by the fact that practically every
African State is in reality multi-national, so that African leaders have been
more absorbed by the political problems of ethnic relations in their
countries and their efforts towards the promotion of unity at the territorial
level, than by the question of realizing an effective form of continental
unity. This perhaps more than any other single factor explains why the
OAU, fashioned out of a compromise at the Addis Ababa Conference of
1963, came to be conceived as a consultative assembly of sovereign states
rather than as a supra-national institution – as a body that enshrines the
nation-state idea in Africa rather than as an instrument designed to transcend it. In these conditions the idea of African unity appears in reality

more as an ideological relic of African nationalism than as a meaningful source of political values and action.

When this development is set against the original involvement of African nationalism with Pan-Africanism, it cannot but strike one as highly paradoxical. For there is a sense in which the Pan-African movement reflected more truly the African situation, showed a more adequate correspondence to the sociological context of nationalism in Africa and therefore to the historical needs of African peoples than the 'territorial' nationalism which appears to have triumphed. Yet it is a development which seems to have been inherent in the very course which African nationalism had to take in the years after the Second World War in order to succeed at all, a course which forced it to diverge from the direction which the Pan-African idea had worked out.

The formal resemblances between nationalist movements in Europe and similar African phenomena have tended to be emphasized by their political objectives – the drive towards statehood, which in the African context is expected to effect the evolution of nations, each with its own individuality. Thus David Kimble, rejecting the suggestion that African nationalism could be a *species sui generis* has observed with some emphasis: 'African nationalism, although it may be precipitated by the domination of alien European powers, is not otherwise fundamentally different in kind from nationalism elsewhere'. (*A Political History of Ghana*, p. xiii.) But while it is important to see the fundamental human basis for the reaction against alien domination, it is also necessary to distinguish the historical and sociological contingencies which determine the forms and directions of such reaction in each particular case.

Thus, the most striking point about African nationalism, when compared with its European precedents and parallels, is the distinctive fact that this was a movement in which the national principle as it was understood in Europe played a minor role. The various manifestations of African nationalism did not, save for exceptional cases, correspond as in Europe to the advocacy of the rights to separate political existence of particular African nationalities, each defined by a common language or a common culture. Seen as a whole, nationalism in Africa developed first as a generalized movement for African freedom from European rule before it acquired political objectives and became variously localized as separate and distinctive currents, each driving towards political independence of a given administrative and territorial unit ruled by the same colonial power.

In its origins, modern nationalism in Africa – as distinct from the earlier forms of resistance to European penetration – was primarily a reaction to the colonial situation, and only secondarily an advocacy of the rights of

particular African peoples to self-determination. The comprehensive transformations in African societies had rendered largely non-operative the
traditional political institutions; the very super-imposition of European
authority over these, even in societies which formed recognizable national
entities, as well as the grouping, however arbitrary, of several linguistic
and cultural communities together within the same administrative and
territorial unit, had created a new sociological reality which superseded
the old. The colonial rulers, by drawing new administrative and juridical
lines around African peoples and societies, had weakened the old political
lines which distinguished them as nations in the ordinary understanding
of the word – that is, in terms of a coincidence between territories and
historically defined peoples.

Moreover, the principal and indeed outstanding point of cleavage in
colonial society was the racial factor, the division between the white ruler
on the one hand, and the oppressed African on the other. Thus, although
the early ideological and nationalist leaders retained their primary affiliations to their language and culture groups, and although their reaction
against colonial rule often sprang from a certain sense of cultural discomfort, the common factor of African peoples ruled by European powers
tended to give a broad continental perspective to their thinking and to
their activities. The fact too that the African élite, whose social frustrations
in colonial society provided the deep motivation for their reaction, often
shared a common European education also helped to foster the sense of
common purpose which lies behind such organizations as Caseley-
Hayford's West African Congress and Solanke's West African Students'
Union, organizations in which nationalist feelings were consistently given
a Pan-African expression in the years before the Second World War. In
other words, the peculiarity of African nationalism derived from the fact
that in its origins, it was caught between the appeal of those tribal and
cultural factors which gave a basis to nationalism in Europe, and the particular pressures of the colonial situation, which created the sentiment of
a shared condition among Africans, and hence a common consciousness.

This common consciousness was however only made distinct and
formulated into an ideology through the Pan-African movement. Although
implicit in the very forms which early African nationalism tended to take,
the Pan-African idea originated from America, where the racial issue
helped to foster among the black population a race consciousness in which
Africa developed into a powerful psychological and ideological symbol.
The black Americans came to acquire a unified vision of Africa that no
primary bonds of language and culture within Africa itself could possibly
interfere with. Their imaginative projection of Africa was all of one piece,
so that for a man like Du Bois, the transfer of immediate loyalty from the

State, to which he technically belonged, to the Black race, led to a consideration of Africa as a 'nation', as a single spiritual entity.

The idea of Africa as a nation in this sense also came to have political implications in view of the almost total subjection of the continent to European domination. The Pan-African movement developed as a double reaction against both white racism as it operated in America, and white imperialism which was its parallel in Africa, and it is through the specific channel of its activities – as led both by Du Bois and Marcus Garvey, in particular – that a definite correlation was established between African nationalism and the Black revolt, and that the idea of African unity was given a sharp focus and endowed with a positive political value and meaning.

The position of Kwame Nkrumah as the living pivot on which the ideological and affective reciprocity between Pan-Africanism and African nationalism revolved is too well known to require here more than a mention. The significance of Nkrumah's role and of his career after the 1945 Manchester Conference is that through him, as Bakpetu Thompson points out, Pan-Africanism as a movement was brought home to Africa, and thus made its transition from the ideological to the political phase. Yet it is precisely to this evolution, this descent from the realm of ideas to that of praxis, of action 'on the ground' as it were, that its gradual disconnection from African nationalism, in real as distinct from theoretical terms, can be traced. The practical divergence between the Pan-African ideal and the concrete objectives of African nationalism which began to take place as soon as the latter took the form of independence movements, took what one might call a 'territorial turn'.

The years that followed immediately upon the Second World War witnessed an intensification of the anti-colonial movement in Africa marked especially by the decisive entry of the African people as a whole into the movement, and the consequent emergence of mass parties. The socio-economic repercussions of the war had ushered in a season of general discontent which created this direct involvement of the masses, and which gave to the nationalist drive a new dimension and quality. Instead of the limited demands for participation in the political life of the colonial system which the élite of the pre-war years had sought, the new nationalism, more radical, called into question the whole system, posing in an acute form the political problem which the principle of colonial rule had held at bay – the problem of self-rule.

In order to assume a more concrete character, to be effective at all, the new nationalism had to focus its attack upon specific issues, and therefore to deal with the particular administrative establishments in each colonial territory. Agitation centred not simply upon abstract rights but upon immediate economic and social problems which created a comprehensive and meaningful framework of political action. In this way, in each territory, a focus of local issues was created around which nationalist activity was organized, so that it was not so much a sense of nationhood emerging in each territory, as that these differentiated areas of discontent and agitation began to break up African nationalism into distinctive territorial currents.

But perhaps the most important factor in this post-war development of territorial nationalism was the political question itself. By the middle of the fifties, the reversal of the colonial system was confidently envisaged by most nationalist leaders, and its replacement by a new political order which would involve self-rule and ultimately independence for the colonies came clearly in sight. Nationalism in Africa began from this time to pursue an explicitly political goal and the attainment of some form of statehood for colonial peoples became its principal concern. This objective called for a geo-political framework for its realization and subsequent organization, and it is one of the most interesting ironies of African history that our leaders came to accept the partition of Africa, decided upon at the Berlin Conference of 1885, as the only workable basis of the new political order.

It is not difficult, however, to understand why this was so. It was clear that a return to the pre-colonial state of affairs was impossible. Moreover, the ideal of a modern state which most African leaders pursued was modelled to a large extent on the political institutions of the West, even though the sociological realities of Africa were signally different. Thus, although ethnic affiliations deriving from the traditional societies were still strong in Africa, they were devalued in favour of a new principle that took the territory as the framework of political association and as the basis for the State, even when it cut across these affiliations, as in the case of the Bakongo and the Ewes. This triumph of the territorial principle underlines the minor role of the national principle in African nationalism, and accounts for the fact that it was possible to integrate Kikuyu nationalism as expressed in the Mau Mau revolution and Yoruba revivalism of the Action Group into a wider territorial consciousness and political purpose in Kenya and Nigeria respectively.

There was then no question of 'unscrambling' Africa, hence the colonial legacy was accepted as the basis of the new political developments in Africa. But although this situation could be considered a progressive one in terms of modern political values, it appears to have been created at the expense of the Pan-African ideal. The inevitable tensions involved in the multi-ethnic composition of African states have created a gulf between the idea of national unity as a political need, and that of African unity as an ideological value; a gulf which began to yawn as the evolution of colonial territories in Africa towards statehood became the exclusive objective of nationalist activity.

The immediate consequence of the concentration of the efforts and thinking of African leaders upon the territory was a significant lull in Pan-African activities, between 1945 and 1957, the year of Ghana's independence. In English-speaking West Africa for example, there was hardly any formal consultation, let alone active collaboration, between Nkrumah and Azikiwe, both of whom had emerged as territorial figures despite their Pan-African beginnings. In the French Colonial empire, the territorial trend was even more marked after the Loi-cadre of 1956, which began the process through which the two federations that constituted the French colonial empire in Africa were dismantled. The cohesive influence of the great political party, the RDA, was worn down, not only by the ideological conflicts that developed within it, but also, and indeed primarily, by the assertion of local territorial interests which stood against the maintenance of the federations. This, more than the example of Togo, as Edward Mortimer has suggested (in his *France and the Africans*, pp. 233–240), was responsible for the fact that Francophone Africa attained independence as a multitude of small states rather than as two large federations campaigned for by Senghor.

The very logic of the territorial emphasis in the final phase of African nationalism was reflected in the action of the leaders themselves after independence. Thus, in order to emphasize Ghana's new status after 1957, Nkrumah expended considerable effort in giving to the state those external attributes of sovereignty that would not only mark its formal break with the colonial past but also foster a new sense of national belonging among the various peoples of the state. In the process, some of the economic ties which bound Ghana to other African countries were dissolved. The same logic obliged Julius Nyerere to abandon his first intention to wait for the other two East African countries with which his country shared common frontiers and services, and to press for independence for Tanganyika.

With these political developments brought about by the territorial trend in African nationalism, a new conception of African unity appeared which gave a semblance of coherence to them. African unity began to be seen as the final stage of the independence movements, rather than as an inherent condition of African nationalism. In political and institutional terms, the Pan-African ideal in its most advanced formulation has now taken the form of a quest for the political union of sovereign states in a continental government, that is to say, an extension of the nation-state.

Despite the progressive aspect of this development of the Pan-African ideal, the fact remains that it does not correspond to the original and more creative movement for an integration of African peoples into larger unions of viable states which was implied by the early phase of Pan-Africanism, and which seems at the moment to have been defeated by the territorial principle. It looks then as if the very force of history, as represented by the colonial fact, has effectively worked against the original Pan-African idea. The present situation in Africa, characterized by small and unstable states, is thus an indication of that passive sufferance of history which nationalism attempted to reverse, and which the Pan-African movement strove to transform, at the international level, into an active confrontation by Africans of the challenge of the modern world.

For the ultimate objective of nationalism, to which the Pan-African movement gave a striking and sometimes dramatic dimension, was the fulfilment of African aspirations to a meaningful place and role in the modern world. The political programme could only be a means to this end, and the attainment of statehood a preparation for the more fundamental objective. That this objective is still as remote as ever seems at the moment fairly clear, despite the formal success of nationalism in Africa. The importance attached today to the idea of African unity among the younger generation of the African intelligentsia is a reflection of the disillusionment with the practical result of the nationalist movement in Africa.

The very tone of Bakpetu Thompson's book is an indication of the profound nature of this disillusionment. It seems certain that this mood will grow with the coming years, and that the attachment to the idea of African unity will come to stand as the emotional foundation for a new form of African 'nationalism', continental in scope, in which the ideas of the Pan-African movement will perhaps be taken up with a new vigour, with a new sense of creative idealism.

Part Three
Literary Studies

7. Literature and Ideology in Martinique: René Maran, Aimé Césaire, Frantz Fanon

▼▼

The Afro-American has three horizons – firstly, that of his immediate American universe; secondly, that provided by the silhouette of Europe, which lies historically and culturally behind America, and of which, as Paul Valéry observed,[1] America itself is an extension; and thirdly, that represented by Africa, the source of his racial origin. It is within this triangular framework of references and responses that his social and emotional life has been taking place in the course of his American existence.

The specific European dimension is perhaps even more sharply outlined in the awareness of the black Caribbean. Britain and France having retained political control for centuries in the West Indies, having shaped directly the history of large areas in this part of the American continent for so long a time, it is only natural that the cultural history of the West Indies, particularly of the French-speaking and the English-speaking parts, should in fact have been dominated by the idea of Europe as the live source of ideas and of values. At the same time, the idea of Africa, even in the negative form it often took, formed part of the consciousness of the Caribbean and intruded upon his social as well as moral vision, keeping alive for him the three poles of awareness that I have outlined above.

It is within this scheme that I would like to examine the development of a new current of social consciousness in Martinique in the twentieth century; tracing its course in the writings of the three outstanding writers that the island has produced so far, namely: René Maran, Aimé Césaire, and Frantz Fanon. For it seems to me that what characterizes the evolution of the ideological awareness that runs in a single progressive course through the writings of these three men is the role played by the opposition between Europe and Africa, with the West Indies in the middle, not only as antithetical terms in the system of social symbols that govern the West Indian collective consciousness, but indeed as social and political realities, as concrete references within the contemporary world order. Furthermore, this evolution has involved a clear shift from the simple expression of attitudes towards an elaboration of ideas, culminating, with Fanon, in the formulation of a world view.

It would be well to begin our discussion by recalling briefly the history of the association of Martinique with France, as well as the social and cultural consequences of this association, as a preliminary background to our discussion. Martinique was 'discovered' by Columbus in 1502, and occupied by France in 1635, and has remained French, with hardly any interruption, ever since. The introduction of the black man into the island dates also from this latter date, and indeed, the political and social history of Martinique has been determined largely by his presence. The three most significant periods of this history can be marked off with reference to him – the slave period which ended with the emancipation of 1848; the colonial period which runs from this date to 1946, when Martinique was integrated into the French nation; and the present period, which can therefore be termed 'the citizen period'. Viewed externally, then, the history of Martinique can be summed up as that of the progressive promotion of the black man on the island.

The social and cultural corollary to this development can also be summed up in the well-worn word: assimilation. It is however on this score that the history of Martinique shows an internal contradiction. Without going into details, I should only like to point out that because this assimilation took place in a typical colonial context, it created the familiar tensions that one has come to associate with the cultural and ideological situation in colonial societies. The racial ideology which, though unofficial, came to underline and to sanction the objective socio-economic division of Martinican society – white upper class, mulatto middle class, black lower class – also acquired a cultural significance in so far as a certain cultural differentiation existed between these three social categories, a differentiation accounted for, as far as the lower class was concerned, by the African element in the way of life of the black population.[2] One significance of this situation, in the context of assimilation in Martinique, is that social symbols crystallized around this objective factor, posing Europe and white culture as synonymous and as the ideal, and Africa and black culture as the negative term of this ideal.

The unilateral character of French assimilation could not but complicate this situation. The social sanction of French culture, inherent in the political ascendancy of the French people, put a pressure upon the black man in Martinique not simply to follow a positive course towards assimilation, but to accompany the process with the negative gesture of the denial of his African antecedents. The social symbols that governed collective life in Martinique were thus wholly weighted against the black man, and the purely social factors of his collective life combined with the cultural in what amounted to his negation by the dominating racial ideology of Martinican society. This process of negation was founded ultimately on an idea of Africa.

If I insist here on this ideological factor rather than on the purely social and economic aspects of the colonial situation in Martinique, it is because of the special importance which it took here, due to the very fact that the official policy practised by the French was one of equality, and so the real conflict in the French-speaking Caribbean situation lay less on the socioeconomic than on the racial level. And in this connection, the negative significance given to Africa contributed to the mental distress of the Antillean in such a way as to emphasize the racial question as his most dramatic problem.

Africa was a troubling presence in the mind and in the imagination of the average Antillean. It represented for him a synonym for savagery, as opposed to the civilization of Europe, the image of blackness which contradicted his dream of total whiteness.[3] For having accepted the norms proposed by his own society and taken as the only valid measure of his humanity the degree of his approximation to the white ideal, he could not escape the fact of his own blackness. His own body remained for him, in an immediate and overwhelming manner, a constant reminder of the global accusation directed against him by his own society. Perhaps nowhere more than in the French Caribbean was the inclination to self-denial as strongly accentuated in the collective attitudes that ruled social life among black people in America. The peculiar form then that colonial alienation took in Martinique, as in the French Caribbean generally, was that the black man lived in a state of permanent dissociation from the social symbols which formed the framework of his social existence and of his emotional life.

The state of alienation, it is said, does not present a problem to the individual until it has permeated to the consciousness, until it is extended from the plane of pure reality to that of felt experience. The situation I have summarized for Martinique was in fact accepted, to the extent that the average Antillean took care to distinguish himself from the African, and came to look upon himself as a Frenchman, whatever his colour. This attitude was justified insofar as the culture that he received was in fact French. However, the energetic refusal of Africa which usually accompanied the Martinican's affirmation of his Frenchness, introduced a problematic factor into this affirmation; it indicated clearly to the Antillean his moral dependence upon the French and consequently his incompleteness, so to speak, as a human being. It created in his psyche an incompleteness of self-identification which tended to engender in him a feeling of being somehow 'abnormal', and fostered the kind of tensions that Fanon has described in his book *Black Skin, White Masks*.[4]

The prevailing overt attitude remained, however, one of total acceptance of 'white' values. This attitude is reflected in the kind of imaginative writing produced in Martinique before the appearance in 1921 of René Maran's first novel, *Batouala*. Before Maran, literary expression conformed in its themes and formal patterns to the French norm. Its tone was dictated exclusively by the prevailing fashion in Paris, its sentiments largely determined by the attitudes of the average Frenchman towards the Antilles. The Caribbean scene features in this literature, particularly in the poetry, as a decorative element, never as a human scene. The French West Indian writer contributed mainly to the Parnassian taste for the exotic, without ever feeling the need to assert any form of individuality. In the years between the end of the nineteenth century and the First World War, Martinique experienced something of a literary renaissance,[5] but produced nothing more than a literature of acquiescence and of what one might call the exterior regard.[6]

René Maran brought a new development into the outlook of Martinican writing, in an indirect but decisive way. It is worth remarking that Maran began his literary career as a symbolist poet, albeit at the decadent stage. Born in 1887 in Martinique of Guyanese parents, Maran did not really get to know his native land and his experience of the colonial situation was to be made in Africa itself. He was taken to France at the age of four and apart from occasional journeys to Central Africa where his father was a colonial officer, spent all his youth in France. He attended College at Bordeaux, and grew up in his education, in his attitudes and in his tastes a Frenchman. His French beginnings in literature were therefore, despite the colour of his skin, perfectly natural. He published two volumes of poetry in his early years in the intimate vein of the later symbolists, and came to be considered a promising regionalist poet, who blended a feeling for landscape with a rare psychological insight. These are qualities which were later to be given forceful expression in his African novels. When it is considered, however, that his second volume of poems, entitled *La Vie intérieure* (1912) was composed almost entirely in Central Africa, where by 1910 Maran had taken up a post in the French colonial administration, the cleavage between the subtle and evanescent inner life to which he gave expression in this volume, and the harsh glare of the African scene which he was later to document in *Batouala*, cannot but strike one as being in every way absolute.

Maran's direct experience of Africa was to change the course of his literary preoccupations and to transform to a considerable extent his own social and human awareness. His correspondence during this period conveys the changes that this experience began to effect in his outlook, and which were to wrench him away from the immaterial vision of his symbolist verse and impel him towards the mindful confrontation with human beings and with events which produced *Batouala*.

The sensitive nature which his lonely youth in France had bred in him did not prepare him for the shock of life in colonial Africa, and it was perhaps because of this that it made such a profound impression upon him. But apart from the immediate psychological impact which his experience had upon him, the fact of his blackness came to have a special significance for him in Africa. Maran does not seem to have been oblivious of this fact even in France, for in a letter to one of his friends, written in connection with an obscure love affair, he leaves us in no doubt as to what the fact of his blackness meant to him:

> And then I am Negro. These five words carry with them all the maledictions, because whatever I do, I remain, secretly, infinitely sensitive.[7]

He may have, as a result, felt a distance separating him from his French colleagues and thereby acquired that measure of detachment necessary to cast an objective and critical eye upon the colonial system. Moreover, the irony of his own position as a black man administering other black men does not seem to have escaped him, and in one of his letters the inevitable feeling of his racial identity that this ironical situation inspired in him is given clear expression. He writes:

> Here, with a French heart, I sense that I am on the soil of my ancestors, ancestors that I reject because I do not share either their primitive mentality or their tastes, but who are nevertheless my ancestors.[8]

Maran's ambivalent attitude towards his African origins implied however a minimum of identification and indicates that his situation was that of a marginal man, placed at the sensitive centre of a conflictual situation. At any rate Maran had precise ideas about what he wanted his novel to do, for it is clear from his correspondence that he conceived it with a critical intent. He spent seven years of careful labour upon it and though he was preoccupied with the problem of style in its elaboration, this preoccupation was in fact largely motivated by his concern to render his expression adequate for the purpose which he attached to the work. Without a doubt, this purpose was to give a testimony of the colonial situation, as he clearly indicates in his correspondence.

Referring to a chapter he was preparing to compose, in one of his letters
he writes:

> I shall bring together in it almost all the grievances that these primitive
> races are accustomed to formulate against Europeans. I will need to ani-
> mate the customs and the dances that I describe in it; finally, employing
> a manner which delights me, I shall bind together, imperceptibly and
> with a knot which at first sight appears loose, the plot to the whole of
> the folklore, the movement and the satires.[9]

Further on in the same letter he writes:

> I am not dealing in exotism in the manner of L . . . (reference obscure)
> or of Loti. The descriptive passages, no more than the others, are not
> imagined.[10]

In considering the work itself, the same ambiguity that we have noted
in Maran's attitude can be discerned in the picture of Africa which he
presents. His image is consciously tainted by the prejudices of the European, and this is demonstrated by the main plot of the work which revolves
around the theme of sexual jealousy and expresses this theme in terms of
an almost animal sensuality.

In an obvious sense and from the purely documentary point of view,
the novel presents an overall picture of African life which is negative. Yet
a close examination of the work, of its levels of meaning, of its narrative
technique and of its symbolic structure reveals the profound identification
which Maran had achieved within his own sensibility with Africa, an
organic sympathy with African life and people which belies the conscious
detachment of Maran's realism.

The first quality that strikes one in this respect is the poetic intensity
of Maran's descriptive passages. The whole work itself can be taken as one
long prose poem in which the African scene is invested with an unac-
customed symbolic power, as in this evocation of sunset:

> Then broad streaks of crimson spread out across space. Decreasing in
> hue, from shade to shade, from transparency to transparency, these
> streaks began to lose their way in the immensity of the sky. And in their
> turn, these shades and transparencies faded until they were no more.
> The undefinable silence which had watched over the agony and the
> death of the sun extended over all the lands.
> A poignant melancholy moved among the stars appearing in the
> horizon. The hot lands exhale mists, and the humid scents of the night
> get on the move. Dew weighs down the forest. One would almost think
> that the feeble odour of the wild mint hums in the wind with the beetle
> and the hairy insects . . .
> Like a canoe brushing its way through watery shrubs – how it glides
> evenly through the clouds – behold Ipeu the moon, all white, appearing.
> She is already six nights old.[11]

I quote this passage at some length, even in my inadequate translation, because such poetry had not before been expended upon the African landscape. It reveals a new feeling of passionate communion with the African scene which we also find in Maran's evocation of the people; such indeed, that even when he intrudes the prejudices he inherited from his French background into this evocation, they give ground before the compelling sincerity of his poetic insight into the communal life of his Africans.

Consider, for example, another extract:

> Dancing and singing are all our life. We dance in honour of the moon, or to celebrate Lolo the sun. We dance on account of everything, on account of nothing, for the joy of it. We dance the dance of the water of the earth and of the water of the sky, the dance of fire, the dance of the wind, the dance of the ant, the dance of the elephant, the dance of the trees, the dance of the leaves, the dance of the stars, the dance of the earth and of what lies within . . .[12]

What a passage like this communicates takes us beyond the simple report of a fact but rather into the sharing of a distinct and especial feeling of life. The immediate and intuitive coincidence of Maran's sensibility with his African subject that these passages reveal also explains his almost total reorganization of the narrative scheme and resources of his novel along new lines which take the direction of the imaginative tradition of Africa itself. The very stylistic traits of the novel participate in its African atmosphere. In his dialogue, he recasts the French language in order to make it capture the very tone and the feel of speech of his African characters. Thus half a century before Achebe, the African proverb had made its appearance in a novel written in a European language.

What is more, the very structure and movement of Maran's prose capture for us those elements in the oral tradition of Africa which give it its distinctive flavour. It is a style full of those insistent repetitions of words and sonal values weaving a pattern of refrains and of alliterations through his narrative, and which we can now recognize as deriving from those elements which compose the essence of the oral tradition of Africa.

Maran could not have achieved these effects unless he had listened with an unusually attentive ear to African speech. In one remarkable passage which indicates how well and closely Maran had observed his Africans to the point of identification, he brings together these distinctive features to recreate the distinctive rhetorical manner of the African countryside and to lend dramatic tension to his narrative.[13]

Batouala, suspecting Bissibi'ngui of designs on his wife Yassigui'ndja, invites his rival to an isolated part of the forest with the intention of killing him. The latter suspects what is in store for him, and prepares himself mentally to give blow for blow. The encounter between the two men takes place in an ominous atmosphere. But as they meet, they greet each other in proverbs and carry on their conversation in allusive speech. They then recount the fables, in which each man conveys his individual sentiment, the folktales expanding on the proverbs, elaborating in figurative language their purport. The two men fence with each other in words in this way until Batouala, unable to restrain himself any longer, makes a pointed statement that uncovers starkly the dread issue that divides the two men.

We have then, in *Batouala*, something far in advance of exotism, something more than a mere outside representation of a foreign atmosphere, but an evocation that goes a long way towards restituting the inner quality of life in a specific human universe. Maran not only portrayed Africa in his novel, but by integrating into the whole design of the work such elements as would break through the confines of an externally contrived representation, takes his readers further into the intimate recesses of African experience.

This, more than the explicit anti-colonial passages, makes Maran an innovator in modern African literature, and indeed, the creator of the modern African novel. He pointed the way by this single work, by its demonstrative value, to those African writers in French who came after him, by achieving a reconversion of the European language to render immediate the atmosphere of Africa. Furthermore, within this scheme of his novel, Maran also created an African, for the first time in French literary history, as a true tragic figure, endowed with an authentic imaginative life. Maran impresses his hero upon our feelings and, indeed, upon our intelligence. The African thus comes alive as a hero, that is, as a man with feeling, with his passions, and above all, with his own manner of apprehending the world.

Batouala also establishes a direct relationship between the lives of his African characters and the colonial situation, between the external framework of African life at a precise historical moment and the destiny of individuals involved in it. It is from this perspective that the novel performs the social function which its author claimed for it in the preface he added to the second edition, published after the work had obtained the Prix Goncourt in 1921. We know that Maran, after the storm provoked by his novel, was dismissed from the colonial service and withdrew into stoic retirement. His writings afterwards indicate that he was agitated by a personal conflict of loyalties. On the one hand, he continued to express his attachment to France and its culture by cultivating a delicate prose, with a dedication reminiscent of Flaubert, and to the French empire by writing four volumes on its heroes and builders. On the other hand, he also cultivated his African vein in a stream of animal and symbolic novels, the most remarkable of which is *Le Livre de la brousse* (1934). In particular, he poured his personal conflicts into an autobiographical novel, *Un Homme pareil aux autres* (1947).

Maran never 'committed' himself politically, but the true import of his career, especially when viewed against his background, resided in the fact that a West Indian, utterly assimilated to French culture, had been confronted with the contradiction of his position and had begun to move towards a view of things outside and beyond the French scheme of values. The critical intelligence which underlies *Batouala*, as well as the imaginative sympathy which he achieved in his novels with the African continent – and which implied a positive valorization of the continent – indicate a reflective consciousness which was bound to affect the vision of the West Indian in his double relation to Europe and to Africa. For Maran had written out of a frame of mind which was not simply moral or liberal, but denoted a sense of concern and involvement, limited perhaps in scope and intensity, but nonetheless real.

This sense of involvement implicit in Maran's work becomes explicit in the work of Aimé Césaire, who was to give a definite figure to the hesitant social vision of his predecessor. In the great poem by Césaire, his first work, *Cahier d'un retour au pays natal* (1939) the contained indignation of Maran explodes into open revolt, and into a new determination. With Césaire, moral concern is transformed into passionate commitment.

Césaire's literary work, especially when considered in conjunction with his political activities, represents more than the expression of an attitude or a symbolic gesture, but rather a privileged form of action – that is, poetic action whose direction is the activation of the mind of the West Indian and whose purpose is the total transformation of his mode of insertion in the world order. Césaire inscribes his poetry within a historical vision and ascribes to it a function – that of formulating for the West Indian a new form of historical existence.

That Césaire was brought to embrace his vocation as a poet of the black consciousness is due not only to his temperament but also to a combination of factors which converged upon him, at a precise moment in history, to determine this vocation for him. Between Maran and Césaire lies a development which gathered force during the inter-war years, and which favoured the emergence of a new current of feeling and of ideas in the French Caribbean. The atmosphere of spiritual distress that settled upon Europe after the carnage of the First World War, and the background of economic difficulties and political tension, determined an intellectual climate in which the old ideas and values that appeared to have sustained European civilization began to be called into question. The surrealist movement is the natural child of those times. The confrontation between

Fascism and Communism which began to split Europe, and the general moral unease that pervaded the European continent left an impression on black intellectuals in Europe: Europe had been shown to be frail and vulnerable. In America, the Negro Renaissance expressed in literature the new mood of affirmation that was spreading through the black population, and in Haiti, the Indigenist movement, led by Dr Price-Mars, had begun to question the primacy of European values in the collective expression of black men whose historical and racial antecedents – and consequently, cultural and spiritual essence – derived more from Africa than from Europe. And of course, the protest theme, in relation to the racial problem, which was the keynote of all this literature, brought home to the French Caribbean the fact of the colonial problem on his island.

It was in Martinique that the immediate follow-up to Maran's gesture was to come, in the form of Etienne Lero's manifesto, *Légitime défense*, which appeared in 1932 in Paris. Lero attacked the lack of relevance of the accepted literature of Martinique:

> A foreigner would look in vain in this literature for an original or profound accent, for the sensual and colourful imagination of the black man, for an echo of the resentment as well as the aspiration of an oppressed people.[14]

Etienne Lero died shortly after, and it was upon Césaire that his mantle came to fall. Césaire, who was a student in Paris at the time, had met Léopold Senghor, also a student, and together they had discovered, each for himself, a new meaning of Africa. For Césaire, Africa meant self-recognition as a West Indian, because it illuminated a whole new dimension of himself which had been obscured; it meant seeing himself anew and aright.

The result is *Cahier d'un retour au pays natal*. The poem cannot, I think, be fully comprehended except in its Caribbean context, that is within the triple frame of reference with which I began this discussion. The dialectic which informs the poet's mental and spiritual progression as it unfolds in the poem is furnished by that historical arrangement which has placed the West Indian in a simultaneous relationship with Europe, America and Africa, constituting them into his poles of social and moral awareness. And it is to set right the lopsidedness of this arrangement that Aimé Césaire sets out on the voyage of self-discovery of which *Cahier* is an account.

For *Cahier* recounts a quest – it reveals itself indeed as the epic of a singular consciousness. It retraces for us the exploration of the tortured landscape of the West Indian mind in an exceptional act of introspection, as well as its movement towards a sense of direction and purpose, its tormented groping towards a sense of fulfilment.

At the beginning of the poem, Césaire unfolds for us a panorama of the incoherence and futility of his native island, enstranged from itself and condemned to a sterile inauthenticity:

> At the end of the dawn, the city – flat, sprawled, tripped up by its common sense, inert, winded under the geometric weight of its eternally renewed cross, at odds with its fate, mute, baffled, unable to circulate the pith of this ground, embarrassed, lopped, reduced, cut off from fauna and flora.[15]

The material squalor of Martinique, conveyed in graphic images of physical degradation, is then seen as being only the outward sign of the moral desolation which has made a waste land of the collective consciousness of its inhabitants and drawn a shroud over their spiritual life:

> At the end of the dawn, the great motionless night, the stars more dead than a perforated balafon.[16]

But it is less in anger than with a motion of love that Césaire descends into this hell in quest of redemption for himself and for his people:

> To flee. My heart was full of generous hopes. To flee ... I should arrive lithe and young in this country of mine and I should say to this land whose mud is flesh of my flesh: 'I wandered for a long time and I am returning to the deserted foulness of your wounds'. I should come back to this land of mine and say to it: 'Embrace me without fear ... If all I can do is speak, at least I shall speak for you.'[17]

Césaire's identification, in a total fusion of body and soul with the tragic fate of his people, has a quality of religious dedication, and his commitment widens his 'open consciousness', defining for him the total area of his passion:

> Mine, these few thousand death-bearers who circle in the gourd of an isle, and mine, too, the archipelago bent like the anxious desire for self-negation as if with maternal concern for the most frail slenderness separating the two Americas; and the womb which spills towards Europe the good liquor of the Gulf Streams, and one of the two incandescent slopes between which the Equator funambulates towards Africa. And my unfenced island, its bold flesh upright at the stern of this Polynesia; and right before it, Guadeloupe slit in two at the dorsal line, and quite as miserable as ourselves; Haiti, where Négritude stood up for the first time and swore by its humanity; and the droll little tail of Florida where a Negro is being lynched, and Africa caterpillaring gigantically up to the Spanish foot of Europe, its nakedness where death cuts a wide swath.[18]

Here is the racial consciousness taken form, amid the far-flung abjection

to which Europe has reduced the black man, and rising to the surface of
the West Indian consciousness. It is Europe that now wears a sinister
mask:

> In leaving Europe wracked with cries and silent currents of despair, in
> leaving Europe which timorously recovers itself and, proud, over-
> estimates itself. I claim this egotism beautiful and adventurous and my
> labour reminds me of an implacable prow.[19]

The very movement of rejection and of revolt to which these words
bring us in the logical progression of Césaire's spiritual adventure initiates
in its turn a new motion towards self-affirmation, for which Césaire in-
vented the word 'Négritude' in the well known passage of his poem:

> My Négritude is not a stone, its deafness thrown against the clamour of
> the day, my Négritude is not a speck of dead water on the dead eye of
> the earth, my Négritude is neither a tower nor a cathedral. It thrusts
> into the red flesh of the soil, it thrusts into the warm flesh of the sky, it
> digs under the opaque dejection of its rightful patience.[20]

It is at this point where we watch the resurgence of the poet's consciousness that the dialectic of Césaire's poem reveals itself most distinctly. The
poet has passed through a succession of phases that are like a purgation,
each phase involving a metamorphosis of the self, and leading to the
definition of a new being. The poem becomes the dramatic exteriorization
of a mental rite of passage, by which the poet gains access to a higher level
of experience both of himself and of the world. The dominant theme here,
as in all Césaire's poetry, is that of a perpetual movement of the self,
realizing ever more fully its integration into a more substantial whole, in
other words an intensification of being. The imagery here also presents us
with a symbolic representation of totality, the poet himself planted at the
live centre of a whole universe of vital responses, so that when he comes
to celebrate his race, it is in terms of a spirituality that draws its energy
from a full, organic and intense cosmic participation:

> truly the elder sons of the world
> porous to all the breath of the world
> fraternal space of all the breath of the world
> bed without drain of all the waters in the
> world spark of the sacred fire of the world
> flesh of the flesh of the world
> panting with the very movement of the world
> Tepid dawn of ancestral virtues
> Blood! Blood! All our blood stirred by the
> male heart of the sun
> Those who know the feminine nature of the
> moon's oily flesh
> the reconciled exultation of the antelope

and the star those whose survival moves in
the germination of grass
Eia! perfect circle of the world and close
concordance![21]

Césaire's Négritude, then, is not only a personal but also a collective
vision, a vision of the race founded upon a novel apprehension of the
meaning of Africa, which serves as the mediating symbol of a new consciousness. Africa has, in an immediate way, a polemical significance – the
contestation of the colonial hierarchy of values implies the glorification of
Africa, the constitution of a counter-myth, a wilful act, in the two senses
of the word, whose purpose, as Césaire puts it, is 'the invention of souls'.[22]

This relative and negative aspect of Négritude explains its excessive
romanticism, its exaggerated emphasis, its irrationalism even. But these
were not without their positive side. If we consider the African myth in
the work of Césaire from the Caribbean perspective, it is easy to recognize
the fact that Africa signified for him a means of mental liberation, as well
as a symbol of spiritual salvation.

For the Martinican wallowing in a quagmire of self-refusal, Africa
offered self-acceptance. The African past came as a historical justification
for his claim to a plenitude of being – it gave a positive dimension to his
historicity by extending his awareness beyond the demoralizing past of
slavery. It also permitted him to recover his authenticity through the recognition of his cultural attachment to Africa. By breaking the vicious
circle of inhibitions set up in the Caribbean mind, it restored him to his
wholeness.

The African myth also has another significance for Césaire, as the source
of his poetic values and the foundation of his poetic vision. Césaire's
African vision is situated within the surrealist philosophy, which can be
summed up as a quest for a fresh mode of experience and of knowledge.
Poetry becomes a vital act, which creates a structure of apprehension of a
mystic, as opposed to a rational, kind. The spirituality of Africa appeared
to Césaire therefore not only as a personal heritage, but also as an ultimate
sanction for his poetic aspiration towards the primary and the elemental.
Africa, in a word, is a symbol which serves as a transcendental reference
for the poetic vision of Aimé Césaire.

The African sentiment of Césaire animates then his messianic vision.
His experience of Africa is imaginative and symbolic, but it has an active
purpose. The poet assumes the role of a prophet, leading his people towards a new world of social experience and human awareness, towards a
new order of existence and of being:

Now I know the sense of the ordeal: my country is the 'night lance' of
my Bambara ancestors.

And I seek for my country not hearts of dates, but hearts of men who
beat the virile blood to enter the cities of silver by the great trapezoid
door . . .[23]

When Césaire's work is considered in its entire range, the distinctive
fact that specifies it can be seen to be social commitment expressing and
realizing itself in imaginative terms. There is at work in it the will to bring
the black man's consciousness to a total coincidence with its historical
determination and thus to illuminate it. Césaire's Négritude, romantic,
passionate, exacerbated even, reveals itself in this light as no more than
the deliberate and lucid assumption by the black man of his destiny.

In this respect, Césaire struck a completely new note in the literature of
Martinique and created a new mode of vision and of expression, the significant aspect of which is the preoccupation that we find henceforth in the
work of a whole new generation of writers with the situation of the black
man in the French Caribbean and in the world. Novelists such as Juminer
and Zobel, poets such as Glissant and Desportes, belong to this generation
who began to work in what I'd like to term 'the heritage of Césaire'.[24]
Frantz Fanon, in his own way, belongs to this heritage. Although not a
creative writer, the new climate of thinking and of sentiment initiated by
Césaire in Martinique is behind his work, which can thus be seen to have
issued directly out of the efforts of Césaire. One has only to point to the
frequent references to Césaire in *Peau noire, masques blancs* to realize that
Fanon's point of departure is the final position of Césaire.

But even with this first work, the emphasis as well as the perspective of
Fanon show a difference. This difference can be accounted for, I think, by
two factors. The first is that Fanon was a rationalist, expressing himself
in dialectical terms, as opposed to Césaire working in images and symbols.
Fanon was casting a clinical eye in fact on the whole complex of emotions
and attitudes that constituted the new racial awareness of his countrymen.
Secondly, Fanon belongs to a later generation than Césaire, with a wider
perspective for viewing things. In this connection, his experience in
Algeria was to have a direct bearing upon his outlook.

An additional factor is the fact that the specifically intellectual structure
of his thought was moulded by the peculiar current of the European
tradition that has produced what one might call 'the revolutionary intellect', represented in modern times by Marx and Engels, Sorel, Lenin
and Sartre. Their influence in various ways led him to elaborate a personal
conception of man which he directed towards a new purpose in relation
to the black man and to the Third World.

The stages of Fanon's intellectual development can now be briefly outlined. His point of departure, as I have remarked, is Négritude. His first

book is an examination of the black man's condition in the context of the colonial situation in the French Caribbean, and in its wider implications. What Fanon attempts here is no less than a phenomenology of Negro existence. He examines the nature of this existence and the various modes of response of the black man to his condition. The reciprocal character of the black man's relation to the white man, who has created him for his use, thus determines these responses so that, in Fanon's view, they constitute no more than a defensive reaction. Fanon's view of Négritude is that it is enclosed within the vicious racial circle initiated by the white man, a compensatory movement generated by the black man's inferiority complex vis-à-vis the white man. He suggests that this is altogether inadequate, and that the real answer to the black man's dilemma is to break the circle by stepping out of it entirely, by revindicating his humanity not as black man, which only reinforces his alienation, but simply as a man. The final peroration in his book illustrates very well his point of view:

> I as a man of colour want only this: That the tool never possesses the man. That the enslavement of man by man cease forever. That is, of one by another. That it be possible for me to discover and to love man wherever he may be.[25]

It is an abstract humanity, however, that Fanon proposes at the end of this study. But what Fanon wanted to stress was the point that the colonial situation was an economic rather than a racial system in essence, that the black man was not oppressed as a black man *per se*, but in his position as belonging to an economic category. This view is obviously an overstatement, but we can understand it to mean that Fanon was seeing, behind and beneath the racial cloak of the colonial situation, the master-slave relationship on which it was founded. And his purpose is not simply to oppose the master, but the world of master and slave, as Albert Camus has put it.[26]

I do not think myself that Fanon was rejecting Négritude outright. He was too perceptive to throw the baby out with the bath water. But he was disconcerted by the vague formulation that it began to receive in the writings of Senghor, while admiring the will that animated the movement, as exemplified in the poetry of his countryman, Césaire. More than anything else he wanted to see in it an original content, perhaps even, at this stage, a clear social as opposed to a mere mystic content – an empirical significance, in a word.

At any rate, his Algerian experience was to give unity and definition to his ideas. In 1952, at the age of 26, Fanon was sent to Algeria, to serve at the French hospital at Blida, as a psychiatrist. The parallel of Fanon's career in the French service with that of Maran is difficult not to make. Like Maran before him, Fanon was brought face to face with the colonial situation, in a new sphere of its effects – the disruption of the psychic life of its victims. His defection to the Algerian rebellion and his subsequent role as the theoretician of the revolutionary thinking of Algerian nationalism reflect, more than his sensitive reaction to the brutal character of the colonial reality, his thirst for a meaningful commitment, through action, to a new image of man.

Fanon's analysis of the colonial situation is inscribed within this humanistic perspective. More concretely, he saw colonialism as the elevation of one set of men at the expense of another set. In the same measure that the colonial master extends his human dimension – through economic advantage and the moral satisfaction that he derives from it – in that same measure is the colonized slave impoverished in body and soul, depersonalized, reduced in his human stature and even nature. Colonial rule tends to drive a wedge between colonized native and his normal adherence to his essential humanity. This is the situation as perceived by Fanon which Sartre in the very first sentence of his preface to *Damnés* sums up in these words:

> Not so very long ago, the earth numbered 2,000 million inhabitants: 500 million men, and 1,500 million natives.[27]

The sharp division between the two categories of individuals that constitute colonial society assumes a moral significance from this point of view. Colonialism is an assault, maintained by force, upon the consciousness of the native.

Fanon's preoccupations in the two books that issued out of his Algerian experience revolve around this problem. As a psychologist, he is concerned, I think, primarily with the subjective states of the colonized peoples. In *L'An V de la révolution algérienne*,[28] he presents a sociological account of the transformations in Algerian society through the changes in social attitudes that are brought about by the necessity of the revolution. Objects acquire new meanings, human relations are modified, new values are created as the Algerians adjust their minds to the revolutionary situation. The structural modifications that he describes take place first in the collective consciousness before they are given objective form. In this sense, Fanon's sociology is of the idealist type.

It is from this point of view that we need to view the discussion of violence in the colonial situation with which he opens his last book, *Damnés*. We can summarize his thought by saying that, for him, violence is a form of psychic therapy which he prescribes, in a literal sense, to cure the sickness brought into the mind of colonized man by his situation.

Inasmuch as the colonizer uses constant force on his victim, he sows in the mind of the latter the seeds of a murderous will which takes root and spreads its poisonous growth, warping and cramping it. Colonial alienation is the introduction here of a sick body into the collective consciousness of the natives. The colonized native is thus a pathological case; in the circumstances, therefore, the only remedy is that the colonized masses take up arms against their overlords in order to recreate themselves as men. The emphasis then is upon the creative role of violence, which dilates the cramped muscles and restores the normal correspondence between the body and the soul in the colonized native.

The rest of Fanon's thesis is devoted to an examination of the political and social implication of this fundamental idea. I cannot render an adequate account of Fanon's political thought in this survey, and I would like simply to limit myself to pointing out what appears to me to be of significance in it, in relation to my general theme, before passing on to some general conclusions.

First, Fanon minimizes the racial factor in favour of the socio-economic, which cuts across ethnic categories. His comments on the national bourgeoisie in the colonial and newly independent countries, and his view of the disinherited peasants of the rural areas as the only authentic revolutionary group, is intended to bring home the fact that the issue at stake is that of privilege and advantage, not race. And precisely because of this standpoint, he discounts an alliance between the masses of the underdeveloped countries and the proletariat of the advanced nations, who enjoy the material fruit of the colonial set-up and therefore have an interest in its maintenance. Hence the class struggle acquires in his thinking a new dimension, indeed a universal character, in which the Third World is opposed to the advanced nations. It is therefore with some justification that Fanon has come to be accepted as a theoretician of the Third World, although only brief allusions are made in his work to the entity.

It is this determination to go beyond the appearance to the reality, from the contingent to the essential, that accounts for his final criticism of Négritude, which was his starting point. Its all-embracing character is belied by the sociological realities, because the condition of black peoples takes on varied and dissimilar forms. More important still, he came to see it as the ideology of the new native ruling class in the post-colonial period, which in its emphasis on the immaterial tended to become in turn an alienating philosophy, in so far as it could not lead on to social action. He came therefore to restore the relative character of the movement, already pointed out by Sartre and against which he himself had protested,[29] but now in a different direction – the social transformation of the emerging

countries. It is in this sense that I consider his thinking to be not so much
a break with Négritude as a transcending of the movement.

We have then in the work of these three dominating figures in the literary
and intellectual history of Martinique a distinct progression. The development that strikes one – when their writings are seen within the historical
perspective that I have attempted here to establish for them – is the manner
in which the social consciousness that they reveal is transformed and extended from one writer to another, its progressive amplification.

René Maran has been hailed by Senghor as a precursor of the Négritude
movement,[30] and rightly so, if one is to judge by his influence. His first
novel is a protest against colonial rule, and served as an initial inspiration
for the literature of revolt of the French-speaking black writers, although
it did not open out to them in an explicit or distinct way the racial perspective of their movement. It was the work of a liberal humanist. More
significant for the influence which Maran was to exercise is the imaginative
sympathy with Africa which he achieved as an artist, as opposed to the
intellectual understanding of the liberal. If we compare his African novels
to those of Joyce Cary, for instance, this distinction becomes clear, as the
validity of Senghor's designation of Maran as the forerunner of a movement he himself and Aimé Césaire have come to incarnate.

For the African vision is at the heart of the affirmation of racial identity
that we associate with Aimé Césaire, for whom the black world appears to
be not only a community of suffering and of interests, but also a community
of values. And in the kind of mystic entity that his poetry celebrates,
Africa, the original motherland of all black people, appears as the ultimate
source of warmth and life.

Frantz Fanon, however, while remaining in the same current of development, takes us from this high point and leads us towards another. He too
had a racial sentiment, and even a vision of the race, but one that becomes
bred to a new awareness, that of the entire humanity of the under-
privileged. There is thus in his work not only a widening of the sociological perspectives of the racial consciousness that was passed on to him,
but also in a fundamental sense, a refinement of vision, in his manner of
giving this consciousness a new relevance with reference to the Third
World.

Thus the development that we observe in the evolution of literary and
ideological expression by natives of Martinique has a qualitative aspect.
This is not without significance in another important respect. We can
observe also in this evolution the movement from collective feeling to
the creation of social ideas. Artistic expression is seen to provide the first
significant indication of a self-consciousness on the part of the blacks –

of a collective affective state – which later crystallizes, as it were, into self-awareness. This in turn finds intellectual projection in ideology. In the particular case of the Négritude movement, of which the developments summarized here constitute an important sector, it is of interest to note the divergent directions which the intellectual activity of the French-speaking black writers has taken, as represented on the other one hand by the conservative social philosophy of Léopold Sédar Senghor,[31] and the revolutionary socialism of Fanon on the other. Both stem from the same original source, and they have a certain unity in the sense that they both represent the outward movement of the black subjectivity towards the objective reality of social factors.

Finally, with relation to our general theme, we might consider the significance of Africa itself as a focus of feeling and of ideas, and indeed of action, for the Martinicans. Their case stands out in the long run as a particular illustration of a more general Afro-American phenomenon. It forms part of a recurrent and consistent pattern of responses that seems today to have become established as an historical cycle. Maran, Césaire, and Fanon belong then to the gallery of figures peopled by other Afro-Americans such as Blyden, Du Bois, Garvey, and in our own day, Malcolm X, who have turned to Africa in quest of a meaning for the collective experience of the black man in the modern age.

We know that this phenomenon of the emotional and intellectual 'return to Africa' by the Afro-American is the result of a reaction to the American experience, or in a wider framework, the western experience. It also bears traces of a certain atavism, although in the case of the intellectuals, an atavism of a positive kind, comparable indeed to the return to the European source by other Americans such as Henry James and T. S. Eliot, and in a sense more relevant than theirs, in its *effective* contribution to the historical and moral resurgence of the African motherland. But the ultimate significance of the phenomenon for Africa seems to me to reside elsewhere.

For when the contribution of these exiled sons of Africa is taken together with that of the western educated Africans in the development of modern African consciousness,[32] it will be seen that in fact the actual spiritual transformation of Africa has been effected through the agency of black men. The entry of Africa into the modern era, though made inevitable by the encounter with western ideas and technology, was made possible historically by the action of her own children, both immediate and remote. Ideology in the black world has a fundamental unity in that it was called into being by the encounter and the resultant clash between Europe and Africa, and in response to the sociological consequences, in

their varied forms, of this historical fact. And out of this global response
has been evolved the new mental universe of the modern African.

Notes and References

1. Paul Valéry, *Régards sur le monde actuel* (Paris, 1945).
2. For a fuller discussion, see M. J. Leiris: *Contacts de civilisations en Martinique et en Guadeloupe* (Paris: Nimègue, 1955); and the present author's doctoral thesis, *Les Origines de la négritude à la Martinique*, University of Paris, 1966.
3. Cf. Leiris, op, cit., and F. Fanon, *Peau noire, masques blancs* (Paris: Editions du Seuil, 1952); tr. *Black Skin, White Masks* (New York: Grove Press, 1967).
4. See F. Fanon, op. cit., in particular chapter 6.
5. Cf. A. Viatte, *Histoire littéraire de l'Amerique française des origines à 1950* (Paris: Presses Universitaires de France, 1954), pp. 482–506.
6. R. Bernabé, 'L'Evolution de la poésie martiniquaise ou les voies de l'authenticité', in *Action* (Fort de France), Nos. 3–4, May 1964.
7. Quoted by C. Kunstler, 'Le Coeur, l'esprit et la raison chez René Maran', in *Hommage à René Maran* (Paris: Présence Africaine, 1965), p. 58.
8. Quoted by L. Bosquet, in the introduction to R. Maran, *Le Petit roi de chimerie* (Paris: A. Michel, 1924), p. 15.
9. Quoted by M. Gahisto, 'La Genèse de *Batouala*', in *Hommage à René Maran*, p. 136.
10. *Ibid.*, p. 137.
11. R. Maran, *Batouala* (Paris: A. Michel, 1921 ed., p.56; English translation *Batouala*, London: Heinemann Educational Books, 1973).
12. Ibid., p. 94.
13. Ibid, pp. 147–60.
14. Quoted by L. Damas, *Poètes d'expression française* (Paris: Editions du Seuil, 1947), pp. 13–15. For a fuller account of these developments, that were to lead to the Négritude movement, see L. Kesteloot, *Les Ecrivains noirs de langue française naissance d'une littérature* (Brussels: Institut de Sociologie, Université libre de Bruxelles, 1965).
15. A. Césaire, *Cahier d'un retour au pays natal* (Paris: Présence Africaine, 1956). This quotation is taken from the bilingual edition, with the English title, *Return to my Native Land* (Paris: Présence Africaine, 1968), p. 13.
16. Ibid., p. 21.
17. Ibid., p. 41.
18. Ibid., p. 47.
19. Ibid., p. 73.
20. Ibid., p. 101.
21. Ibid., p. 103.
22. A. Césaire, 'L'Homme de culture noir et ses responsabilitiés', in *Deuxième Congress des écrivains et artistes noirs* (Paris: Présence Africaine, 1959), p. 118.

23. *Cahier*, 1968, p. 127.
24. Cf. B. Juminer, *Les Bâtards* (Paris: 1961), and *Au Seuil d'un nouveau cri* (Paris: 1963); J. Zobel, *La Rue cases-nègres* (Paris: 1955; English translation *Black Shack Alley*, Washington DC: Three Continents Press and London: Heinemann Educational Books, 1980). *Le Soleil partagé* (Paris: 1964); E. Glissant, *La Lézarde* (Paris: 1958), *Le Quatrieme siècle* (Paris: 1964), and the volume, *Poèmes* (Paris: 1965), containing his principal collections of poems; G. Desportes, *Sous l'Oeil fixe du soleil* (Paris: 1961), and anthologized poems in Damas, *op. cit.*
25. F. Fanon, *op. cit.*, p. 231.
26. A. Camus, *L'Homme revolté* (Paris: Gallimard, 1951), tr. A. Bower, *The Rebel* (London: Hamish Hamilton, 1953).
27. J-P. Sartre, preface to *The Wretched of the Earth* (Harmondsworth: Penguin, 1967), p. 7.
28. Translated into English by H. Chevalier under the title, *Studies in a Dying Colonialism* (New York: Monthly Review Press, 1965).
29. *Black Skin, White Masks*, pp. 132–5.
30. L. S. Senghor, 'René Maran, précurseur de la négritude', in *Hommage à René Maran*, pp. 9–13.
31. Cf. L. S. Senghor, *On African Socialism*, tr. (New York: M. Cook and London: Pall Mall Press, 1964).
32. Cf. R. July, *The Origins of Modern African Thought* (London: Faber & Faber, 1968).

8. French African Narrative Prose and the Colonial Experience

▼▼

Creative writing has been so consistently employed by French-speaking black intellectuals to express their particular social consciousness and to give persuasive form and force to their ideological position that it is justifiable to see their literature, especially when viewed through its themes and its attitudes (both explicit and implicit), as very largely a complement to their ideological writings. The development of French African prose, and of the novel in particular, has to be seen in this perspective for its immediate significance to be understood.

Such an approach carries with it, however, the danger of missing important details that give the modern literature of francophone Africa its specific character. For it is also a move towards the creation of a new literary tradition, which though related to the French is distinguished from it by its African frame of reference. It owes its originality to being a reflection of the African continent and the African mind. As far as the novels are concerned, their value as works which contain an enduring human interest can easily be obscured by what appears at first sight to be their documentary significance. The originality of each writer can be missed, together with the rich variety offered by contrasts in thematic viewpoints and formal approaches to a common subject. But the more accomplished among French African prose-writers are able to bestow upon their imaginative creation a clear human image. The documentary and ideological interest of their works makes it easy to overlook the fact that also, through their handling of a language and of a tradition inherited from the French, they have succeeded in adapting the novel to the realities of their own world of experience.

French African prose can be given a beginning with the publication in 1921 of the novel *Batouala* by René Maran, a West Indian in the French colonial administration in Central Africa. The impact of this novel, which won the famous Prix Goncourt, was due mainly to the vigour of its exposure of the effects of colonial rule in the French colonies in some of its passages. But its sensitive portrayal of African life, coupled with its evocation of the natural environment, could not but make a profound impression upon its African readers and offer a vivid example of what an African novel in French could be. Maran designated the novel, *roman nègre*, thus declaring his intention to present an inside picture of African life. He followed it up later with an even more impressive novel, *Le Livre de la brousse* (1934), in which the tropical world, personified, acquires the character of an active force in the human world, and attains the dimension of a dynamic imaginative symbol. In another work, an autobiographical novel entitled *Un Homme pareil aux autres* (1947), Maran dramatizes, with an intense pathos, the psychological conflict of the individual in quest of spiritual belonging. These are themes that were later to reappear in different guises in both the poetry and the prose of francophone African writers. René Maran was not only an important forerunner of the Négritude movement and hailed as such by Senghor, but his work, like that of his compatriot, Aimé Césaire, constitutes a link between the literatures of French-speaking Caribbeans and Africans.

More important for the development of French African prose was the demonstrative value of Maran's African novels. Not only had he created in Batouala, the principal character of his first novel, and Kossi, the hero of *Le Livre de la brousse*, African characters whose destinies are central to the narrative plot, but his integration of the African scene into the narrative and symbolic structure of his novels as essential elements of their total scheme was a departure from the decorative role it had played in the exotic novels of previous French writers who had used Africa as a setting. Maran was thus the first to make Africa a living presence in an imaginative work in the French language.

The influence of Maran is palpable in French African prose works published in the wake of *Batouala* in the twenties and thirties. His attentive description of African life, with human characters involved with the vegetation and wild life, may have recalled to his African readers the elements and atmosphere of their traditional tales. It also explains, at least in part, the fact that the most notable work in prose to come out of francophone Africa before the war should have been an ethnological novel, *Doguicimi*, written by a Dahomean scholar, Paul Hazoumé, and published in 1938. In this novel, an epic narrative of pre-colonial Dahomey, the reference is to traditional society as regards content, and to some extent, to traditional chronicles and legends as regards the narrative form. But although *Doguicimi* is interesting as an experiment in recasting the oral literature of Africa within the form of a French novel, it fails to achieve a satisfactory degree of literary interest independent of its academic appeal. It is significant that *Doguicimi* was in fact published in an ethnological collection. Paul Hazoumé's lead has been followed in more recent times by such writers as Djibril Tamsir Niane, whose book *Soundiata* (1960) retells in French the legendary foundation of the Mandingo empire, and Nazi Boni, with his chronicle of the Voltaïque past, *Crépuscule des temps anciens* (1962). Both writers display a measure of literary skill, but their works fail to come alive in terms of their human as distinct from their historical content. This failure is all the more apparent when set against the success of those writers who turned rather to the folk-tales for inspiration, recreating them in French to give them new life.

The work of Birago Diop remains unequalled in the respect. His first collection of stories, *Les Contes d'Amadou Koumba*, appeared in 1942 and Diop was immediately acclaimed as an original African talent. Senghor is said to have exclaimed, upon first reading Diop's stories: 'Voilà de la pensée nègre!' Diop's subsequent collections, *Les Nouveaux contes d'Amadou Koumba* (1958) and *Contes et lavanes* (1963), have not only confirmed the vitality of Birago Diop's special genius but also established the *conte* as a viable genre in modern African literature.

In their essential features, Birago Diop's *contes* derive from the folk-tale tradition in Africa. Diop himself disclaims authorship of the tales, ascribing them rather to Amadou Koumba, an old sage of his natal village, and claiming for himself the sole merit of having transcribed and rendered them into French. In their content as in their form and general feel, they retain an authentic quality that bears out his desire to be considered as the faithful perpetuator of an age-old tradition.

Diop's fidelity to the original material does not, however, preclude an originality of style and presentation by which he puts a personal seal upon the tales. The *contes*, as they exist in his versions, amount in fact to a restitution in French, a transposition that captures the spirit and movement of the African folk-tale, while employing to the full the resources of the French language. Indeed, the most engaging quality of Diop's writing is the gentle humour with which these tales are rendered in French and which constitutes not only his distinctive contribution to the maintenance of the folk-tale tradition but also a reflection of his essentially humane outlook upon men and upon the world. The diversity of situations in his stories reveals Diop's penetrating insight into the many facets of human nature, while his animal characters reinforce with their allegorical implications his vision of the human condition. In a manner free from self-consciousness, he captures and transmits the atmosphere of the traditional setting of the West African savannah, with its customs and values, and gives to his stories through the blend of realism and fantasy, the stamp of an authentic and deeply felt African universe. Birago Diop is also a poet who has shown in his verse an attachment to classical convention. This concern for structure is reflected in his *contes* in the elegance of his

language and his sensitive exploitation of the formal pattern of an essentially oral genre, thus transforming the folk-tale into a new means of
literary expression. Diop unites in his *contes* an individual awareness and
a feeling for the symbolic connotations of the natural world, enlarging the
scope of the traditional model and giving it a resonance beyond its immediate local context.

Birago Diop has been closely followed in this direction by another
writer, Bernard Dadié of the Ivory Coast, who has published two collections, *Légendes africaines* (1950) and *Le Pagne noir* (1955). A different
atmosphere prevails in Dadié's stories, which emphasize more than Diop's
the element of fantasy in the folk-tales and reflect a different aspect of the
West African scene, that of the coastal forest belt. Dadié also writes with
a deep understanding of his traditional background and it is significant
that in his book, *Un Nègre à Paris* (1959) he emphasizes the African perspective of his commentary on French life by constantly drawing parallels
and making comparisons between the values and customs of the French,
and those of his original culture. Another collection worthy of note is
Ousmane Socé Diop's *Contes et légendes* (1951). In these and other
renderings of African tales in French, there is a clear intention to recreate
them as literature, to portray through them Africa in its most authentic
vein, and in doing so, to employ an essentially African form.

For all these writers, who can be termed traditionalist, Africa as a source
of inspiration is not the social reality of the colonial situation but rather
the setting of the traditional world, presenting itself to the imagination as a
differentiated and self-contained universe. Only within this realm of experience, it seemed to them, could they truly reflect an original African mind
and feeling in their works, and their preoccupation in deriving their means
of expression from an African tradition (even while using the French
language to enlarge their audience) reflects further this desire to address
the world in an authentic voice. It cannot be said, however, that these
efforts to create a new form of French African prose by reviving traditional
oral literature in the French language have offered a serious challenge to
the conventional western novel. The modern African situation forces itself
upon the attention of any contemporary artist almost by necessity, and to
treat such realities in an extended manner in fiction demanded a literary
medium more suited to a realistic presentation while offering ample scope
for individual expression: such a medium existed in the conventional
form of the western novel.

Already in 1926 a Senegalese, Bakary Diallo, had published a novel,
Force bonté, which owed nothing to traditional models. The novel is a
comment upon French colonial rule, which it glorifies; it has little literary
merit to recommend it. In a different vein was a novel by another

Senegalese, Ousmane Socé Diop, *Karim* (1935), which touches upon the disruptive influence of contact with a foreign way of life. No criticism of colonial rule is made or suggested in this novel; rather, its author emphasizes the inadequacy of the African's adaptation to changing values. But in his second novel, *Mirages de Paris* (1937), Socé Diop sets the action in France itself, where his African hero, Fara, breaks down under the strain of his physical and mental exile and commits suicide. This novel looks forward to Cheikh Hamidou Kane's *L'Aventure ambiguë* (1961). Another important novel of this early period is Abdoulaye Sadji's *Nini* (1954) which deals with the subject of the half-caste who symbolizes physically the encounter between Europe and Africa, and Sadji attempts to portray in the novel the social pressures and psychological problems arising out of this encounter. His second novel, *Maïmouna* (1958) describes the destructive effect of city life on a naïve village girl.

From a technical point of view, none of these novels is satisfactory, but they indicate the direction which French African literature in prose had begun to take : towards an attentive exploration of the shifts in the social situation and in the mental universe of the African after contact with western culture. Although these early writers were unable sufficiently to break free from the conventions established by French colonial writers, they write nonetheless from an African point of view, and their themes point to the social consciousness arising out of a specific historical situation – colonialism and the corresponding transformations in African life – which has so dominated modern African literature. This particular awareness underlies the work that can with justice be regarded as having brought French African narrative prose finally into its own – Camara Laye's autobiography, *L'Enfant noir*, which appeared in 1953. The sustained excellence of Laye's writing in this book is in marked contrast to earlier attempts by Africans to write an extended prose work in French, and although in retrospect *L'Enfant noir* appears a relatively slight work, it indicated at the time of its publication the growing assurance of the African writer in his assimilation of the French prose tradition. Laye's success was also to mark the beginning of a particularly productive period in the development of the novel in francophone Africa, and the fact that this development coincided with a period of intense nationalist activity in the erstwhile French colonies is not without relevance to the themes and the concerns of the novelists during this period.

Laye's autobiography owes its extraordinary success to both its theme and the style in which it is written. His account of an African childhood derives its primary interest from the fascination which an inside picture of the growth and development of a personality normally holds for us, but this interest is heightened in Laye's case by its specific reconstitution of the background which is the framework of his early life. Laye's work is not only a personal recollection of his childhood but also a nostalgic record of a way of life in the process of profound change, but to which he remains deeply attached: his purpose is not only to express the quality of life he knew as a child but also to affirm his appreciation of and fidelity to his origins.

It is to these elements in his autobiography that Laye's style gives point and effect. The winning simplicity of his writing is in accord with the theme of childhood which he develops throughout in the work. But even more engaging is the way in which he presents the social life of his people, conveys the warmth of personal relationships among them, and expresses the sense of the values which animate their existence. These descriptions are charged with an intense romantic note imparted by the author's passionate prose which sometimes partakes of the quality of poetry. Thus, although the image of his African childhood which Laye offers is indeed an idealized one, the personal feeling that he maintains throughout gives his account a compelling note of sincerity. In evoking the life of his people and the quality with which it is lived, Laye offers an intimate picture of traditional Africa from a personal point of view and through an individual sensibility.

L'Enfant noir in its content and atmosphere is far removed from any specific political orientation and does not appear to be inspired by any definite social purpose, such as animates the novels of Laye's contemporaries. But it is written out of an attitude, and its general tone reflects the viewpoint from which it is conceived. Although at one level the book relates the growing-up process of an African boy moving from the security of his indigenous society to an outside world dominated by European values, the sense of deprivation which pervades Laye's portrait of his African background, presented as an integrated community, alerts us to the plea which, at another level, he introduces underneath his factual account for the preservation of its spiritual heritage. The work is thus not only the record of an individual response to the forces of change, but also a subtle affirmation of the positive values of traditional Africa. This aspect of *L'Enfant noir* is given a more elaborate development in Laye's second book, *Le Regard du roi* (1954), a symbolic novel in which he vindicates his conception of an African viewpoint of life all the more emphatically by deliberately opposing it to the rational attitude of western man, represented by a European character, Clarence. Laye has written a third novel, *Dramouss* (1966) in which his visionary themes are centred upon the contemporary political situation.

Laye's insistence on the inner life stands out more clearly when *L'Enfant noir* is contrasted to Dadié's autobiographical novel, *Climbié*

(1956). The progress of the African child towards assimilation into European culture through Western education is described in both, but Dadié's emphasis falls on the external forces that create trials on this route, so that his novel gets progressively more bitter and even polemical. A similar course is also charted in Cheikh Hamidou Kane's single novel to date, *L'Aventure ambiguë* (1961). Here however the subjective element in Laye's autobiography is carried a stage further and deepened into an introspective method.

L'Aventure ambiguë is indeed in many respects a unique work. In its structure, style and overall feeling, no other work in the whole body of African writing – save perhaps Laye's *Le Regard du roi* – offers a close parallel to it. Yet, for all its singularity, it is a work that summarizes and brings into brilliant focus the ideas, sentiments and attitudes that lie at the centre of inspiration of all French African writing. It can thus be considered to represent the most characteristic statement in imaginative terms of the fundamental outlook of the French African intellectual in the colonial situation.

What gives *L'Aventure ambiguë* its character of uniqueness is the balance which Kane has striven to achieve in the work between pure fiction, in which the intellectual content emerges out of the imaginative scheme to give it an effective significance, and philosophical dialogue, in which the imaginative content is developed as a function of the ideas which it serves to illustrate. The result is a narrative in which these ideas are not simply dramatized – given flesh or represented by the characters – but given conscious articulation in a consistent and coherent way, even in abstract terms, by the characters who inhabit Kane's fictional world.

The novel deals with a religious theme which is narrowly circumscribed for most of its development – the conflict between the Islamic faith and the way of life it determines within an African community on one hand, and on the other, the impact of western conquest whose social and cultural consequences threaten the spiritual basis of that community's existence. Yet, as its title indicates, the area of reference of the novel goes beyond the religious theme to embrace the whole question of the relation between western and African values in the wake of the colonial encounter. In Samba Diallo, his tragic hero, Kane offers what amounts to an archetypal figure of the burdened *assimilé*, torn between two conflicting frames of moral and spiritual reference. Around this figure, Kane has gathered up and woven into a significant whole all the elements of the conflict within the divided consciousness of the westernized African: between his acquired image in a new world of thought and effects, and his sense of an original self and aspiration to an original identity. The narrative thus serves to provide a functional context of situations and of meaning for a personal and inward drama, but the intensity with which Samba Diallo's mind and emotions are seen to be engaged in his individual problem reflects the hold which this problem has had on the imagination of the French African intellectuals as a whole, as is evidenced by other novels on the same or related theme such as Aké Loba's *Kocoumbo, L'étudiant noir* (1960) or John Malonga's *Cour d'Aryenne* (1955), though none of these works carries the same force of suggestion as *l'Aventure ambiguë*.

The tone of Kane's novel derives indeed from the fact that it is essentially a meditative work. Throughout the novel, Kane maintains a gravity of style which accords with his noble conception of his characters. Samba Diallo in particular appears as an idealist whose faculties, both intellectual and affective, are so involved in his quest for spiritual resolution as to make him something of a mystic. Kane's style thus underlines the profound seriousness of the subject with which he deals.

But depite its austere and dispassionate manner of presentation, the novel must be read as a critique of European civilization for its intention to be wholly grasped. Like Camara Laye, Chiekh Hamidou Kane sets the profound harmony evolved out of an adherence to shared values and an understanding between man and the universe which he discerns in traditional society, against what he sees as the materialist emphasis of western civilization which is incapable of offering to man his full measure of fulfilment.

Both Laye and Kane use the novel then as a vehicle for expressing their vision of an African mode of existence. They are aware that the African's spiritual foundation is threatened with dissolution by a new dispensation which may not provide him with a satisfactory alternative. They can be considered traditionalists in the sense in which their works are meant to promote a sense of the integrity of the African self amidst the flow of change. Their stand does not however exclude compromise with the new order – indeed, they both seem resigned to the inevitable – but they seek to embrace this within an all-encompassing mental universe that remains fundamentally rooted in the old order. What they deplore is not change, but the cleavage it has produced in the mind of the African; seen in this light, their works take on an added value as the vivid reflection within the individual consciousness of the process of transformation.

Camara Laye, C. H. Kane and Birago Diop come closest in their themes and in the attitudes that underlie them to the poets of Négritude, and their prose even exhibits this affinity in stylistic traits. Laye's warm lyricism and Kane's compelling imagery are both complementary aspects of the same design: to give sensuous life to their perception of the African setting, and to give a vivid immediacy to their feeling for its values.

A distance separates the works of Laye and Kane from that of the other writers of this period in French African writing – the distance between the literature of imagination and that of realities. In the novels of Mongo Beti,[1] Ferdinand Oyono and Sembène Ousmane, a pronounced social consciousness dominates. They direct their attention mainly to the conflicts of the colonial situation, seen in its broader social and political aspects, and although as novelists the reaction of individuals to colonial rule forms an inseparable part of their narrative scheme, they emphasize more the external conditioning of their characters rather than their inner responses. A firm social commitment dictates their themes and the desire to call into question the entire ideological structure of the colonial system is behind their choice of the human situations in their work. Theirs is a literature of open revolt, which Oyono and Beti express through critical satire, while Ousmane's polemical radicalism leads him to place his opposition to colonial rule in the wider perspective of an ideology that calls for the transformation and updating of African society.

Mongo Beti's output as a novelist began with the publication in 1953 of a short novel, *Ville Cruelle* as part of a collective volume. The main interest of this novel, which was issued separately a year later, lies in the creation of a type of youthful hero at odds with his changing world and sensitive to the pressures of the colonial order, a type that reappears in truly memorable form in his third novel, *Mission terminée* (1956). But already with his second novel, *Le pauvre Christ de Bomba* (1955), Beti had found his characteristic satirical tone and manner – it is significant that with it, he dropped his earlier pseudonym for his present one. The preoccupation with the colonial situation finds in this second novel a fully realized expression in its critical assessment of the peculiar connection between the political and economic aspects of colonial rule and its social and cultural implications. Through the brilliantly contrived ingenuousness of the point of view of an African mission boy on Christian missionary activity in colonial Africa, the novel presents the way in which the association existing in the minds of the African population between the new religion and their subordination to the white man conditions their reactions. It is thus out of the imperfect understanding of African attitudes on the part of his hero, the white missionary Father Drummont, that Beti has derived the satirical humour and human interest of his novel.

The collapse of Father Drummont's missionary effort in the novel and his final discomfiture are direct indications that *Le pauvre Christ de Bomba* is meant to represent an attack on missionary activity in Africa as part of the entire colonial system. But depite its unequivocal stance, the actual development of this theme in the novel is by no means simplistic. Beti explores with real feeling and insight the contradictions of the white missionary's situation, which are made to unfold both in his actions and in the growing awareness of the character himself to their wider impli- cations within the framework of the colonial relationship. Thus Father Drummont gropes towards an understanding of his true position and goes through a real process of mental development.

This observation is even more true of Jean-Marie Medza, the hero of *Mission terminée*, whose journey into the hinterland turns out for him to be a means to the revelation of his own nature. In this novel, Beti makes a notable departure from the usual approach to the colonial question. In- stead of a direct attack upon colonial rule through a presentation of its workings – of its agents and their actions – Beti turns his attention to African society seen on its own terms rather than in its immediate re- lationship to the colonial order. The novel focuses entirely upon the lives of backwoods Africans whose social and moral context of existence has been rendered incoherent as a result of the ascendancy of a foreign culture over their traditional intitutions. The picture that emerges is one of a society in decay, of the absurdity of life in a situation where individuals are left to their own devices due to a confusion of values in a world whose foundations have been undermined.

Beti develops the colonial theme through his narration of the adventure of Jean-Marie Medza, a young *assimilé*, into this hinterland, on a mission which brings him into contact with the realities of life in the backwoods of colonial Africa. The experience opens his eyes to the degenerate state of his society and to the extent of his estrangement from his African back- ground caused by his western education. The adventure leads ultimately to a crisis of adolescence which takes on a larger social and moral meaning as the hero turns both against his world and the whole colonial order in a gesture of revolt. Jean-Marie Medza's journey thus acquires the value of a quest ending with self-discovery and inspiring a final gesture of self- affirmation. But the only kind of liberation that he can obtain is one that can lead nowhere, and his ending up as an aimless vagrant is by no means a triumph. The kind of individual that he becomes is indicated in the portrayal of the selfish cynic, Kris, another youthful character who appears in Beti's fourth novel, *Le Roi miraculé* (1958) and who is in many ways the counterpart of Jean-Marie Medza.

Mission terminée is undoubtedly Mongo Beti's most accomplished work. His satire is at its most cutting in this novel in which the verve and exuberance of the writing are given the fullest play in an unrelenting interrogation of the traumas and frustrations of the colonial experience. And in the way in which the novel captures the atmosphere of the African setting, Beti gives a special effect to the indirectness of his attack on the colonial system.

These same qualities are to some extent in evidence in *Le Roi miraculé*

in which Beti returns to the subject of missionary activity in Africa and
its disruptive effect on African life. From the 'technical' point of view, this
novel must be considered the best constructed of all his fictional works:
the plot moves through a definite progression from an initial situation of
dilemma which develops into a crisis, leading to a final resolution. Indeed,
through the very structuring of the novel, Beti presents an admirable
canvas of the web of human relations and the values with which they are
invested in traditional society, and demonstrates how Christian evangelical
effort strikes as it were at the very heart of this structure at once complex
and delicate. The theme of the novel is thus firmly integrated into the
narrative scheme through which it is expounded, so that, in a sense, the
resolution which occurs at the end of the novel in favour of the traditional
society may be considered a vindication of African social arrangements.
Nonetheless, the novel cannot be taken as a celebration of African values,
for although the prevailing mood contrasts appreciably with that of
Mission terminée, the ironic tone and the satirical mode employed in *Le
Roi miraculé* precludes any suggestion of a romantic identification on the
part of the novelist with the characters he portrays and the world he
evokes.

This observation is of particular significance in an assessment of Mongo
Beti's view of the African situation during the colonial period. The essence
of the African's condition as presented in Beti's novels resides in his complete spiritual confusion, the moral isolation of individuals consequent
upon the breakdown of the traditional order under the impact of colonialism. The ambiguity of the African described by Beti implies neither the
romantic glance cast back at the old order, as in Laye, nor the severe and
noble self-doubt of Kane's hero, but rather a situation of total disorientation in which it is impossible to discern any positive perspective. The
colonial alienation as seen by him is not touched with any light, but is
marked by the moral desolation of African society by a system which
emancipates men from their traditions but is incapable of making them
anew, of giving them a foundation on which to base their lives. Beti's
novels thus express a revolt against the colonial situation that arises from
a deep mood of disenchantment.

Ferdinand Oyono concentrates on this mood by showing that colonial
society by its very nature vitiates normal human understanding. His emphasis is on the institutional barriers to communication, and he brings out
his point by presenting characters who seek an accommodation with the
white man but who fail because of the values which the colonial system
presupposes and the attitudes which it determines. That this can be the
cause not only of misunderstanding but also of tragedy is shown in *Une
Vie de boy* (1956) which, though written in a satirical vein, is far removed

from comedy in its total effect. Oyono's satire is a sour pitiless one which pervades the entire work with an atmosphere of malaise and foreboding. Indeed, few African novels contain a more bitter denunciation of colonial rule than *Une Vie de boy*. The acid tones and the harsh realism of Oyono's writing, underscored by his laconic manner, give the narrative throughout an undercurrent of violence that comes to the surface, and to a head, in the final scenes. The contrast between the naïve faith of Toundi (of whose tragic experience the novel is a record) in the agents of colonial rule and the system they represent on the one hand, and on the other the brutal nature of his victimization, emphasizes the essential antagonism between the two racial categories that make up colonial society and the impossibility of bridging the gap of human feelings and relations between them. At the same time, Oyono's dramatization of the colonial tragedy is not merely an indictment of a particular system but a portrayal of human passions when they are unleashed; the tragedy depicted is as much a matter of racial or ideological concerns as a moral assessment of human weakness.

Oyono's second novel, *Le vieux Nègre et la médaille* (1956) offers a contrast to *Une Vie de boy*, of which it is something of a sequel: in its structure, characterization and narrative style, and consequently in its mood, which is less oppressive. However, both novels have the same theme and deal with colonial society, which is presented in each from different perspectives and probed as it were at different levels. The differences in the kinds of situations which they explore and the characters which they portray determine the change in tone and mood from one novel to the other in Oyono's presentation of the colonial experience as lived by the African.

Where in the previous novel the principal character is a rootless individual with no clear consciousness of his personal worth, the hero of *Le vieux Nègre et la médaille*, old Meka, is something of a notable with a deep and firm attachment to his indigenous culture and society but who seeks a compromise with the colonial order in the belief that he can find within it a place equivalent to that which he holds within the indigenous system. Oyono's satirical probing of the ambivalent social and cultural situation in which as a result Meka finds himself, focuses as much on the uncertain mental state of the character as on the absurdity of his exterior life and behaviour through which that ambivalence is reflected and which provides the comic strain of the narrative. Yet Oyono's lightheartedness is constantly felt to be on the verge of indignation at a situation which can reduce a man to the ridiculous and abject state in which we see old Meka for most of the novel. When therefore at the end of the novel old Meka returns after his final humiliation to his people and to his traditions, we understand that the ideas and attitudes on which the colonial order is based and which give a rigorous definition of the respective positions of Africans and Europeans within the social system, preclude any kind of real human understanding between individuals caught up in it.

The common theme of disillusionment in Oyono's first two novels leads the main character in each to some form of illumination – tragic in the case of Toundi, and resigned in the case of Meka – upon the real nature of the colonial situation and its implications for the African. The same theme reappears in a different form in his third and last novel to date, *Chemin d'Europe* (1960) in which Oyono has come close to Beti by creating in Aki Barnabas a youthful character who is able to survive only by acting out of self-interest. The disillusionment is placed at the very beginning of the novel, for the character's determined effort at social ascension is marked by a profound distrust in the colonial system itself and in its agents: there is no little irony in the fact that this consciousness leads to a cynical will to turn the system to personal advantage and to employ its representatives as tools for self-advancement. Furthermore, the hero's progress is oriented towards a physical withdrawal from a society in which he can find no satisfaction, and informed by an ideal of self-fulfilment that is represented by the continent of Europe itself. But as in the case of Jean-Marie Medza, his final departure leads him into a spiritual exile from which there is no possibility of return. *Chemin d'Europe* has none of the tension that marks *Une Vie de boy*, nor the comic expansiveness of *Le vieux Nègre et la médaille* – qualities which give powerful effect to Oyono's point in both novels – but it prolongs the polemical demonstration of the negating principle of colonial domination.

It has been suggested that the peculiarily sharp critical sense of Beti and Oyono may have been the consequence of the more varied and intense character which the colonial experience took in the Cameroun than in any other African country.[2] The suggestion may well be true, but although the two writers have a common approach, they differ in a number of respects. Beti attempts to explore the psychology of his characters more fully, and the situations he presents are more complex than is the case with Oyono. His characters appear therefore more rounded and more human, because they are seen to be more involved in their fates and more responsible for their actions. The kind of development one observes in them is lacking in Oyono's characters, who are denied any initiative and, faced as they are with a rigid situation, can only be passive sufferers of their fate. And where Beti's satire unfolds progressively, and is to some extent employed as an instrument of reflection, Oyono's is sharp and direct, aimed at an immediate effect. Both are in their different ways effective and brilliant writers, infusing into their indictment of colonialism considerable passion, but Beti's method is through critical analysis, Oyono's through bitter demonstration.

If the keynote of the novels of the two Camerounian writers is scepticism, in the work of the Senegalese Sembène Ousmane the operative principle around which his view of the African situation is organized is a progressive radicalism. Ousmane occupies a special place among French African novelists by reason both of his personal history and of the specific social purpose in his writing. An ex-serviceman and one-time docker and trade-union leader in Marseilles, he alone among the more accomplished writers of francophone Africa has not received a formal education. He does not write, therefore, from the perspective of the assimilated élite but with a pronounced bias for the ordinary people to whom he feels an unbroken belonging. He is much less concerned with the spiritual problems of the colonial conflict than with the specific social and economic aspects of this conflict. Further, his project extends beyond the limited sphere of the confrontation between Europe and Africa, and takes in the whole problem of social transition in contemporary Africa.

This project is explicitly formulated by Sembène Ousmane in his preface to *L'Harmattan* (1964), in which he makes clear his conception of the African novelist's relation to the social background which provides the framework of his imaginative world. He compares the modern African writer to the traditional *griot*, a chronicler who must remain close to the people and to real events in their history so as to record the impact of these events upon their lives. The writer, like the *griot*, thus becomes a committed witness whose duty it is to report the people's collective experience from the inside, seeing it with their own eyes and giving voice to their inner responses to external circumstances.

In modern terms, Ousmane's work can be best understood as an illustration of the theory of socialist realism – that is, as a work whose conscious direction is towards the attainment of a social ideal established through the presentation of exemplary characters and situations. The artist's role in this conception becomes that of both witness and reformer, and Ousmane has progressively entered more fully into this role as his literary career has developed. His first novel, *Le Docker noir* (1956) is straightforward protest denouncing racial injustice and the prejudices by which it is fostered; despite the strong sense of conviction which it conveys, it cannot be considered an effective work. In his second novel, *O Pays, mon beau peuple* (1957) he turns his attention to African society not so much to uphold the right of the colonized African as to challenge the adequacy of traditional ways and mentality, overtly advocating the adoption of western ideas for modern progress. The work has some interest in its indication of Ousmane's development as a writer and man of ideas, but its merits as a novel capable of engaging the reader's feelings are limited. This was followed by *Les Bouts de bois de Dieu* (1960), the work which established Ousmane's reputation as a novelist and in which his artistic ideas were first given effective realization. In its imaginative recreation of a real event – the strike of the railwaymen of the Dakar–Bamako line in 1947 – Ousmane's novel presents an impressive array of varied characters related to a common action, and his realism is employed both to present the broad outlines of the social conflict which is the theme of the novel and to explore the tensions generated by this conflict and the requirements of the action. We are thus offered a complete picture of life and experience in the colonial situation which adds a dimension of depth and gives conviction to Ousmane's celebration of the collective heroism of a whole African population in revolt against colonial exploitation. As much in its demonstration of Ousmane's growing competence in the use of the narrative mode as in the clarity of the social vision which it projects, the novel marked a definite advance in Ousmane's writing.

This development was confirmed with the appearance of *Voltaïque* (1962), a collection of short stories which must be counted among Ousmane's most successful works. The fact indeed is of great interest, as the short story (*nouvelle*) in its orthodox western sense – as distinct from the tale (*conte*) – is a form which has not found much favour with African writers using the European languages. In such stories as 'Un amour de la rue sablonneuse', 'La Noire de . . .' and the title story itself, Ousmane is revealed as an accomplished practitioner of the genre who may be contributing to its establishment as a significant part of modern African literature. These stories are marked by a fineness of insight into situations and individuals which is not often given sufficient scope in the novels, dominated as they are by their author's preoccupation with dramatizing social issues in their external configurations. The significant point then about Ousmane's short stories is the way in which his directness of style and realistic approach are effectively applied to the more restricted and intimate form of the short story.

With respect to both its theme and narrative technique, *L'Harmattan*, Ousmane's next work, is a development upon *Les Bouts de bois de Dieu*, and the novel provides perhaps the most striking illustration of the conception of the writer as advanced in the preface. Taking once again a real event as his point of departure – the historic referendum in French colonial Africa in 1958 – he portrays the reaction of the African population in something of a composite colony to the event. Ousmane describes the atmosphere in which this referendum is to take place – the different pressures that are brought to bear upon the people and the varied range of reactions which they provoke. He is thus able not only to convey the impression of a typical situation but also to indicate the social and political issues with which the novel is concerned. By examining the different social classes through his main characters, he shows how their reaction to the campaign on the referendum is conditioned by their social position and interests as well as by their degree of understanding of the issues involved in the referendum.

Although *L'Harmattan* is primarily a political novel, it clearly has a more properly social dimension as well, and the structure reflects the author's purpose in this respect. Extending the scope of the narrative technique in *Les Bouts de bois de Dieu*, Ousmane employs a method carried over from the cinema, an art form in which he has earned a solid reputation. The succession of tableaux which constitute the novel centre around a succession of characters, with flashbacks sometimes recalling their backgrounds and with isolated sequences detaching significant personages or actions in the complex web of situations and events. The main purpose of this method is to encompass within the narrative the whole range of people involved in it while keeping the principal actors constantly in focus; to produce the effect of a panorama showing these people in their various modes of involvement with external events.

L'Harmattan is characteristic of Ousmane's style and of the way one feels his presence in all his work, shaping situations and characters according to his personal attitudes. It therefore has some of the characteristic weaknesses of a partisan novel, but it is not a poor one. The characters are often vividly drawn and almost always convincing, and the narrative style gives an impression of constant movement to the story. It may indeed be reckoned Ousmane's best single work, for in it he achieves at moments such a concentration of narrative style as to give dramatic power to his work. *L'Harmattan* and more recently *Vehi ciosane suivi du mandat* (1966) have thus brought Ousmane's writing to a new level of competence and revealed the ever-widening range of his social vision.[3] But while his work develops in technical skill and deepens in its human conception, Ousmane's greatest asset as a writer remains his gift as a story-teller, with a directness of appeal which lends conviction to his knowledge of and sympathy for the ordinary African.

Sembène Ousmane's ambition is to record the progress of African society, to provide an inside picture of its evolution as it is being lived, while at the same time opening out purposeful perspectives for collective life on the continent. His work represents the ultimate point in the kind of commitment, inherent in the majority of French African novels, to the use of fiction as a means not only of capturing and transmitting the various currents in African life at their moment in time, but also of anticipating the future, and even of demonstrating an ideal future. This prospective ideal has been summed up in a single novel, *Cette Afrique-là* (1963), written by a Camerounian, Jean Ikellé-Matiba, who attempts to chart the full course of the movement of history in his country from pre-colonial days to the present, and, through the life history of his principal character, to elucidate the logic of this movement.

It is this consideration, this will to grasp the meaning of history in imaginative terms, which has governed the whole approach to fiction among French African writers to the extent that one can discern a single purpose and a single direction in the development of the French African novel. And it is precisely the importance these writers attach to the larger problems of their social and political situation which has given impetus to this development and urged them decisively to adopt the conventional forms of the western novel. Those writers who have attempted to revive the narrative forms of traditional Africa have been unable, with the notable exception of Birago Diop, to solve the problems involved by their transference from one climate of expression to another. The subjects normally associated with the legends and epic in oral literature are more appropriate to romantic rather than realistic themes, and to verse narratives rather than to the novel as it has come to be understood.

It is true that the novel in Europe is now, with regard to certain developments in its themes and techniques, returning to the mythical and heroic structures from which it evolved. It is not impossible, therefore, that works like *Doguicimi* and *Soundiata* may come in future to be regarded as the forerunners of a similar development for the African novel. That such a development cannot be ruled out is suggested by the example of the *contes* of Birago Diop, who has been favoured both by his genius and the circumscribed nature of the folk-tales in converting them into an original form of short narrative. And in some respects, despite the obvious debt that Laye owes to Kafka, his symbolic novel can also be considered an extended form of the traditional fable and, therefore, to be essentially of African inspiration. A detailed analysis of *Le Regard du roi* from this point of view has still to be done, but there are clear indications in the novel that Laye conceived the novel as a synthesis of Kafka and the African folk-tale. However, the atmosphere that prevails in these works is too remote from the immediate concerns that have claimed the attention of most African novelists and is at odds with the realistic orientation of the French Africans in particular. They appear, therefore, at the moment as isolated experiments.

Meanwhile, French African writers have chosen as a rule to appropriate the tradition of fiction in Europe, contenting themselves in the main with adapting it to meet their own purposes. Each writer has adopted an individual viewpoint to the common theme, and consequently they have chosen to employ different narrative methods. French African prose is therefore not uniform, for apart from the differences in style which are to be expected, it is also diversified by the multiple perspectives and the varied means of expression of the writers. Their range covers practically all the genres and manners employed in story-telling, including diaries, letters and the reflective and the symbolic novel, in addition to the straightforward realistic novel. As we have seen, one writer, Sembène Ousmane, has with great success practised the particularly demanding form of the short story. Within this range, moreover, many individual works are, in their structures, a compound of various narrative methods. But although such diversity in the conception and execution of works of fiction by French African writers would seem to be a deterrent to any attempt to impose unity on them other than that of subject-matter, it is nonetheless safe to say that these writers tend to handle situations for their dramatic rather than psychological interest, and that characterization is developed as a function of a definite plot, of the progression of events, rather than as a exploration of individual sensibility. The two possible exceptions to this observation are Kane and Laye, but even they raise issues related to a public theme, the problems they examine are felt to be typical, and the experience they describe are representative rather than individual. The novel of pure mental states, or of the singular experience unrelated to a collective situation, has still to find favour with the writers of francophone Africa.

French African novelists have also shown a marked reluctance to depart from the standard structures of the French language. Their position in this regard is, however, understandable. The violence done to English by Amos Tutuola gives to his novels the appeal of novelty of language in addition to that of theme, but his procedure has remained an exceptional phenomenon. A similar break-up of the European tongue was even less likely to be carried out among French African writers, almost all of whom received a regular French education which emphasizes respect for grammatical norms. Their fidelity to these norms has indeed contributed to the mastery of language and the sure sense of style often displayed by the French African writer, and which in prose are best exemplified by the classicism of Birago Diop, the rigorous precision of Kane, and even, in its own way, the extravagant vitality of Mongo Beti.

Furthermore, a wholesale recasting of the adopted language in the mould of an African syntax, comparable to that attempted in English by Gabriel Okara in *The Voice*, does not seem possible in French, for the language is not by its nature permissive of such experimentation, and *petit nègre*, the equivalent in francophone Africa to our pidgin English, is not developed or widespread enough to furnish the writer with a narrative medium. It is possible, too, that the indifferent results obtained by some Caribbean writers who have used Creole as a medium of expression may have further discouraged their African counterparts from similar attempts. But despite the severe limitations imposed on them by their linguistic medium, French African writers have nonetheless attempted to Africanize their works not only by the occasional introduction of local terms but also by habitually adapting French to African forms of phrasing in the speech spoken by their characters. Sembène Ousmane and Ferdinand Oyono are the most consistent in this practice, producing in the language they put in the mouths of some of their characters turns of phrase that distinguish them, and using such devices as a means of registering various types and levels of characters and sometimes even of situations. So effectively indeed has Oyono employed language in this way to particularize his characters, and, especially in *Le vieux Nègre et la médaille*, to create the atmosphere of his novel, that he must be considered on this point the counterpart of Chinua Achebe among French African novelists.

The parallel between Oyono and Achebe has another significance which is of a more general application. African novelists have tended to make such demands upon the novel as have been adequately provided for by the conventional forms of the narrative in the European novel. Such experiments as they have attempted have to do either with stretching the expressive range of their medium sufficiently to embrace African realities, or with evolving a compromise between traditional African narrative forms and the western novel when dealing with themes lying outside the field of modern experience in Africa. Where this experience is at the centre of the novelist's preoccupation, however, the African novel is distinguished from the western tradition not only in its perspective but also in its content, for the need to offer an African perspective has urged the novelist to relate his work in a fundamental way to its African context. The high social content which characterizes the French African novel in its development illustrates particularly well this relation of modern fiction in Africa to social inspiration, making clear the cycle of responses which brought into being and has sustained so far a new African expression through the novel. For the French African novelist only found his true voice by speaking out from within the tensions of his society.

In their efforts, therefore, to create an appropriate and meaningful context for their perspective, to give a quality of truth to their vision, the French African novelists have, since Maran's *Batouala* showed the way, succeeded in breaking away from the limitations of exoticism and imitation, and in projecting in their works an authentic picture of the African world. Whatever formal links, forged by a common language and inherited techniques, remain between the French African novel and the French tradition, it is undeniable that a distance, that of their respective areas of reference, separates them today. For all its derivation from Zola, Ousmane's realism is fully integrated to a contemporary African experience, and it is indeed a far cry from Maupassant's *Une Vie* to Oyono's *Une Vie de boy*.

Having thus established a distinctive tone of address, the novel in francophone Africa can now be expected to progress beyond the bounds of preoccupations arising out of colonialism which events have now overtaken, into new areas of experience and thus perhaps to develop in range and complexity. That this process has already begun – that new issues are calling forth new concerns and, therefore, a new approach – has already been indicated by the emergence in 1967 of a new novelist, the Senegalese Malick Fall, in whose novel *La Plaie* the theme of the social outcast possessed by a morbid obsession has made its appearance in the African novel.

If then, in its first phase of development, the principal concerns revealed in the French African novel have revolved around the encounter with Europe and the colonial question, this is because these have been major factors in the modern experience of Africans which have driven in upon themselves those minds upon which they have impinged most profoundly. French African writers have reacted most vigorously to this experience by seeking out and giving expression to a new awareness of their identity and of their destiny as Africans in relation both to their past and their present. The novelists have sought in particular to come to grips with the immediate problems of the colonial situation by exploring its contradictions and by delving into the inner strains it produced. The prose literature of French African writers thus complements their poetry – both are parallel currents in a single, forceful movement.

The novel appears to have been the medium which has offered these writers the most comprehensive and most effective means of carrying out the social function which seems inseparable from their conception of literature. For if in poetry their sentiments and attitudes are given an articulation than often rises to heights of fervour and passion, in the novels they are referred back to their foundations in real experience in all its implications and extensions – demonstrated concretely, as it were – and thus given a vital significance.

Notes *and* References

The following titles mentioned in this chapter are available in English translation in the African Writers Series (London: Heinemann Educational Books):

Mongo Beti *Mission to Kala* (AWS 13), *King Lazarus* (AWS 77) and *The Poor Christ of Bomba* (AWS 88)

Bernard Dadié *Climbié* (AWS 87)

Malick Fall *The Wound* (AWS 144)

Cheikh Hamidou Kane *Ambiguous Adventure* (AWS 119)

René Maran *Batouala* (AWS 135)

Gabriel Okara *The Voice* (AWS 68)

Sembène Ousmane *God's Bits of Wood* (AWS 63), *The Money Order* with *White Genesis* (AWS 92), *Tribal Scars* – English version of *Voltaïque* (AWS 142) and *Xala* (AWS 175)

Ferdinand Oyono *Houseboy* (AWS 29) and *The Old Man and the Medal* (AWS 39)

An English translation of Camara Laye's *The African Child* is published by Fontana/Collins.

1. As is well known, Mongo Beti's real name is Alexandre Biyidi.
2. Judith Gleason, *This Africa* (Evanston: Northwestern University Press, 1965), p. 149.
3. Since the original version of this text was written, Sembène Ousmane has published another novel, *Xala* (Paris: Présence Africaine, 1974; English translation, London: Heinemann Educational Books, 1976).

9. Faith and Exile: Cheikh Hamidou Kane and the Theme of Alienation

▼▼

There are at least two senses in which *L'Aventure ambiguë*, Cheikh Hamidou Kane's only novel to date, can be said to have attained the status of a classic. First, in the way in which it brings a distinctive treatment and a 'high seriousness' to a problem that is central to contemporary African writing and to modern African awareness, namely the problem of cultural conflict, the novel stands out as an exemplary work, a prototype as it were of African expression in our times. Secondly, the art that informs and shapes this work proceeds from an imaginative spirit that is essentially classical. The severe restraint and austerity of the style, the soberness that marks the presentation of the human problems and the moral and spiritual issues with which the novel is concerned; the conscious architecture of characters and situations employed in the novel to translate ideas for which the narrative scheme serves largely as a framework of development: all these features of the novel reflect an intention behind the work, directing its meaning towards a large statement upon the African condition and in a more general way, upon human fate. *L'Aventure ambiguë* is palpably an allegory derived from a meditation upon the African situation, a work in which the balance is finely held between the contemplative function of imaginative inspiration and the reflective significance of a conscious and deliberate art.

The key to the allegorical character of the novel is furnished by the central character. In Samba Diallo, we have, like in the novels of André Malraux, an 'articulate hero', that is, a character who expresses the ideas that he stands for and who at every moment is engaged in taking a measure of the forces involved in his individual fate. Samba Diallo combines an intense self-consciousness with a lucid introspection. Like Malraux again, Kane calls his work a 'récit', that is, not a novel in the ordinary sense, a story issuing largely from the play of fancy, but rather, a narrative that is barely removed from a direct reporting from fact. Whether or not the novel is a transposition in imaginative terms of the author's life, as suggested by Vincent Monteil,[1] there seems little doubt that a large measure of direct involvement by the author with his principal character supplies to the work much of its moving power. In Kane's designation of his novel as a *récit*, as indeed in the whole manner of Kane's writing, one discerns at all events an insistence on his part on the representative value of Diallo's adventure; *L'Aventure ambiguë* can be said to present itself as a case-study and its hero as a model.

But if, in this view, Samba Diallo appears to us somewhat of an abstraction, he is nonetheless a credible creation, the radical representation of a recognizable type of individual temperament and destiny. Indeed, the emphasis on individual consciousness in this work is unusual in the general run of African novels. In other words, Samba Diallo is far from being a stock figure, a disincarnated symbol. We respond to him as to an individual who is implicated in an intense personal drama, and our interest in him is commanded by what we understand immediately as the character's peculiar form of response to the burden of existence. And it is through the intensity of this response that the character acquires his representative value and that we are drawn into an involvement with the author's exploration of the alienated condition and sensibility. Thus it is the intimate correlation between the hero and the situation which he symbolizes that brings alive for us the total significance of the novel.

L'Aventure ambiguë is unusual among African novels in its special approach to the common theme of cultural conflict. The theme of exile is situated in this novel at two levels and within a double perspective. There is, first, the religious subject which carries the emphasis of the author's treatment throughout and which is rigorously particularized, but which is nonetheless inscribed within the larger context of the colonial situation. Kane's explicit focus on the religious crisis accords with the general scheme of the novel: religion is felt here as being both a subjective state and an objective factor, as both a matter of personal experience and as a social force. The novel can be seen, from a narrow point of view, to reduce itself to an examination of the crisis of religious belief, the tensions that build up within the religious personality that William James has called 'the divided self'.[2] But this examination is prolonged and extended by the specific context defined by the historical and cultural references that give to the particular religious theme its ample resonance. In other words, presented in its religious form, the spiritual conflict inherent in the colonial situation acquires a new and lively edge.

In *L'Aventure ambiguë*, as in Laye's *L'Enfant noir*, the personal drama of the hero resides in a radical change from a positive to a negative state. The tragic implication of his adventure derives from the process that forces him out of a familiar and hospitable world into an exterior and hostile world. In both works the spiritual conflict is related to the interruption in the normal process of growth and maturity within its natural habitat of a young and sensitive soul. The disruption in the hero's awareness and his consequent sense of frustration, follow upon his removal – in both a physical and moral sense – from his own native background. The mood of nostalgia that dominates in Laye's account of his African childhood is determined by an acute sense of loss. A similar mood pervades Kane's novel and affects his hero, but the nostalgia of Samba Diallo is not simply a hankering after the moral and psychological comforts of his early background, but after the live sense of integration with the universe which its spiritual life provided him. Both Laye's autobiography and Kane's novel involve the drama of separation, but in *L'Aventure ambiguë* this drama assumes a metaphysical dimension.

The religious factor gives a special character to Samba Diallo's drama. The two phases of his adventure mark an opposition between an anterior state of grace and coherence of being, on one hand, and on the other, a spiritual fall, the decline into an alienated condition. His movement is from faith and a certain knowledge that it brings from an assured hold upon the world, to doubt, loss of faith and the despair of religious and spiritual exile. His estrangement from his community is also for him an estrangement from the world. His personal drama also symbolizes the passage from one historical moment to another, the one defined by a stable world order and collective vision in his African society, the other by the breakdown of this collective state of harmony and the ensuing deterioration in the collective apprehension.

The kind of sustained development of character that one is used to in the traditional novel is absent in *L'Aventure ambiguë*. Samba Diallo does not evolve properly speaking; we are not presented with anything like a continued progression in the mental process of the character as he goes through his adventure. What we witness rather is an abrupt shift from one part of the novel to the other, a sudden rupture in his attitudes and transformation in his mental constitution. In keeping with the allegorical character of the novel, Samba Diallo serves to point out in this dramatic development the cumulative effect of the obscure forces at work in the society he represents. Viewed from the formal angle, the hero serves primarily as a focal point in the internal organization of the novel: in the interconnections between the various characters that affect his fate, and the evolving pattern of situations through which the author conveys the relationship between the various pressures in the historical situation he examines.

In the presentation of the 'pays des Diallobé' in the first part of the novel, Kane defines for us a particular moral and spiritual universe to serve as a point of reference for Samba Diallo's adventure. The other characters are presented in direct relation to his place within that universe and, consequently, as a function of his eventual fate. They represent the varied facets of that universe, the values that combine and interact with the common adherence to Islam to form a living wholeness. The austere mysticism of Thierno, the Most Royal Lady, the grave nobility of the Chevalier, are not merely the personal attributes of these three characters but also the moral qualities that inform life in the society: significant elements in its total spiritual essence in which Samba Diallo himself in varied measures participates. They compose together the distinctive style of existence to which his being in its fundamental nature has become attuned:

> *Vivre dans l'ombre. Vivre humblement et paisiblement au coeur obscur du monde, de sa substance et de sa sagesse* ...[3]

This total acquiescence to the solicitations of the obscure forces of the universe has all the marks of an ecstatic quietism. But it is not an altogether negative approach to life, for it reflects an integrative vision of the world, and it is the contemplative attitude which this vision implies that accounts for the remarkable composure with which life is lived in the community. In this attitude, Islam and African animism have combined to produce an intense mysticism, the constant awareness of a spiritual principle in the universe, immediate to the consciousness, and which binds man to nature in the essential unity of the cosmic life. Such an attitude moreover provides a means by which the anguish that attaches to the fact of death can be exorcised; it allows man to accept the inescapable reality of death with grace, in the religious acceptance of the word.

The obsession with the image of death as a structural theme in Kane's novel[4] thus reveals itself as a means of expression of his profound concern with the problems of living. The society that he depicts is ideal in the true sense of the word; it is not simply a matter of a romantic and idealized presentation of the African background, but rather the proposing through this presentation of the deeper implications of the values of life that enter what he understands as the spirit of the society he depicts.

In the immediate context of the novel, the presentation serves to establish the first phase of Samba Diallo's experience as it develops in the novel, set against the second phase which corresponds to his departure from his native community to Europe. There is an obvious paradox in the fact that when Samba Diallo enters the university, it is philosophy that he chooses to study. His choice appears an apt one in view of the image we have of him, of his early training and of the personal disposition towards meditation fashioned in him by his background. His decision to study philosophy thus grows naturally out of his earlier experience within his own environment. Yet it is through philosophy that he makes full contact with the rational tradition of Europe which, by driving an intellectual wedge between his individual awareness and the life and religion of his people, leads to that inner disengagement that is the essence of his ambiguity. The paradox deepens into a tragic irony in his failure to achieve a reconciliation between this intellectual disengagement and his continued emotional attachment to his antecedents.

His failure is indeed a mark of a high degree of sensitivity which prevents a full involvement on his part with the European reality and conception of life. Against the African conception of a personalized universe with which man establishes a familiar and warm relationship, Samba Diallo meets the European conception in which the universe is an objective, impersonal factor, removed from consciousness by the very opacity of its material structure, and without any meaning for man except as a means to the expression of his conquering spirit. There is every indication that this harsh view both repels and fascinates him: offends his sensibility and yet forces upon him a recognition of its validity both as an intellectual proposition and as a real historical force. The ambivalence that sets in within Samba Diallo is made of a conflict between two sets of impulses: on one hand, between an instinctive allegiance to a way of life that has shaped his very being, but whose passive character and essential fragility he is forced to acknowledge; on the other, between his respect and admiration for the metaphysical courage involved in the European position and his horror at the historical result it has engendered – the estrangement of man from the world of nature. The two sets of impulses work against each other and cancel out, leaving him without any firm point of reference for his moral and spiritual orientation. It is his clear-sighted realization of this dilemma that inspires one of his most significant observations in the novel:

> *Il arrive que nous soyons capturés au bout de notre itinéraire, vaincus par notre aventure même. Il nous apparaît soudain que, tout au long de notre cheminement, nous n'avons cessé de nous métamorphoser, et que nous voilà devenus autres. Quelquefois, la métamorphose ne s'achève pas, elle nous installe dans l'hybride et nous y laisse. Alors, nous nous cachons, remplis de honte.*[5]

The quotation given resumes the sense of Samba Diallo's adventure, and the note of anguish that it transmits comes from his awareness that his ambiguity stems from the conflict between two principles that he has internalized at two different levels of his personality. The tension here is thus between emotion and intelligence, faculties with which Samba Diallo is endowed to an unusual degree.

Samba Diallo's ambivalence develops into an alienation that is both affective and intellectual. His senses and his psychic life no longer offer to his intellect any experience capable of engaging it in a full and vital way. His separation from the world is compounded of a lucid disregard for meaning in the pattern of his experience, and a psychological and moral disenchantment that approaches physical disgust. As he walks down the crowded Paris boulevards, the material world assumes an exterior character that is bewildering, if not nightmarish:

> *Ces rues sont nues, percevait-il. Non, elles ne sont pas vides. On y recontre des objets de chair, ainsi que des objets de fer. A part cela, elles sont vides. Ah! on y recontre aussi des événements. Leur consécution encombre le temps, comme les objets encombrent la rue. Le temps est obstrué par leur enchevêtrement mécanique. On ne perçoit pas le fond du temps et son courant lent. Je marche. Un pied devant, un pied derrière, un pied devant, un pied derrière. un ... deux ... un ... deux ...*[6]

Here we have the very antithesis of his earlier experience, the reverse side of his mysticism, manifested before as a feeling of direct and spontaneous communication with the world, now as an acute sense of radical disparity between his individual self and consciousness, and the world around him. The loss of his own identity reflected back to him in his full participation and involvement in a culture becomes the loss of a live sense of a relationship between himself and the world. Loss of faith leads then to a deadness of the soul, to an insensitivity that overwhelms his entire being. His return to his native country takes place at a point where the effect of his adventure has become practically irreversible; the tiredness of the body that marks the end of his return becomes a concrete metaphor for his mental and spiritual state. His exile is complete, and his adventure has run its full course even before his death at the hands of the madman.

L'Aventure ambiguë is built on a structure of oppositions that accords with its overt theme. This structure is not articulated through a simple polarization of characters and situations around the two terms of the antinomy implied in the theme, but involves a more complex pattern of relationships. Some of the aspects of this structure have been touched upon in this discussion in order to show its broad outline, but they could be developed further to show the complexity that Kane introduces into the matter. Thus, for example, Samba Diallo and Thierno are identified at the beginning of the novel, and at the end stand at opposite poles, while the Chevalier stands mid-way between the two in so far as his situation prefigures that of his son in both directions. In a similar way, towards the end of the novel, the madman is introduced into the scheme as both a parallel and as a foil to Samba Diallo.

It is through this kind of varied presentation that Kane develops the symbolism of his work. His evocation of the free, open and intense perspectives of African landscape contrasts in its vigour with the presentation of Europe; at the same time, the human drama that unfolds in the novel implies the force of the European presence in the lives of his African characters. In short, in the pattern of relationships between characters and situations and even in his style, Kane weaves an elaborate framework of suggestions that furnish the thought of the novel and give substance to the statement which Kane appears to be at pains to make through it.

In its very simplest expression, this statement seems to be to the effect that faith is a spiritual necesstiy. The final chapter of the novel – coming as a kind of coda to a drama in two movements – seems to be designed as a device for achieving in this novel some final sense of resolution. Samba Diallo finds ultimate fulfilment in this return to the mystic participation, in this total reintegration into the living substance of the cosmos. The terms in which this final triumph is presented indicate an intention on Kane's part to vindicate the position of faith as a poetic and spiritual condition.

At the same time, Kane remains faithful in this novel to the truth of the African situation and in a more general way, to the reality of the contemporary world. His novel is a recognition of the proposition that man cannot live by faith alone. It dramatizes the conflict between the two positions in which is summed up not merely the dilemma with which Africa is faced in its contact with the West, but indeed the pathos that attaches to the condition of modern man: the commitment to the immediate life and the concern with the soul. In this sense, *L'Aventure ambiguë* provides a specific and original comment upon the crisis of the modern consciousness.

Notes and References

1. In the preface to the first edition of the novel (Paris: Juilliard, 1961; English translation, London: Heinemann Educational Books, 1972).
2. William James, *Varieties of Religious Experience*, Lecture VIII.
3. *L'Aventure ambiguë*, p. 89.
4. See S. Anozie, *Sociologie du roman africain* (Paris: Aubier-Montaigne, 1970), pp. 148–59.
5. *L'Aventure ambiguë*, p. 133.
6. Ibid., p. 151.

10. Tradition and the Yoruba Writer: D. O. Fagunwa, Amos Tutuola and Wole Soyinka

▼▼▼

The title of this paper is a deliberate echo of that of one of the most cele-brated of T. S. Eliot's essays, namely, 'Tradition and the Individual Talent'. In that essay, Eliot defined the relationship of the European writer to the entire literary tradition of European civilization, and sought to clarify the manner in which the work of the significant new talent coheres, as it were, with that tradition and creates a new pattern of meaning within its total framework. Eliot's idea offers, I believe, an extremely profitable perspective for a comprehensive view of European literature not merely with respect to its historical development, but also, and perhaps primarily, with respect to its essential spirit. But what strikes one as significant about this essay is the original understanding which it offers of the meaning of 'tradition' – as not so much an abiding, permanent, immutable stock of beliefs and symbols, but as the constant refinement and extension of these in a way which relates them to an experience that is felt as being at once continuous and significantly new.

I have taken Eliot's idea as my point of departure here because of what I believe to be its immediate relevance to a consideration of the literary situation in Africa in our times. It is my personal belief that what gives a special character to literary creation in Africa today is the movement to establish and to maintain the sense of tradition in the sense that Eliot gives to the word. The essential direction of modern African writing, of the work of the truly significant writers, is towards the definition, in and through literature, of a distinctive mode of thought and feeling, towards an imaginative apprehension and embodiment of an African spirit. And the main motive power in this movement proceeds from the endeavour of the African writers to work out a new spiritual coherence from the historical disconnection between their African heritage and their modern experience. In no other area of Africa is the current along which this elaboration in literature of a continuous stream of the collective conscious-ness, from the traditional to the modern, so clearly evident and so well marked out, as in Yorubaland. For while it is true to say that, in other parts of Africa, the writer has been aware of the compelling reality and importance of the essential structure of traditional patterns of life for his experience and for his artistic expression, and has sought either a thematic or formal integration of his work to the specific mode of literary expression which has been associated with these traditional patterns of life, it is only among Yoruba writers that, to my knowledge, the various levels of this transition from the traditional to the modern can be illustrated to bring out its full implications. In Yorubaland we have the extraordinary situation where the vast folk literature, alive and vigorously contemporary, remains available to provide a constant support for new forms – for the literate culture developing within the language itself as a result of its reduction to writing, as well as for the new popular arts that sociological factors have brought into being, particularly the so-called 'folk opera'; and beyond these, to provide a source for the new literature in English, the language through which the modern technological world made its entry into the awareness of Yoruba people and constituted itself part of their mental universe.

Perhaps the most remarkable feature of the evolution of Yoruba culture over the past century or so has been the way in which it has been able to afford a stable institutional and spiritual groundwork for the transformation of collective life and feeling for the individual within this culture, at the critical moment when western civilization introduced an element of tension into African societies. Yoruba culture has played an integrative role in the process of acculturation which all African societies have undergone, in such a way that this process can be seen today as one largely of adaptation, the adjustment of the native culture with the foreign, the harmonization of two ways of life into a new entity.

The integrative role of Yoruba culture in the situation of contact created by the advent of western culture is fully reflected in the work of the Yoruba writer, not only at the level of content analysis of individual works, which reveals the direct working-out of the process, but more significantly in the pattern of evolution established by the inter-connections between the various levels of literary expression in Yorubaland. It is in this perspective that I would now like to discuss the theme I have chosen, by reference to the work of three outstanding Yoruba writers, D. O. Fagunwa, Amos Tutuola and Wole Soyinka. If I have chosen these three, it is because of the intimate relationship that exists in their work not only by their derivation from a common back-cloth (to echo Soyinka himself) but also through the active influences at work from one writer to another all along the line of development which can be seen running through their writings.

The death of D. O. Fagunwa on the very day on which his article on vernacular literature appeared in one of the Nigerian dailies (December, 1963) is surely one of the most tragic coincidences in literary history. By an obscure irony of fate, this writer, whose work was steeped in the mystical world of Yoruba folklore, seemed to have felt a premonition of his departure, and to have wanted to leave behind a final testament of the faith in his vocation which animated his literary career.

But not only his end, his whole career now appears as an irony. While his works enjoyed an immense popularity among the Yoruba public as evidenced by the publication history of his novels, each one of which has been reprinted no less than ten times, he does not seem to have attracted until very recently the kind of serious attention that lesser writers working in English have had. Even now, the recognition that he is beginning to get as a writer is a grudging one. There is interest in him as a vague forerunner of Tutuola, and in a mention of this connection, in his *History of Neo-African Literature*, Janheinz Jahn is able to affirm confidently: 'Tutuola's source, everyone agrees, is the oral Yoruba tradition, and he is closer to it than the author Fagunwa, who wrote in the Yoruba language and influenced him.'[1] In an earlier article by Beier, from which Jahn probably derived his impression, we read, after an analysis of a passage of Fagunwa, this surprising comment: 'It is in passages like this that Fagunwa is closest to Tutuola. *The Palm-Wine Drinkard* and *My Life in the Bush of Ghosts* abound with descriptions like this, and they may well have been influenced by Fagunwa'.[2] The whole tone of that comment, as of the article itself, suggests that Beier was concerned primarily with pointing out the achievement of Fagunwa, while taking care to safeguard the foreign reputation of Amos Tutuola. But the ultimate injustice to the memory of Fagunwa and to the nature of his achievement comes however from his own publishers who seem to have appreciated his value as a source of profitable business rather than as a writer in his own right. In the translation of Fagunwa's novel, *Ogboju Ode*, prepared by Wole Soyinka and published by Nelson, the title page and blurb are designed to relegate Fagunwa into the background as much as possible, and to bring the translator into focus; obviously, Nelson are more interested in having Soyinka on their list (with the prospect of good sales that this entails) than in giving the wider world a taste of Fagunwa's creative genius. The cynical attitude of Fagunwa's original publishers with regard to his work is seen at its height in one advertisement of Soyinka's translation I have seen in which they have gone so far as to suppress Fagunwa's name altogether.

I have insisted at this length on Fagunwa's fate at the hands of critics and of his own publishers not simply to give vent to personal indignation, but rather to make a point which needs to be vehemently made, that his work stands at the head of creative writing in the Yoruba language and exerts the most pervasive influence on every category of Yoruba literary expression; to highlight the extreme importance of a proper and serious consideration of his work within the development of a new tradition of Yoruba literary expression.

The achievement of Fagunwa has been by all accounts a remarkable one. He responded early to the need for a literature in the vernacular, at a moment when a new cultural consciousness began to emerge out of changing social conditions. His work appeared at the appropriate phase in the development of the language itself, from a purely oral to a written one. With about a hundred years of work already expended upon the task of devising a graphic form for the language, and thus giving it, as it were, a more stable character, Fagunwa arrived to consolidate the work already done by furnishing the language with a literature in the secondary (literal) sense of the word – by translating the oral tradition into a written form, and laying the basis for its transformation into a literate culture. In the sense that he was the first to make a new and significant literature of the language, to have given the oral tradition an *extended* literary form, he was a pioneer.

But the term 'pioneer' is inadequate to describe Fagunwa, a writer who was nothing less than a complete artist and indeed a master in his own full and independent right. In an original situation such as that of Fagunwa, it is especially important to consider the exact nature of the relationship between the work of the writer and the particular context in which it occurs, and from this point of view, the achievement of Fagunwa in creating a new literature within the Yoruba language must be taken as being indeed a considerable one. But beyond this simple fact of Fagunwa's originality, his work needs to be measured in terms of its coherence as a whole, and of the levels of meaning revealed by his use of language, and in this light, he appears to be more than the simple initiator of a forward movement in the development of Yoruba literature. He is indeed the creator of a particular insight into life. In his work, Fagunwa did more than give new life and effect to the oral tradition which he inherited from his culture; he also created out of the communal material it offered him a distinct personal statement in artistic terms upon the issues of human life.

Thus it would be a grave error to dismiss his work as simple fantasies, or more seriously, as naïve childish productions. On the contrary, there is maturity of expression and of vision in his work which is as fully adult as the most modern novel, and a seriousness of purpose which fully engages the imagination and the intelligence. For the primary element in the achievement of Fagunwa was the way in which he was able to fill out the restricted outline of the folk tale and to give it the dimension of a developed narrative form, which retains its essence – its allegorical and symbolic quality – while giving it an enduring relevance. This new and original medium one can only call, for want of a better term, the 'mythic novel'.

The novels of Fagunwa are constructed in relation not only to a definite cosmology. His narrative technique flows directly out of the oral tradition; at the same time, it is evident that he strove, even with noticeable strain, to get beyond the limitations of the tradition in the context of an extended literary medium. What Fagunwa has sought in each of his novels is to create a unified sequence rather than a juxtaposition of motifs from the Yoruba narrative tradition. Indeed, in the series of adventures that make up the narrative scheme of each novel, it is not so much a question of the author putting together separate, recognizable motifs into a sequence, as his drawing upon the raw materials in the tradition to create a single extended narrative. There is a genuine attempt at a more elaborate construction of situation, and a certain measure of concern for realizing character more fully than in the folk tales. Both his human and supernatural characters are endowed with life, and clearly individualized in such a way that their actions, though proceeding from moral or spiritual attributes that are given at the outset rather than developed, assume that measure of interest necessary to engage the reader. Thus, in *Igbo Olodumare*, the formidable spirit, Esu-Kekere-ode, with which the hunter Olowo-Aiye has to wrestle, is so vividly realized that the outcome of the contest becomes important for the reader. Moreover, an attempt to give a central unity to the conception of character is apparent in the link between Akara Ogun and Olowo-Aiye, (the central figures respectively in the first two novels, *Ogboju-Ode* and *Igbo Olodumare*), who are both hunters of the same family. Above all, in making the transition from the oral tradition to a written literature, Fagunwa brought into play his considerable descriptive power in order to give the necessary imaginative scope to the situations he creates and to sustain his narratives. The opening pages of *Igbo Olodumare* represent a remarkable example of this aspect of his art.

This last observation points at once to what remains the most striking merit of Fagunwa's art – his way with language. He possessed the Yoruba language to a high degree and employed it with intimate mastery. The tone of his language, as has already been observed, is that of oral narrative which not only gives to his writing an immediate freshness, but reinforced by the use of imagery, contributes to what Wole Soyinka has called Fagunwa's 'vivid sense of event'. The various shades of living speech give full value to the style of the author who draws the most surprising effects from the structure of the language itself. Repetition, balance of tonal forms, word-building, and sustained phrasing in whole passages, build up in his works a distinctive idiom in which Fagunwa's personal feeling for language and the rhetoric of Yoruba oral literature have become intimately fused. Thus, what is significant about his personal use of language is his resourceful exploitation of the communal medium and his ultimate fidelity to its nature, his individual illustration of its peculiar blend of exuberance and gravity.

It should become clear that a consideration of Fagunwa's narrative technique and use of language provide a lead into the profound meaning of his work as a whole. His language in particular expresses an attitude, which reveals itself in these novels in the extraordinary sense of humour with which he treats his subject matter. The atmosphere in each novel despite its 'ghostly' character, is constantly lightened by touches of warm, familiar humour; the most grisly character is damned from the outset by a laughable name, the most harrowing situation relieved by some comic interlude. The lightness of touch confers a certain emotional ease not only to the individual situations but to the whole narrative train, so that the mind moves freely in the world of Fagunwa's novels.

This quality of Fagunwa's work is not without significance. For the humour, the apparent lightness of the imaginative discourse in his novels are an inherent part of their moral purpose. It is not simply in the didactic strain of these novels – which in itself constitutes a value for the Yoruba – that this significance must be sought, but rather in the total world view which the novels reveal. Fagunwa's work reflects a vision of man and his place in the universe. This is admittedly not a deliberately worked out and consciously articulated structuring of his novels, but something inherent in their symbolic scheme and resonance, and which derives ultimately from the culture that stands as the foundation of his individual imaginative world.

The most obvious characteristic of Fagunwa's world is its fusion into a comprehensive theatre of human drama of the natural and supernatural realms. His characters exist and move within an imaginative framework whose frontiers are wider and more extensive than that of the conventional, realistic novel, a universe in which the 'normal' barriers between the physical and the spiritual world have been dissolved. He has created the universe of his novels directly out of the African, and specifically Yoruba, conception which sees the supernatural not merely as a prolongation of the natural world, but as co-existing actively with it. Given such a cosmology, the role of the traditional artist has consisted in transposing the real world in his work in such a way as to reveal its essential connection with the unseen, in giving to the everyday and the finite the quality of the numinous and infinite.

The special position of Fagunwa in this respect is that while his work relates to this tradition, his art goes beyond it by giving a freshness to the old materials with which it was carried on. His knowledge of Yoruba life and customs, combined with the particular effect of his descriptive and narrative power, gives vividness to the settings of his novels and lend a strange and compelling quality of truth to his evocations. The world of spirits, the realm of fantasy, is made familiar and alive, because it proceeds, in these novels, from an individual understanding of human life and of the varied moral situations in which it takes place. It is this element in Fagunwa's art, the continuous extension of human fate and responsibility beyond the confines of the immediate social world into the spiritual, which lends to his work its total impact.

The significance of his work is thus inherent in the symbolic framework and connotations of his novels. A simple but valid interpretation of the pattern of situation in his novels suggests that his forest stands for the universe, inhabited by obscure forces to which man stands in a dynamic moral and spiritual relationship and with which his destiny is involved; in short, a mythical representation of the existential condition of man as expressed in Yoruba thinking. The tremendous adventure of existence in which man is engaged is dramatized by the adventures of Fagunwa's hunters who go through trials and dangers in which they must justify and affirm their human essence.

The very choice of the hunter as the central figure in Fagunwa's principal novels and in the human scheme of his narratives is of great importance, for the hunter represents the ideal of manhood in traditional Yoruba society. There is a real sense in which the hunter can be said to be a 'given' hero in the Yoruba imagination, as exemplified not only in numerous folk tales, but especially in the *ìjálá* poetry, the themes of which are specifically organized in relation to the hunter's perception of the world of nature, and which express the particular ideal that he pursues: the unique combination of physical and spiritual energy that is the privilege of man in the universal order, and which the traditional image of the hunter represents in the highest degree.

There is, then, a humanist vision of a special kind inherent in the symbolic foundation of Fagunwa's novels. They express a sharp awareness of the necessity implied by man's precarious existence for an active confrontation of the world, as well as a triumphant affirmation of man's central place in the entire scheme of creation. It is to this attitude that Olowo Aiye gives expression in a passage from *Igbo Olodumare*:

ebora ti o ba fi oju di mi, yio ma ti orun de orun, emi okunrin ni mo wi be, oni ni ng o so fun eyin ebora Igbo Olodumare wipe, nigbati Eleda da ohun gbogbo ti mbe ninu aiye tan, o fi enia se olori gbogbo won.[3]

Take care, you daemons, that none of you show defiance towards me, lest he spend his days wandering without rest through the spheres. Daemons of the forest of Olodumare, hear this today from a man, that when the Creator created everything in the universe, He placed man as master over all.

It needs to be emphasized that we are dealing here not with an influence from an outside source – that Fagunwa's humanism is not Western or Christian – but that this is an element that proceeds directly from the very structure of the imaginative tradition from which his work derives. Contrary to the theories that anthropologists have peddled, depicting the traditional African as so saddled with the weight of his existence as to be crushed by it and therefore inclined to a passive attitude to the universe, the cosmologies of the different African cultures reveal an intelligence of the world centred upon the privileged position of man, an imaginative and symbolic organization of the world not simply in human terms, but in a comprehensive relation to man.

For the Yoruba, the balance of human life, the very sense of human existence, consists in the dynamic correlation of individual responsibility and the pressure of external events and forces. In the oral literature, the understanding that human fate is as much a matter of chance as of conscious moral choice is what determines its social function – their illustration of the moral and spiritual attributes needed by the individual to wrest a human meaning out of his life. In the folk tale, in particular, the imagination is led precisely towards a vision of the world that privileges the part of human will and responsibility, and by the same token reduces the force of the arbitrary and the hazardous. It is this element of the folk tradition that is so vividly drawn out by Fagunwa in his novels. The trials and terrors, the forces that his heroes confront in their adventures, set off on the one hand the fragility of man, but on the other, by an ironic reversal, emphasize the very strength of his moral and spiritual resources through which he triumphs over nature.

When the testamental import of these novels is grasped, the relevance of Fagunwa's fantastic world becomes clear. Our very notion of fantasy as opposed to reality undergoes a drastic revision, and we are in a position to understand more adequately the nature of Fagunwa's art, and to enter more fully into his world. We cannot then demand from him a narrow realism, either in his theme or in his construction of character. His imagination is operating at a more profound and more fundamental level than that of the realistic novel. It is on this account that one would reject as too narrow the criticism made by Ayo Bamgbose, that Fagunwa does not develop the psychology of his characters.[4] Psychology in relation to character belongs to the nineteenth century European novel, and has even now been abandoned by the modern writer, in favour of a probing of the deeper layers of the human consciousness. It is the work of Kafka, not Flaubert, that is most representative of the creative development that is responsible for the peculiar strength of the European novel today: the withdrawal from a surface exploration of human motivations and their implication in social issues to a more comprehensive and more fundamental concern with the total spiritual atmosphere in which the human condition itself is shrouded. The spirits and figures that inhabit Fagunwa's forest and cross paths with his strong-willed hunters (Ogboju ode), are clearly projections of the terrors and obsessions that have haunted the imagination and consciousness of man from the beginning of time, and which remain the active characters of the collective dream of humanity. To this dream of mankind, Fagunwa gives a localization within Yoruba culture. More than this, he has invested it with a direct immediacy in his individual transformation of its elements within his personal vision.

Fagunwa's work belongs then to the great tradition of allegorical and symbolic literature, set within the framework of a particular complex of cultural references. His achievement resides in his creation of a form in which the Yoruba imaginative tradition can be given a translation in modern terms, and in the process acquire new vitality. It is this achievement that lies directly behind the work of Amos Tutuola who exploited the medium of expression forged by Fagunwa and, because he wrote in English, thereby won international acclaim.

There is a great amount of misunderstanding involved in the reputation that Tutuola has enjoyed outside Nigeria, and especially in Western countries. It was thought that he had created a new form of expression, a new kind of novel, whereas in fact, as has been shown, he merely took over a form developed out of the folk tradition to a new level of expressiveness by Fagunwa. It was even imagined that the universe of his narratives bore some kind of relationships to that which the surrealists, each in his own way, sought to evoke from the subliminal reaches of the individual consciousness. His limitations with regard to the English language in which he expressed his works were also valorized. I suspect myself that on this point, an element of prejudice was combined in a number of cases with ignorance: one commentator for example welcomed the English of Tutuola as a welcome change from what he considered the 'pretentious' rhetoric of his more thoroughly Westernized compatriots, as if there was necessarily merit in doing violence to English, and a corresponding demerit in using that language with an acceptable measure of competence! In short, Tutuola has been admired for his 'quaintness', for the apparent ingenuousness of his style and of the content of his novels.

Now, quaintness, as such, is not and cannot be a value. To make matters even clearer, we must go further and say that on the specific point of language, the limitations of Tutuola are limitations and constitute a real barrier, sometimes even a formidable one, both for him as an artist, and for his readers. Tutuola obviously does not dominate his linguistic medium and there is no use pretending that this is an advantage. The truth is that we arrive at an appreciation of Tutuola's genuine merit, *in spite of* his imperfect handling of English, not because of it.

It is clearly useless to speculate at this stage what the exact nature of Tutuola's work would have been like, and what his standing, if he had chosen to write in Yoruba rather than in English. There is however no question that the Yoruba language lies much nearer the heart of his inspiration and of his sensibility than English, and one cannot help feeling that it would have been preferable if he had written his works in the language that came most easily to him and most naturally, as it were, to his material. The very pressure of the Yoruba language upon the peculiar idiom which Tutuola wrung out of the English language may have a fascination for some of his foreign readers, but it is not, to my mind, a satisfactorily creative tension between the two languages that it produces, but rather an imbalance, and a resultant break between the content of his work and its medium of expression which must be considered a serious shortcoming.

There is nothing to wonder at therefore in the poor and often hostile reception which his work has received in Nigeria, especially among literate Yoruba. This is something that has surprised and worried Tutuola's foreign admirers. A good part of this reception has admittedly been obtuse, but a little reflection and some understanding of the cultural context in which Tutuola's work has been received at this end is enough to show that the sudden acclaim showered on Tutuola could not but make little impression upon a public long familiar with the works of Fagunwa – in other words, with the original thing, presented in the singular felicities of Fagunwa's handling of Yoruba. It needs to be said and recognized that the shift from Fagunwa in Yoruba to Tutuola in English cannot but represent, at least at the first flush, a disappointing experience for the Yoruba-speaking reader familiar with the work of Fagunwa, so that it needs closer attention to arrive at a response to the writings of Tutuola adequate to his peculiar genius. The temptation to disregard the many pointers to this genius, and thus to miss the true value of his work, is made all the stronger not only by the divorce of the material from its original setting by Tutuola's use of English but indeed by the very peculiarities of this English which tend to obscure the real qualities and the strength of Tutuola's imagination. It is but a short step from the initial disappoint-

ment to the conclusion that, set beside Fagunwa, Tutuola is nothing but
a poor imitator, an inferior artist who has taken advantage of the historical
prestige of English to overshadow the creator and master of the new
Yoruba novel.

This view of the relationship between Fagunwa and Tutuola is not
without a certain element of truth. It is clear that much of the praise and
acclaim that have been lavished upon Tutuola belong more properly to
Fagunwa who provided not only the original inspiration but indeed a good
measure of the material for Tutuola's novels. The echoes of Fagunwa in
Tutuola's works are numerous enough to indicate that the latter was consciously creating from a model provided by the former. In some cases,
these echoes have the sound of straightforward transcriptions, not to say
plagiarisms. But having said this, it is important to make the only point
that seems to me to be significant in the current examination of Tutuola's
debt to Fagunwa, that despite its derivation from the work of Fagunwa,
Tutuola's work achieves an independent status that it owes essentially to
the force of his individual genius. The development that he has given to
the form he took over from the earlier writer has the character of a
brilliant confirmation. It is pertinent here to observe that a writer's use of
a medium created before him is of course the most normal thing in literary
history – the very essence of the continuity of a literary tradition resides
in the passing of forms and means of expression from one writer to another
in successive generations. There is thus no disparagement of Tutuola's
achievement implied in pointing out the immediate derivation of his work
from that of Fagunwa. It would indeed have been to Tutuola's advantage
if this connection had been discovered earlier, and when subsequently
noticed, more overtly acknowledged. This omission in Beier's consideration of the two writers appears to me particularly regrettable, for a more
rigorous examination which insisted upon this connection would have
brought out the special vigour of Tutuola's imagination, its considerable
sharpness, as it is inscribed within the mythical framework in which, after
Fagunwa, he too operates. The point then is that Tutuola needs to have
his case more scrupulously made for him by the critic. For the fact that
needs to be made more evident is that Tutuola possesses a power of the
imagination which breaks though the limitations of his language and
which, properly considered, compels our adhesion to his vision and our
recognition of him as an original artist.

Tutuola has been discussed enough by competent critics to save me the
labour of going over his work, and it would appear to me sufficient to
indicate here his particular contribution to the Yoruba narrative tradition
within the perspective I have adopted for this discussion. The distinction
of Tutuola, as Gerald Moore has observed, resides in his visionary

powers.[5] The Orphic significance which Moore has drawn out of his writing is indeed important, and it is useful to observe that it lies at the end of the high road of myth which his imagination, at one in this respect with that of his culture, traverses with such zest and assurance. But its importance also arises from the fact that it is the dominant element in the individual apprehension of Tutuola the artist and not, as is the case with Fagunwa, in the individual expression of a collective consciousness. The difference I am making between the two writers may perhaps appear a specious one, particularly to readers who have a direct acquaintance with Fagunwa in the original. But I believe it to be real, and that it is fair to say that where Fagunwa achieves a personal reorganization of the traditional material, and is thus able to put his stamp on this material in his own writings – aided especially by his gift of language – one feels that with Tutuola, there is a total *reliving* of the collective myth within the individual consciousness. The artist is here at the very centre of his material and of the experience that it communicates. It is not so much a matter of authenticity, of a literal fidelity to the details of the tradition, as of the degree to which the artist has assumed the tradition and so interiorized its elements, its very spirit, as to bring to it, in his own work, a new and original dimension.

It is perhaps possible to articulate this impression that one receives from Tutuola's novels in a more precise way by pointing to the imagery that he employs. The most cursory study of his works shows the constant recurrence of images built upon the play of light through the entire range of the colour spectrum. His imagination can indeed be qualified as being characteristically luminous, for his visual imagery constantly communicates a sense of brilliant intensity for which the only parallels one can think of in modern African literature belong to the work of Senghor and Okigbo. One can point for example to a passage such as the following from *The Palm-Wine Drinkard* to illustrate this special quality of Tutuola's imagery and its peculiar fascination:

> She was the Red-smaller-tree who was at the front of the bigger Red-tree, and the bigger Red-tree was the Red-king of the Red-people of Red-town and the Red-bush and also the Red-leaves on the bigger Red-tree were the Red-people of the Red-town in the Red-bush.

The 'Television-handed ghostess' of *My Life in the Bush of Ghosts* affords another memorable example, among many others, of this constant engagement of Tutuola's perceptions and sensibility with the phenomenon of light.

Tutuola's imagery suggests the nature of his experience and gives an indication of the temper of his imagination. His vision is that of a dreamer, in the sense in which Eliot described Dante as a dreamer; that is, of a seer of visions. The imagery reflects an unusual capacity for perceiving and realizing in concretely sensuous terms a certain order of experience that lies beyond the range of the ordinarily 'visible'. And in this ability to give body to the fruits of his unusually productive imagination, Tutuola also displays the multiple facets of a sensibility keenly attuned to the marvellous and the mysterious.

Tutuola cannot be considered a mystic in the ordinary Western understanding of the word because although his visions are personal, they do not involve a withdrawal from the world, but on the contrary, in terms of the culture in which his mind functions, a more active involvement with that scheme of reality that binds the everyday to the extraordinary in a lively reciprocity. The faculty that generates the kind of events that we meet with in Tutuola's work is one that is favoured and in specific cases cultivated in the environment which has shaped his mind, so that we can accept Tutuola's testimony that he set down these events in his books in the order in which he saw them – that his visions are, in truth, *literal*. His novels prolong, in the clearer perspective afforded by art, a feature of the culture to which he belongs and that stands out as a norm.

The heightened capacity for vision in this primary sense also accounts for that other aspect of Tutuola's imagination that impresses itself upon our attention, what one might term its expansiveness. Tutuola's imagination is not only 'outsize', it tends towards a constant comprehensiveness; it seizes with energy upon any aspect of experience within its range in order to integrate it into the particular tenacity of feeling determined by its own mode of apprehension. There is a cumulative effect in Tutuola's way with imagery which is akin to the manner of much of African music, which often progresses by an insistent building up of tension. The inner intensity of seeing in the individual progression of his images derives from the extreme precision with which they reveal themselves, and combine with an outer expansiveness to create that impression of a living variousness that we get from his works. There is at work in the densely packed atmosphere of his narratives an unrestricted play of the imagination and at the same time a strong sense of artistic involvement, a deep identification on the part of the writer with the products of his imagining spirit. Tutuola's individuality resides in this constant movement of his own mind, in this fundamental response of his own creative spirit, to the whole expanse of his imagined universe as it presents itself in his novels.

It is this keen participation by Tutuola in his own evocations that seems to me to set him off from Fagunwa. In all Fagunwa's stories, a distance seems to separate the characters and events that he presents from the deepest feelings of the author himself. This impression of a dissociation between the narrative content and the writer's response is reinforced by Fagunwa's habit of didactic reflections and constant asides to his audience. The result is that the world Fagunwa presents, despite its vivid realization, acquires a certain objectivity and the drama that he depicts a certain explicitness whose meaning seems to stand apart from any activity of his own artistic consciousness upon his material. With Tutuola, on the other hand, we get the impression that he is himself the hero of his own stories, and we feel that they relate primarily to his own immediate sense of humanity and proceed from his own immeasurable appetite for experience rather than from a more general social and moral awareness. There is thus a sense in which one can speak of a contemplative quality that is implicit and immediate in Tutuola's evocations, and which goes deeper into the spirit of the mythical language which he employs than the works of Fagunwa. In other words, the heroic implication of the traditional mythical vision that informs Fagunwa's work finds in Tutuola's development the kind of concrete and fully felt realization that was necessary to give it a new artistic dimension. In his exploration of the governing symbols that translate the Yoruba perception of the forces that are active in the life of humanity, Tutuola does not merely provide the general framework of an allegory in which the essential tensions of human life are more or less explicitly denoted, but in the fuller penetration of his creating mind into the very texture of these symbols, restores for us a sense of the fluid connotations that wrap round their central meaning.

Tutuola's experience, then, is very personal, and his vision particularized; nonetheless, the elements that furnish the substance of his writings derive in a recognizable way from his culture. His work relates in a much freer and more dynamic way to the Yoruba narrative tradition than that of Fagunwa, but there is the channelling of the elements through the form created by his great predecessor. It is this newly creative use of his inheritance that redeems Tutuola from the snare into which he put himself by his use of a language which he so imperfectly commands, and which constitutes his work into an important stage in the development of a new literary tradition within Yoruba culture. Fagunwa has had imitators and followers writing in the Yoruba language, but none of them manifests the genius of Amos Tutuola. The point, then, is that it was not imperative that Fagunwa's work should be continued in the Yoruba language; what was important was that the direction of his work should be maintained, and the true significance of the communal spirit which it embodied.

Thus, despite the varying degrees and different manners in which they express this communal spirit, the works of Fagunwa and Tutuola belong very much together and complement each other admirably in their reference to a common stock of symbols and their foundation in a world view

that is culturally bound. Their work flows out of a distinctive manner of
envisaging the world and of comprehending it, and it is precisely in their
attachment to this essential foundation that they acquire their universal
resonance.

Much of the effort of interpreting and understanding the writings of
Tutuola in Western circles has turned on the application of certain categories of myth analysis, and were Fagunwa to be made more accessible
in these circles, there is no doubt that the same approach to his work
would be adopted. Clearly these works do provide a striking illustration of
the mythical imagination at work, and as such, a fertile hunting ground
for the avid Jungian; it is even quite conceivable that they could yield
material for a typology of archetypes and their transformations. But it is
well to bear in mind that the specific forms of transformation that these
symbols undergo in the work of Fagunwa and Tutuola are determined by
their cultural context which gives them their particular shapes and shades,
and which, combined with their artistic presentation, brings them alive.
It must also be remembered that any direct and automatic assignment of
Jungian 'tags' to these symbols as they appear in the works of Fagunwa
and Tutuola gives them a false transparency, which reduces the force of
the very meaning that is sought in them. They are not just details in a
general and abstract scheme, they build up together to express that affirma-
tive purpose which Jung himself recognized as the ultimate purpose of
myth. In other words, the significance of the creations and evocations of
Fagunwa and Tutuola lies not so much in their literal correspondence to
aspects of the universal mental processes as in their global representation
of the complexity of the lived texture of human life: of the human condition in its existential fullness.

If the relationship between the work of Fagunwa and Tutuola to the
Yoruba narrative tradition and world view can be considered direct, due
to the close situation of the two writers to the well-springs of the culture,
no such direct link can be said to underlie the work of Wole Soyinka, in
which elements of the traditional system are integrated into the writer's
vision through the mediation of a highly conscious art. This means that in
the case of Soyinka, the relationship of the work to the communal spirit
passes through a process of personal rediscovery of traditional values and
the progressive approximation of the individual artistic personality to the
determinations of the collective consciousness.

It is however not an accident that Wole Soyinka should have come to
undertake the only English translation of a Fagunwa novel. Apart from
the esteem which the older writer has long enjoyed in his homeland, and
which has made his name, in the popular parlance, a 'household word',

his novels do reflect the pervasive influence of the culture on all its members: which the fact of Western education has, paradoxically, helped to throw into high relief in the awareness of its most sensitive members.

Soyinka's preface to his English version of Fagunwa's first novel[6] is a testimony of his admiration for the work of his great predecessor in the tradition. The two qualities that Soyinka singles out for special praise in Fagunwa's writing are his sense of drama – 'his vivid sense of event', as he puts it – and his use of language, qualities that one recognizes as belonging also to Soyinka's own works, in which the dramatic effect is carried through a sensitive exploration of language, in this case English, in its various shades. Moreover, the special trait that Soyinka shares with Fagunwa on this question of the artist's response to his means of expression is the same blend of humour and seriousness characteristic of Yoruba itself, the working out of the deep artistic meaning of the work by taking language through a wide range of expression.

We know that Soyinka's admiration for Amos Tutuola is also considerable. The relationship of the two writers, who employ English, towards the older writer, who employs Yoruba, seems therefore to turn upon Tutuola himself as a kind of link between Fagunwa and Soyinka, who can be considered the spiritual heir of Fagunwa, and spiritual brother of Tutuola. This is not to say, however, that Soyinka's work contains any distinct direct echoes of the work of the other two writers. The exception to this is perhaps *A Dance of the Forests*, where the symbolic setting of the dramatic action is the same as in Fagunwa's novels, and where the figure of the 'Half-child' may have been taken over from Tutuola's *The Palm-Wine Drinkard*. Even here, these are elements that also belong directly to the Yoruba imaginative tradition.

Where Soyinka stands apart from the two is the extreme individuality of his own art, which proceeds from a developed awareness of the multiple meanings that this art achieves. There is not only an intuitive participation of the artist in his own symbols, but an intellectual direction given to them, as a means of an integrated and conscious artistic statement.

This method of directly employing the materials of the traditional cosmology to engage in a clearly articulate discourse, to make an individual point, is best illustrated in his play, *A Dance of the Forests*. This was his first 'serious' play – in it, Soyinka effected a notable transition from a superficial satirical approach to social problems, towards a deeper concern with the great moral and spiritual issues. His elaborate use of Yoruba mythology in this play can be explained partly by the need he began to feel from this period onwards to give resonance to his handling of the larger problems of existence, and partly also by the evolution in him as an artist toward some kind of comprehensive framework of thought that would provide a foundation for his own spiritual needs and imaginative vision.

Although *A Dance of the Forests* is not a satisfactory play, it remains a very important work in the development of Soyinka's art, for what he initiates in this play begins henceforth to achieve a refinement both in the expression and in the greater coherence of the experience. The personal elaboration of elements drawn from tradition into a new pattern of meanings attests not simply to a desire on the writer's part to give originality to his work but to a more important artistic preoccupation; it registers Soyinka's quest for fundamental human and spiritual values as they are expressed in the traditional world-view. There is thus an immediate connection between the use of traditional material in his expression, and the development of his individual artistic experience. In this last respect, it appears indeed, from the evidence of *Idanre*, that Soyinka's exploration of tradition has led him to evolve a personal relationship with the tradition, a kind of poetic mysticism derived from Yoruba cosmology.

This development begins to unfold in an explicit way in *A Dance of the Forests*. If in this play he does not appear to be in full control of his symbolic scheme – for the dramatic medium certainly does not sustain it adequately – he does succeed in making a statement of importance. It is the first work in which the troubled awareness of the human scene, as exemplified by the African situation, which has emerged as the dominant theme of Soyinka's work, is given expression at a serious meditative level. The immediate reference of the play, the celebration of Nigerian independence, is presented as a paradigm of not only the African society, marked explicitly by the fact that it is poised at a turning point in time, but also of human society generally, whose moral progress is inscribed within a historical perspective. The play is a consideration of the chances of Africa, in which this historical perspective has taken on an acutely felt dimension, of fulfilling the promise of the moment by a universal renewal of moral and spiritual values. The historical moment assumes, as it were, a cosmic significance.

The direction of Soyinka's meditation in this play has been indicated by a statement which occurs in one of his essays in which, calling for what he calls a 'historic vision' on the part of the African writer, he develops his point as follows:

> A historic vision is of necessity universal and any pretence to it must first accept the demand for a total re-examination of the human phenomenon.

This clearly is the objective that he set himself in *A Dance of the Forests*. Soyinka presents a somewhat Voltairean view of history as a record of human follies, of mankind imprisoned within an absurd cycle of blind passions. Forest Head who represents the Supreme Deity in this play also acts as a kind of objective judge of human condition, and it is through him that the essential point of the play is put across most clearly:

> ... The fooleries of beings whom I have fashioned closer to me weary and distress me. Yet I must persist, knowing that nothing is ever altered. ... Yet I must do this alone, and no more, since to intervene is to be guilty of contradiction, and yet to remain altogether unfelt is to make my long-rumoured ineffectuality complete; hoping that when I have tortured awareness from their souls, that perhaps, only perhaps, in new beginnings. ...

The true significance of the moment should be the fulfilment of the little in the past that is genuinely creative, a spiritual regeneration, in a word. Demoke, the carver and ward of the god Ogun only dimly understands this, but he is nonetheless significant as the image of the artist which Soyinka begins to conceive. The 'historic vision' is lodged in the consciousness and sensibility of the true artist, who affords society those momentary insights into the nature of existence by which a moral and spiritual intelligence of the world is built up. And it is such intelligence that gives power to man to master his condition in a meaningful way. The play's theme points them to the larger issues of human experience: time and human will, man's relationship to the universe, the great mystery of life.

With such a weighty theme, it was only natural that the dramatist should seek for an appropriate and adequate symbolic scheme with which to represent it. His turning to the Yoruba 'forest of symbols' for his presentation of the drama of existence arises specifically from the local focus of the play, but beyond this fact, the very handling of the material shows a new understanding of the traditional world beginning to emerge in Soyinka's writing. This understanding turns on his progressive elaboration of a vision of the artist in society, and of his relationship to its organic life. In *A Dance of the Forests*, it is through the character of Demoke that we are presented with the first clear outline of Soyinka's conception of the privileged position of the artist, of the creative and sensitive individual, within the human community. As the central human character in the play – a position highlighted by his role in the final scenes of the play in which he appears as the turning point of the choices open to his society – Demoke serves principally to provide a moral and symbolic focus for the multiple interactions between events past and present, and between the characters, human and supernatural, through which the implications of the play are unfolded. In the very ambiguity of his two portrayals, there seems to lie a confirmation of the primary value of his position in the final drama. Demoke maintains a sinister continuity through a repeated crime between his previous life as official poet in the court of Mata Kharibu, in which he plays a role as the purveyor of mindless rhetoric which serves to justify a destructive course,[7] and his reincarnation as a carver. But a new light is thrown upon his new existence which transforms his dramatic personality and restores his earlier significance in a more positive perspective. In his link with Ogun in his new existence, he partakes of the same boundless impulse associated with the god and shares the same spiritual endowment of the hunter, the creative energy which is fundamental to his vocation as an artist. There is the suggestion that the contradictions of his existence resolve themselves finally into a new insight into his own individual nature and that of his fellow men, a development which transforms him into a true artist, into the live centre of the communal consciousness. Art in its deepest sense implies not only a surge of the senses, but also an introspective process.

The myth of the artist as it develops in Soyinka's writings rests on an idea of his role as the mediator of the inner truths that sustain the collective life, and on his function in renewing the fundamental values that govern it. This myth is demonstrated in *The Interpreters*, Soyinka's only novel to date,[8] and a kind of sequel to the play, *A Dance of the Forests*. The novel gives a dimension to the social satires of Soyinka, for where the satirical plays, especially *Brother Jero*, focus upon manners which are the external signs of the disturbing spiritual state of the society, the novel is a direct and comprehensive analysis of that state itself. It seems that Soyinka needed to turn to the narrative form in order to work out this intention, for it allows him extensive scope for analysis and presentation which the dramatic form does not.

The burden of the novel is carried by the character Egbo, in whose spiritual adventure the problem that Soyinka wants to demonstrate is developed. Egbo is presented as an individual who is also unusually endowed, and who is seeking for some kind of fulfilment. His quest all through the course of the novel does not however find any form of adequate realization not only because his innate strength is never allowed full outer expression, and thus spends itself in inconclusive mystical strivings, but also because he does not himself have a clear understanding of his own powers. His dilemma is not however without meaning, for it not only indicates the means to that complete reformation of the spirit through which, as Soyinka says in an essay, 'the salvation of ideals' can be achieved in social life, but it also emphasizes the heroic and exacting nature of the process. In the tragic divorce of human action from a governing source of values which characterizes the social world that Soyinka depicts in the novel, Egbo's groping towards some form of profound and abiding measure of living takes on an exemplary value. His intimations are those of the true artist as Soyinka conceives him – the relentless seeker after the profound meaning of existence.

The Professor, in *The Road*, is a character who also corresponds to this conception, and his quest for the 'word' is, in a sense, an articulation of Egbo's strivings. *The Road* takes up the themes of *A Dance of the Forests* and *The Interpreters* where they touch upon metaphysical issues. The central problem of life and death dominates the dramatic action, and the whole play turns upon the idea of death as a form of revelation upon life. It is significant that the central character, the Professor, is presented as a kind of cross between a quack and a madman, and therefore, as essentially an individual outside the norm of society. He does not live or act by the same references as other men, but is moved rather by the force of his inner vision. His progression towards the 'essence of death' seems therefore to be prepared by some kind of illumination of the spirit.

More important still, the world of the Professor is that of the dream, which extends to the universe of myth. His relationship with Murano, the dead Agemo cult masquerader, seems to be his means of insight into a world beyond the visible, and into the connection between life and death, and their essential unity. As with *A Dance of the Forests*, Wole Soyinka is using in *The Road* the traditional collective myth as the organizing principle of his individual symbolic framework and as a channel for his artistic vision. Beyond this immediate factor, the issues upon which Soyinka touches in these plays have a profound human significance which has been perceived and symbolized in the traditional thought systems of the Yoruba, hence the ready availability of the material with which Soyinka represents his concerns. Thus, without seeking a point by point correspondence between Yoruba thought and Soyinka's work, we can say that the former serves as a foundation for the latter, that the collective system represents a global reference for the individual artist's expression.

The Road is a kind of fantasy in which the inner questionings and obsessions of the playwright are exteriorized and interwoven with elements of reality in a dramatic 'condensation' of multiple levels of action and symbols. It would be difficult to unravel these adequately for the purposes of elucidation especially as the play itself does not provide a constant framework of references which could serve as reliable pointers to the various stages and direction in the unfolding of Soyinka's meditation. However, what appears to constitute its basic symbolic structure is the fusion of the image of the road with the Yoruba belief in a transitional stage between life and death expressed in the Agemo cult.[9] The obvious and general connotation of the road as the symbol of the journey through life is merged with the idea of death as a process, a gradual transformation into another form and essence, contained in the Yoruba myth, to give a broader, more intense conception of life and death as connected and transitional phases in a single and vast movement of the spirit. In other words, *The Road* expresses the idea of existence as a becoming, as one long rite of passage. The Professor's search for the 'word' is not only equivalent to the artist's groping towards its profound meaning, his effort to grasp its hidden principle, but represents as well man's eternal quest for ultimate knowledge.

The general theme of the road as a symbol of human experience – as an image of life seen as a trial and a progression towards some kind of fulfilment and revelation – seems to command more and more Wole Soyinka's imagination. His poetry in particular can be summarized as a varied expression – in significant fragments – of this single theme. The first section of the volume *Idanre and other poems* is entitled 'of the road' and the poems in that section are intimately related to those in the third section, entitled 'of birth and death'. Human experience seems to be presented as consisting of a cycle involving life in the constant passage from one stage of organic development to the other, a development that is shot through with spiritual implications. One poem in particular from the third section of the volume holds a special meaning in relation to this general idea – it is the poem entitled 'Dedication'. It is cast in the form of the prayer at the naming ceremony of the new child (ìkomọ́ jáde), and gathers up in powerful organic imagery some of the traditional ideas associated with the mystery of birth in the framework of the cosmic order:

> Camwood round the heart, chalk for flight
> Of blemish – see? it dawns! – antimony beneath
> Armpits like a goddess, and leave this taste
>
> Long on your lips, of salt, that you may seek
> None from tears. This, rain-water, is the gift
> of gods – drink of its purity, bear fruits in season.
>
> Fruits then to your lips; haste to repay
> The debt of birth. Yield man-tides like the sea
> And ebbing, leave a meaning on the fossilled sands.

In this poem, the vitalism intimated in the previous works is given full expression, and the artist's imagination and consciousness are directed towards an intimate coincidence with the elemental.

It is in the long poem, *Idanre*, that we see most clearly this movement of Soyinka's artistic spirit and the role of tradition in its most developed expression in all his work. The poem itself is the record of a personal experience which recalls and extends that of Egbo in *The Interpreters*. In the poem, the natural world becomes a more expressive symbol of vital values:

the landscape itself is suffused with the presence of the primal and the elemental, and *Idanre* stands as the concrete embodiment of the Yoruba myth of origin.

The central section of the poem is an evocation of the saga of Ogun, whose power is for Soyinka the archetype of the artistic endowment, of that intense energy of the mind and of the senses which is the privilege of the creative individual. This evocation indicates the essential spirit of the poem, for the re-enactment of the traditional myth is equivalent to the ritual recall of the gods in the Yoruba festivals, whose essential purpose is to revitalize the world of creation. The poem represents for the modern artist a means of recapturing that full sense of life, that intense organic feeling for the universe which the myth expresses, and which forms the basis of Yoruba religion and world view. Thus, the experience of *Idanre* is a mystical one, in which the poet enters into communion with the land and with its moving spirit. The poem marks a high point in Soyinka's relationship to tradition and in his spiritual development. The collective myth has entered so fully into his awareness, has been so profoundly interiorized as to provide the very substance of his intimate experience. For Soyinka, artistic creation has become a medium for realizing his individual sensibility in and through the collective consciousness.

The great French poet, Baudelaire, once remarked that he could admire only three categories of men: the warrior, the priest, and the poet. This is a remarkably 'African' point of view, and more precisely, these three categories represent exactly the great points of cohesion in the Yoruba world view, which is reflected in the work of the three Yoruba writers I have been considering, and particularly in the writing of Wole Soyinka. They embody those qualities, and their characteristic vocations dramatize those traits that stand out as illustrative of a conception of life which seems to serve as the organizing principle of the collective mode of being and of the existential posture in the fundamental African society. This conception manifests itself specifically in the Yoruba context in the discernible cult of intense vitality that permeates every aspect of the culture and its social articulations, in the active celebration of the sense of a constant and forceful connection of man with the springs of life latent in the universe.

But if I have made the reference to Baudelaire, it is not to stress a similarity of outlook between him and Soyinka, but rather the difference in their situations. Baudelaire strove to take French poetry beyond the rhetorical limits within which it was confined when he began to write, to make it a means of knowledge. Neither he nor those poets who followed his lead – from Rimbaud right up to the surrealists – were able to find a truly coherent cultural reference for their visionary aspirations. The col-

lapse of Christianity as the great myth of Western culture has forced these
poets to create an individual mythology, each one for himself. In English
poetry, the most striking example is that of W. B. Yeats; and Eliot's efforts
to give a new relevance to Christian cosmology as the source of poetic
thought and feeling for the modern world have not met with any kind of
general response.[10]

The great fortune of African writers is that the world views which
shape the experience of the individual in traditional society are still very
much alive and continue to provide a comprehensive frame of reference
for communal life. The African gods continue to function within the realm
of the inner consciousness of the majority of our societies, and the symbols attached to them continue to inform in an active way the communal
sensibility. It has thus been possible for our poets in particular to evoke
them as a proper, and indeed integral element of their individual
imaginings.

It is of course possible to take the view that one of the functions which
this return to the African source has served in the work of some African
writers has been to effect a cultural differentiation of their creations from
those of the metropolitan writers, and thus to afford some kind of psychological satisfaction to the African writer in his striving for an original
idiom. There is no doubt that this kind of Africanization of the content of
the literary work implies in some cases no more than a literary pose, a
mere decking out of the material employed, lacking the force of a full and
genuine commitment of the artistic personality to the African system of
ideas and symbols. It is however an entirely different matter where such
a commitment can be discerned, where the writer is felt to be creating out
of a sense of a responsive connection of his individual imagination to the
communal spirit.

I venture to say that the links between the three writers discussed here
demonstrate just this latter kind of situation. The work of Fagunwa and
Tutuola grow out of a living tradition, and in the writings of Wole Soyinka,
we find a personal appropriation and reinterpretation in new terms of
Yoruba cosmology, so that it exists in his work as an authentic mode of
vision. The artistic experience of the three writers, taken together, represents a development of the common stock of images in a way that is not
only a restatement of their significance in the context of the traditional
experience, but also of their continuing truth for modern man. Their work
expresses the essence of myth as a comprehensive metaphor of life: as a
re-formulation of experience at the level of image and symbol so as to
endow it with an intense spiritual significance.

Notes and References

1. Janheinz Jahn, *A History of Neo-African Literature: Writing on Two Continents* (London: Faber & Faber, 1968 and New York: Grove Press, 1969), p. 23.

2. Ulli Beier (ed.), 'D. O. Fagunwa, A Yoruba Novelist' in *Introduction to African Literature* (London: Longman, 1967) p. 191

3. D. O. Fagunwa, *Igbo Olodumare* (London: Nelson, 1949), p. 1.

4. See his article 'Yoruba Studies today' in *Odu*, New Series, No. 1, April 1969.

5. See his article 'Amos Tutuola, a Nigerian Visionary' in Ulli Beier (ed.) *Introduction to African Literature* op. cit.

6. *Ogboju Ode ninu Igbo Irunmale* (London: Nelson, 1950) translated as *The Forest of a Thousand Daemons* (London: Nelson, 1968).

7. Demoke's role in this connection calls to mind the character of Demokos, whose name he echoes, in Jean Giraudoux's *Tiger at the Gates* (*La Guerre de Troie n'aura pas lieu*).

8. Since this was first written, Soyinka has published another novel, *Season of Anomy* (London: Rex Collings, 1973).

9. For an extensive discussion of this point, see Oyin Ogunba, 'The Traditional Content of the Plays of Wole Soyinka', *African Literature Today* No. 4 (London: Heinemann Educational Books, 1972, Omnibus ed. 1–4) and No. 5 (London: Heinemann Educational Books, 1971).

10. For a fuller discussion of this point, see George Steiner, *The Death of Tragedy*, Chapter IX.

11. The Season of a Mind: Wole Soyinka and the Nigerian Crisis

▼▼▼

No serious consideration of Soyinka's writings can fail to perceive the central position and even the explicit character of the social awareness that runs through all his work. The social dimension of Soyinka's imaginative expression manifests itself as a conscious direction of the writer's meditation towards the nature of the collective experience in his society and as a full engagement of his artistic mind with the immediate issues and problems involved in life as it is carried on around him. And it is the logical development from this fundamental interest in the realities of social experience implicit in his writings to an active sense of social responsibility, that seems to define the relationship of Soyinka himself to his own work as well as the elements of his individual career and indeed, of his personal drama.

Soyinka's social concern first found expression in his work through the satirical vein of his early comedies, such as *The Lion and the Jewel* and *The Trials of Brother Jero*. But the same awareness and purpose revealed in these comedies are also at work in the first group of serious plays, like *The Swamp Dwellers* and *The Strong Breed*. These two plays in fact complement the comedies by providing an admirable balance to them in viewpoint, treatment of character and situations, as well as expression. Taken together, these early plays attest to the same activity of a creative mind whose primary inclination is toward a critical appraisal of individual action and identity, in the broad perspective of a general enquiry into the conditions that define an authentic moral and spiritual universe for human life. In *A Dance of the Forests* in particular, Soyinka attempts a comprehensive examination in symbolic terms of the total African situation, caught at a significant point in time – for which Nigerian independence stands as an appropriate paradigm – by reference to a definite scheme of moral values.

The inspiration that lies behind the imaginative understanding of human affairs which this play reveals is essentially a spiritual one, for although the play contains no explicit message, and indeed ends on a certain note of irresolution, there is no doubt that Soyinka sets the negative picture of collective purpose and experience which he presents in this play against an ideal background of positive values that we are to understand should determine the shape and course of the historical process as it unfolds in the concrete pursuit and realization of human needs, in the immediate responses of men to the pressures of experience. For all its bewildering complexity, *A Dance of the Forests* emphasizes that aspect in Soyinka's artistic consciousness that has perhaps most forcefully informed his creative efforts – the constant quest for moral significance in human action.

It is in the same perspective that the novel *The Interpreters* takes on its positive meaning. In its documentation of a general climate of moral disorientation in the new social environment that the writer perceives building up around him, the novel presents a more immediate and more concrete exploration of the theme of *A Dance of the Forests*. More than a portrait of a demoralized group of individuals, it is the image of a depressed moral world – of the negative conditioning of individuals – that Soyinka offers, with the clear suggestion that in a situation of spiritual void that the social world around him is beginning to create, no meaningful individual gesture can be expected to emerge or make a difference to the pattern of communal life. It is possible to read into this novel the presentation of a situation of a futile heroism, the expression of a vision of that ambiguity that has set in as the characteristic trait of the contemporary African condition.

With *Kongi's Harvest*, Soyinka's critical intent demonstrated in the preceding works acquires an explicit political statement, a development that relates his general moral and social concern to public events. This play however does more than confirm a steady direction in the unfolding of the writer's social awareness; it marks as well a clear dividing line between an earlier attitude of satiric detachment and of a certain distance between the author's moral consciousness and the objective reality that provides a reference for this imaginative perceptions on one hand; and on the other, the heightened sense of involvement in events, the line of real commitment to social reform opening out to political activism that has declared itself in his work and marked his personal career in recent times. The appearance of this play at about the period of his first act of political involvement and the cynical realism of its whole mood seem in fact to be directly related to the specific climate of political violence that began to prevail in Nigeria from the middle of 1965 onwards. *Kongi's Harvest* thus provides an indication of a new realization of social experience imposing itself upon the mind of Soyinka as an artist, and which he has expressed in his controversial statement on 'The Writer in an African State'. In the peculiar circumstances of its formulation, that statement needs to be taken as Soyinka's manifesto for social commitment.

It is thus a critical regard that Soyinka has, from the very beginning, projected upon the world and upon events, and it is well in the very nature of his viewpoint and in the very meaning of his work that his social concern should have developed into a definite sense of responsibility for the state of his own society. It is as if the full implications of his imaginative awareness had grown upon him and, aided by the pressure of events, led him to a confrontation of his immediate social and political environment. There is a sense then in which the significant progression in Soyinka's work can be said to reside in the continuous extension of his social awareness to a point and to a degree where it could no longer be contained within the formal bounds of artistic expression, but was ready to seek a direct connection with life and events in the real world, and indeed, an outlet in action.

It is against the background provided by this development in Soyinka's work and thinking that his recent writings related to the Nigerian situation need to be seen to appreciate their special significance. For one thing, the tragic sequence of events ushered in by the military coup of January 1966 came to provide him with an immediate frame of reference for the disturbed apprehension of the African situation to which he had given expression in his previous writings, especially in its progression along the line of vision that connects *A Dance of the Forests* with *Kongi's Harvest*. By creating around him a collective drama, the general shape and direction of which he had intimated in his writings, these events had the effect of lending a terrible relevance to his intimations, and of giving a new quality of desperate urgency to his social vision. Generally, in the very reaction of his social consciousness and his artistic sensibility to the disquieting process of history as it began to emerge starkly from these events, Soyinka's sense of responsibility seems to have acquired a new edge and complexity. It would of course be too simple to say that he could have derived the slightest satisfaction from seeing his worst fears confirmed in the drama that engulfed the country, or that from the events that compounded this drama the sense of mission implicit in his work and beginning to emerge in his actions at the time received a new impetus and justification. Either view would appear to give too sharp a relief to the confused welter of emotions and responses that most people in the grip of such events are likely to experience; in the particular case of Soyinka, it appears indeed that they had the effect of implanting within his consciousness a kind of ambivalence that has continued to affect his writing ever since with its peculiar sombreness.

The six poems grouped under the heading 'October '66' in the volume

Idanre and Other Poems afford the first indication of this gathering darkness of Soyinka's mind. They are strictly poems of circumstance, written as an instant response to the agonizing impact of a collective tragedy on the individual sensibility, and intended to register the immediate horror of the historical moment. Only one poem of the group 'Civilian and Soldier', in its sardonic variation on a theme supplied by Wilfred Owen's 'Strange Meeting', maintains a certain distance between the creating mind and the occasion to which it relates. The remaining poems in the group serve to convey as much as possible the terrible resonance of events in the poet's consciousness. The major piece in the group, 'Massacre, October 1966' illustrates this essential character of the poems in the way its meditative cast and exterior and its formal complexity emphasize rather than diminish its emotional hold on the mind. Placed at a distance to the scene of events, the poet is not led to a reformulation of the tragic experience, but rather to a more intimate identification. All the elements of the new environment enter into his consciousness of the awful enormity of the experience he has sought to flee, and establish for him a tenacious relationship between the new environment and the tragedy he has left behind in Nigeria:

> I borrow seasons of an alien land
> In brotherhood of ill, pride of race around me
> Strewn in sunlit strands. I borrow alien lands
> To stay the season of a mind[1]

There is here an intense dwelling of the poet's mind on the moment in a way that keeps the experience associated with it within the confines of the immediate consciousness. It is perhaps a paradox that it is in the very whirl of consciousness around a single experience that he achieves the steadying of the mind that he looks for. At the same time, the fact that he refuses or is unable to go beyond the shock of the events that he is caught in seems to have determined in Soyinka's work an intense dejection that has evolved decidedly into a radical cynicism. For since Soyinka wrote these lines, his work has moved deeper into the atmosphere of gloomy despair to which the 1966 poems give expression.

It was of course not to be expected that his arrest in August 1967 and his subsequent detention for over two years would have done anything to lighten his mind or brighten his vision. It was thus predictable that his personal experience of imprisonment should have had the effect of intensifying the temper of his mind and of his imagination as reflected in these poems. But the fact that all his published work since his release from prison in 1969 should not merely bear the severe imprint of the collective crisis but also that their entire mood should proceed from a fundamental despondency seems to indicate the particular intensity of that adherence of the writer's mind to events as we begin to observe the process in the 1966 poems.

In this respect, *Madmen and Specialists*,[2] his first published work after the civil war, holds a special significance within the body of Soyinka's work, not simply as his form of commentary on the war itself, but also as an indication of the new dimension that his awareness has acquired. We have here no longer a direct preoccupation with social problems and human types, but rather a passionate and consuming obsession with the problem of evil. That element of his outlook on human affairs which has been described as an 'ontological pessimism'[3] and which had hitherto cast a long shadow over his imaginative universe now moves forward to the very centre of his vision of the world.

Thus the civil war features in the play less as a realistic context for the action than as a general reference for its dark and brooding theme, and as a suggestive background for its prevailing atmosphere of acute moral and spiritual discomfort. Although the play maintains a recognizable connection to the historical circumstances of its inspiration, Soyinka is engaged in it in a meditation upon the human phenomenon that proceeds beyond the contingent factors of a given and definite social and political situation to a more fundamental concern with the quality and purpose of human existence.

The playwright uses here the negative approach of his earlier works to an absolute degree. The play offers hardly more than the disturbing spectre of a world in which action parts company with purpose, and words with meaning, and relationships have lost their natural setting and broken up into pure incoherence. The world that Soyinka presents is a nightmarish one that is merely the setting for a mindless round of savage impulses.

What I have called Soyinka's ambivalence as discernible in the attitude of his 1966 sequence is given its full development in the play that has emerged out of the paroxysm to which the earlier disturbances were to lead. The studied ambiguity of the character Dr Bero is not only a reflection of the incoherence of the world as Soyinka sees and portrays it, but also of Soyinka's new mood. Dr Bero represents the paradox involved in the situation of universal chaos that the writer intimates, a paradox that produces the weird irony of his conscious and articulate acceptance of the inhuman as a norm. It is quite clear of course that the character is not to be identified with his creator, but he reflects the way in which Soyinka's moral vision tends in this play towards a global manicheism underscored by a profound cynicism. The world may be a stage for a duel between positive and negative values, but individuals are rarely endowed with an active sense of values sufficient to maintain under all circumstances the line between good and evil. In such a situation, the exacting demands of the good yield ground and advantage to the forces of evil; at best, the kind of innocence represented by Si Bero appears to be nothing more than a naïve understanding of the tremendous power of evil, insufficient to provide a rampart against them, or a protection for the humane sensibility.

It needs to be stressed that the play does not by any means contain any indication of Soyinka's acquiescence in the universe he has created, and his cynicism does not imply that he is no longer intent on keeping his moral sights steady. In a sense, the presentation, as remarked earlier, is in the nature of a negative demonstration. This, the writer appears to say, is the awful prospect that awaits mankind if the facts of the experience represented by the civil war are pressed relentlessly to their full implications. The play remains in this sense a deliberate prod at the moral conscience and interest of us all. It offers an inverted image of a world that could be moved by compassion and humane considerations, rather than by the pure rationality of limited and finite objectives, of an assiduously cultivated humanity which alone is able to justify the constraints of social existence by providing a secure framework of moral principles for individual lives.

It must be admitted however, that this view of the play represents something of an extrapolation – the drawing out of a hopeful message from a work which has absolutely none. For if the ambivalence that runs through the play does not imply on the part of the writer an absolute moral neutrality, it nonetheless reflects an acute sense of despair. The play draws its essential impulse from Soyinka's pessimistic insistence on the fundamental perverseness of human nature. He seems indeed to have fastened upon the fact of the Nigerian civil war as an indication of the unredeemable condition of human nature, in order to give a metaphysical sweep to his characteristically negative conception of history as no more than the accumulation of the record of human folly. Thus the civil war itself seems to stand behind this play as a pervasive symbol not merely of moral collapse but indeed of an original state of inherent barbarity. Evil assumes the dimension of an overwhelming primal force, with the dreadful suggestion that, in the only world which man knows, the only form of transcendence that makes any sense is self-fulfilment through brutality and crime. The play achieves something of an allegorical quality that places its relevance beyond its specific historical reference: it presents a sombre image of human nature as its concrete manifestations have impinged upon a reflective consciousness. From its encounter with the historical circumstances of the Nigerian civil war, Soyinka's imagination has emerged upon the desolate perspectives of the absurd.

The path taken by this new development through Soyinka's consciousness is retraced for us in the two works that have followed the production of *Madmen and Specialists*. In the essay *The Man Died*[4] and the collection of poems *A Shuttle in the Crypt*,[5] Soyinka presents a record of his personal experience of the Nigerian crisis as a detainee of the Federal government, and the circumstances of his singular physical and mental ordeal. The two books together thus provide an admirable guide to the present state of Soyinka's mind as it has evolved from this experience, and help us in a significant way to a further understanding of the dominant mood of his recent writings.

A certain misunderstanding concerning the nature and purpose of *The Man Died* seems to have beclouded discussions of the book. Despite the intensely personal nature of the book, it seems to have been received as a statement of Soyinka's involvement in the civil war. The book is however not a political document in the ordinary sense of the word. It is both less and more than this: less, because it is neither an exposition of the author's political views nor a systematic analysis of the issues involved in the civil war; more, because it is an individual testimony and in its political aspects which are incidental to that testimony, a pure act of indictment.

It remains true of course that *The Man Died* has an immediate political significance, if not a documentary interest, with regard to Soyinka's role in the civil war. In his narration of the details of his arrest and detention, Soyinka seems to have intended the book first and foremost as an exposure of the structure and operations of the security system in Nigeria, and his point of view on the general political and social situation in the country is central to the undertaking. To put the matter clearly, it is his own way of calling into question the whole fabric of authority and power as constituted in the past few years and as presently maintained in Nigeria.

In considering this aspect of the book, it is important to make considerable allowances for the feeling of personal grievance that Soyinka retained from his prison experience, and which he has allowed to seep heavily into the writing of the book. The whole tone and character of his discussion of public events proceed from a sense of outrage which seems to have been exacerbated in the circumstances by a feeling of resentment and anger arising from his personal experience of humiliation and mental suffering. The acid tone of his comments on individuals and on the workings of certain organs of State cannot be explained otherwise. There is such a general air of wilful petulance about these comments that one is forced to conclude that they are inspired as much by a dedication to principle as by a provocative intention, the clearest manifestation of which is the rather coarse-grained raillery of identified personages into which Soyinka unfortunately allows his writing to descend at some points. The effect of this is not only to distract attention from the serious issues of the book but worse, to suggest a spitefulness and a personal interest on the part of the author that detract from the force of his public attitude. The danger of this has been well brought out in some reactions to the book in Nigeria, which indicate that it is having the effect of arousing passions rather than mobilizing minds.[6]

A more important weakness of the book in its political aspect is its general lack of concreteness. Apart from the fact that Soyinka's focus on the Nigerian scene is too negative and possibly too narrow to give his discussions that measure of balance needed to carry conviction, his approach to the precise issues raised by the Nigerian crisis – which after all provide the immediate context of his reflections – as well as his viewpoint on the general political situation in Nigeria, appear to me to be too personal to have more than a very general significance. These issues are evoked in a glancing way, and the author never seems to feel that his elusiveness on them could be a source of dissatisfaction to his readers. His disregard for the concrete framework of events, and his refusal of a clear sociological or ideological conception of the forces present in the Nigerian conflict leave one with the impression of insubstantiality. The book takes too much for granted on the part of the readers by assuming a common viewpoint on events, which needed in the first place to be established by a close consideration of these same events.

In this connection, Soyinka's book offers a striking contrast to its closest parallel, Mongo Beti's *Main basse sur le Cameroun*.[7] The two books have a number of common features which derive from the polemical passion that governs their conception and execution. But Beti makes a sustained attempt to give substance to his denunciation of the present Camerounian regime by a comprehensive and detailed examination of the facts on the ground, so that the roots of his indignation are laid bare for our consideration and judgement. It is this concrete dimension that is lacking in Soyinka's work.

The political perspective of *The Man Died* has perhaps been kept vague by design, but the reference of the book dictated a more definite and more forthcoming approach. This is particularly true of the hints that Soyinka gives of the presence of new forces at work to effect a new order, hints which have a conspiratorial air about them simply because they never seem to be grounded upon any discernible sense of actuality, or a considered appraisal of the character and potential of these forces of renewal. At best, Soyinka's identification with them seems more to be dictated by an emotional warming to individuals for whom he has conceived an instinctive sympathy, than derived from a hard-headed social and political understanding. If there is anything more to that identification than pure idealism, the book does not give any indication of it.

These observations are not meant however to minimize the importance
of the book; if anything, they serve to emphasize the fact that its significance as a political document is such that Soyinka needed to put more into
it to give it the full impact it deserved. And on the particular question
of its revelations, it has a shock interest which cannot be underestimated.
Many Nigerians on reading the book must have been surprised to learn
that they are surrounded by an elaborate security organization which has
a potential of intruding into their lives to a degree of arbitrariness that
could in effect significantly damage their status as free citizens. The contemplation of the uses to which such an organization could be put in
ordinary times can only be a profoundly disquieting one. *The Man Died*
brings to us the realization that the world of Kafka's *The Trial,* of
Koestler's *Darkness at Noon* and of Solzhenitsyn's *A Day in the Life of
Ivan Denisovich,* may not be as remote from our immediate reality as we
had tended hitherto to imagine. Soyinka's testimony thus has the value of
an admonition that has not come too soon, and to which it is impossible to
remain indifferent.

In a more general way, it is probably unfair to insist on a certain order
of limitation in a book whose obvious purpose is less a detached analysis
than the expression of a general mood of dissidence, and the declaration of
a moral stand. Soyinka's urgent preoccupation with the human implication
of the situation he is dealing with not only precludes a detached approach
but secures him from the danger of falling into a moral trap. For too often,
analysis in its clinical function has the effect of draining passion and thus
leading the mind to rationalizations which dull its sensitive edge. Soyinka
in this book is viewing public issues with the eye of a writer, and with a
heart warmed by a concern for the effect of events on the spiritual condition of the community and on the quality of collective life. The moral
perspective of the book is characteristic, and is summed up in a single
sentence: 'For me, justice is the first condition of humanity'.

To qualify the immediate political value of *The Man Died* in this way
is, however, to indicate the direction from which its true significance must
be sought, that is, its outstanding quality as a human document. Seldom
has it been given to a writer to have a direct experience of extreme situations which his imagination is able to call up, as has happened in the
particular case of Soyinka, and few writers would be capable of reproduc-
ing such experience in so memorable a way as he has done. There is a
stringent paradox involved in the realization of the parallel between the
ordeal of the character Emman in Soyinka's *The Strong Breed,* and that
of Soyinka himself as reported in this book; of the total assumption by the
writer in his flesh and blood of the exacting imperatives of his imaginative
perceptions:

Again and again, I recognize this territory of existence. I know that I have come to this point of the cycle more than once, and now that memories are so acute that I wonder if it has not been truly in a mere prophetic expectation of it all, in the waiting upon it in captive attendance, wondering merely when.

From the recognition of this correspondence between his profound intimations and the reality of his actual experience, Soyinka has acquired a sharpening of his tragic sense of life. *The Man Died* describes in vivid terms the movement of his mind towards a new insight into the arduous task of giving a meaning to human existence, and the difficulty of adjusting human aspiration to the devastating conditions imposed upon the individual fate by the elementary forces by which it is governed. But if this is the ground base on which Soyinka develops the reflections on human life dictated to him by his ordeal, it is less a wider understanding of the general humanity that has been the object of his artistic preoccupation that he seems in this book to have striven for, than a sense of fulfilment through a private spiritual experience.

There is indeed a real sense in which, on the evidence of this book, confinement seems to have had the effect of making the man sink into his deeper self, and involved him in the drama of a lone mind thrown upon itself and in danger of turning its formidable resources upon itself. In the isolation of his prison cell, his mind seems to have reached the depths of a despondency that in its particular intensity attains the quality of a metaphysical despair. And it is this impression that seems to me to account for the fact that, despite the trenchant power and brilliance of the passages that relate to his feelings, they convey such a note of incommensurable pathos. These passages build up an account of a *via dolorosa* to the inner reaches of the individual being: they suggest a deliberate but pained withdrawal into the contemplation of a private realm of consciousness and of life that borders on quietism.

We have a clear and final confirmation of the source in Soyinka's personal disposition of the mystical inclination that some of his characters have always exhibited – such as Egbo in *The Interpreters*, and the Professor in *The Road* – and which expresses itself as a form of contemplative vitalism in the poem *Idanre*. In *The Man Died* Soyinka describes a situation in which this inclination is given free rein: oppressed by the tensions of the moment but at the same time liberated from the constraints of an actual engagement upon active issues, his mind turns away from a consideration of its connection with other human minds and their common implication in the actualities of existence to pursue a singular trail of cosmic integration.

It is impossible to judge the value of the kind of experience that Soyinka relates on a level beyond the personal, except by accepting that such an experience holds a representative significance as the vindication of the human mind in the fulfilment of the particular. Even here, there is a paradox that affects a good part of Soyinka's work and which emerges with particular force in *The Man Died*. The paradox resides in the contradiction between his declared attitude of critical confrontation of the world, which implies an active interest in its affairs in an objective sense, and the tendency to a subjectivism which in principle excludes such an interest and in any case inhibits the kind of interpenetration of minds on which alone collective action can be predicated. And this paradox, this fundamental contradiction, seems to me to create an awkward tension between the political parts of Soyinka's book, and its purely personal parts.

The poems of *A Shuttle in the Crypt* strike a much more satisfactory balance between the public and the individual lines of the introspective process that Soyinka's mind was engaged in while in detention. They present a much wider scale of thoughts and ideas, of feelings and sensations, and of attitudes and perception, than the prose work, and enable us to grasp more clearly the way all these elements resolve themselves into a new consciousness with the framework of a comprehensive outlook upon the world.

These poems have in the first instance a personal significance as the fruits of the poet's effort to hold his mind together during his ordeal. The surest evidence of this effort is the care for technical execution manifested in their formal structure. Soyinka clearly sought through deliberate versification to impose a bracing discipline on his mind in order to keep it from floundering. The result is a striking perfection of his poetic idiom, a new lyricism in which his characteristic feeling for words is put to forceful effect:

> I wait on the winnowing run
> of breezes, on songs gathered
> To green ears in a field of sap
> I wait on footpads of the rain

The greater surveillance of means of expression and the greater coherence in the development of the poetic elements in this volume as compared to his earlier work certainly reflect the energy of a mind turning over its contents and striving more purposefully to order them into a fine intelligence. As Soyinka says:

> Thought is hallowed in the lean
> Oil of Solitude

Thus, although many of these poems speak of an intense dwelling of the poet's mind upon his experience – upon incidents and upon moments that represent his varied states of being and are the privileged landmarks of his spiritual adventure – they maintain a constant relation to the world in the way they signify the extraction from a long contemplation of rare perceptions that are fitted into a controlling scheme of awareness:

> Shape the clean ascetic silo
> Long travelled in dimensions of the loom
> The bird of pressed wings may come to rest
> The tapestry of cycles, rolled
> And hoarded to a chosen germ
> Within the silent sentinel may wake
> To lonely chimes of rain.

In other words, contemplation is felt as a gathering of new strength for greater purposes, and the essential reciprocity between the singular sensibility and the social reference becomes more firmly established in this perspective. More than of a political friend, it is of himself that Soyinka writes in these lines that express most fully the significance of his new visionary posture:

> He wandered in a treasure-house
> Of inward prizes, strove to bring
> Fleeting messages of time
> To tall expressions, to granite arches
> Spanned across landslides of the past.

Social criticism springs from a sentiment' of dissatisfaction with the world as it is given and as it impresses itself upon the awakened consciousness. Soyinka's work has consistently communicated a strong sense of disquiet at the direction which African life in our times has been taking, but it is only in his recent work that this feeling has clarified itself and evolved from the vague premonition of disaster and general uneasiness in his outlook into a definite and clear-cut disaffection. The fleeting pointers of a fundamental imperfection in our situation have now gathered in his imagination around his individual perception of actual events to create a comprehensive climate of gloom in his work. Because of the consistency and a certain inflexible bent of its critical stand, there is a possibility that his work might be disengaged from its objective reference in the lived reality of our contemporary situation, and taken as the expression of a purely literary attitude. And it is true that the single-minded pursuit of the negative aspects of life tends to impose a certain restriction upon a writer's perception and to narrow his angle of vision. Moreover, the peculiar character of his social vision has undoubtedly been affected by his personal orientation, and the very nature of its expression a factor of his individual temperament.

Yet, it would be a clearly insufficient appreciation of his work to consider it as being solely derived from a mere inclination to morose contemplation, or worse still, as simply the gratuitous exercise of a perverse penchant for negation. For there can be no doubt that it stands in a relation that is palpably concrete to the actual conditions of our collective life. Soyinka's work stands out as the most comprehensive exploration of the contemporary African situation and draws its overall meaning from the sustained application of a sensitive intelligence upon the African experience.

There are obvious limitations to the overall meaning that we get from this work and which are inherent not only in his medium but in his particular employment of it. Literature is a poor vehicle of social thought, and literary images cannot have the same clarity as ideas worked out in the framework of a social philosophy. In the case of Soyinka, this disadvantage is aggravated by the evidence in all his work of an insufficient attention to the objective forces that make the living tissue of history. His gaze is too intent upon the spiritual dimension of the human condition to take in the pressures of the immediate existence, and however admirable the high-mindedness that this attitude implies, it ignores the fundamental fact that men are often caught in the grip of actual forces, and so leaves little room for sympathy.

But perhaps the most serious weakness in his work, a weakness that is emphasized by his recent writings, is the persistent climate of irresolution which betrays the lack of a clear sense of direction. It is always with caution that a writer needs to approach 'ideology' taken in its usual sense of a body of ideas designed for organized action on the social and political plane. It is thus with reason that Soyinka has, until very recently, manifested a distrust of ideology in this sense. But it is not asking a writer to write to set prescriptions, to expect to derive from his work a clear idea of what he represents beyond a merely circumstantial relevance. This requirement is all the more important now that Soyinka's role has evolved from that of a 'pure artist' which he seemed in the early days of his career to have wanted for himself, into that of a committed writer and political activist, a new role that demands an adherence to identifiable options. This implies that Soyinka needs to give an intellectual direction to his work, for at the moment what he has to express does not strike one yet as arising from a defined groundwork of ideas to which his outlook on the world can be said to relate in a fundamental way. If Soyinka's work can be said to fit into any kind of framework of ideas at all, the best that can be found for it is a romantic anarchism, which expresses itself as an extreme attachment to the abstract ideals of the liberal individualism of the nineteenth century European intellectual tradition. It is not clear by any means how an outlook on the world and an attitude to collective life derived from this tradition can be given a concrete and dynamic significance in the immediate African context. The point here is that, as Soyinka begins to assume the role of social reformer, intent upon action, the lack of a definite and positive orientation to his imaginative vision begins to make itself more strongly felt. This limitation seems to me to be responsible for the impression his work often gives of swinging without a middle term between tragic pessimism and lyrical idealism.

But to speak of the limitations of Soyinka's work in this way is to recognize its singular importance for us at this time, and to acknowledge his particular strength as a writer. For his work has about it that special quality of greatness that transcends the limitations and imposes itself upon our minds and upon our feelings with a rare power. It is not only a matter of the supreme mastery of expression that Soyinka displays in his writings, but also the urgent tone of his work which attests to a radical sincerity of his concern, and a fundamental rightness of his vision. For however diffuse in terms of their objective political and social significations, it must be granted that his feelings, responses and attitudes as they declare themselves in his work spring from a humane and generous acceptance of the moral imperatives that he considers as binding upon him as a writer. And if Soyinka is the creator of a disquieting awareness, it is as a means to the illumination of our collective consciousness in this our 'age of anxiety' as Africans, and as an invitation to a lucid understanding of our situation. His work assumes then a special significance which is resumed in his determination to see through the superficialities and accommodations that constitute collective life to a moral intelligence of the world around him.

In the final analysis, the relevance of Soyinka's work and the truth of his vision are inherent in and derive from his passionate and obstinate quest for a full and responsible awareness of fundamental values.

Notes and References

1. *Idanre and Other Poems* (London: Methuen, 1967), pp. 40–55. For a fuller analysis of this poem, see Eldred Jones, *The Writings of Wole Soyinka* (London: Heinemann Educational Books, 1973), pp. 11–12 and 137–47.
2. *Madmen and Specialists* (London: Methuen, 1971).
3. Alain Ricard, *Théâtre et nationalisme: Wole Soyinka et Leroi Jones* (Paris: Présence Africaine, 1972).
4. *The Man Died* (London: Rex Collings, 1972).
5. *A Shuttle in the Crypt* (London: Rex Collings/Eyre Methuen, 1972). The volume contains two poems previously published in a leaflet entitled *Poems from Prison* and issued by Rex Collings in 1969 while Soyinka was still in detention.
6. For example, the review by Sowemimo in the newspaper *Nigerian Observer*, Benin City.
7. *Main basse sur le Cameroun* (Paris: François Maspéro, 1972).

Index

▼▼▼

Martinique 125–45
Marxism 78–9, 102, 107, 108
Melone, Thomas 22
Mirages de Paris (Socé Diop) 150
Mission terminée (Beti) 154, 155, 156
as *Mission to Kala* 166
Mphahlele, Professor Ezekiel 109–10
My Life in the Bush of Ghosts (Tutuola) 176, 185
mysticism, African, 77–8, 83, 100

nationalism 11, 97, 102–5
Négritude and 68, 72, 82–3, 85–6, 91, 101
Nkrumah's concept of 105–9
Pan-Africanism and African 117–24
territorial 121–4
see also African personality
Nationalism in Tropical Africa (Hodgkin) 117
Nègre à Paris, Un (Dadié) 149
Négritude 5, 54, 110, 142, 143, 153
African socialism and 78–9
black consciousness and 67, 69, 73, 74, 76, 80, 82, 86
Césaire's concept of 136–8
criticisms/objections 83–6, 111–12
definition and origin 67–8
Fanon's theory of 138, 139, 141–2
literature of 13, 68–9, 110–12
Senghor's theory of 69–78, 80–86 *passim*, 107, 108–9
see also African personality; nationalism
Niane, Djibril Tamsir 148, 162
Nigeria 6, 14, 122, 198–211
Nini (Sadji) 150
Nkrumah 79, 90, 102, 105–9, 118, 121
Nouveaux contes d'Amadou Koumba, Les (Diop), 148
novels 128–33, 163–4
Nyerere, Julius 79, 107, 123

O Pays, mon beau peuple (Ousmane) 159–60

Obiechina, Emmanuel 23
Ogboju-Ode (Fagunwa) 176, 178
Okara, Gabriel 51, 110, 163, 166
Okigbo, Christopher 21, 22, 111
oral literature 12–13, 16–17, 45–6
formal analysis 18–24
oral tradition 11, 12, 13, 15, 17–21
'Orphée noir' essay (Sartre) 69–70, 83
Osadebay, Denis 110
Ousmane, Sembène 63n, 154, 159–61, 163–5, 166
Oyono, Ferdinand 33, 154, 156–9, 164–5, 166
Ozidi (Clark) 21, 36

Palm-Wine Drinkard, The (Tutuola) 176, 185, 189
Pagne noir, Le (Dadié), 149
Pan-Africanism 68, 90, 91, 102
and African nationlism 117–24
Pan-Negro 68, 72, 90, 105, 106, 108
Path of Thunder (Okigbo), 22
Pauvre Christ de Bomba, Le (Beti) 154–5
Placide Tempels, Fra 80
Plaie, La (Fall), 165
as *The Wound* 166
poetry 15, 17–20, 22, 110–12, 136–8
political consciousness 117–18
politics 11, 56, 78–9, 84, 96, 141
nationalism and 102–9 *passim*
Nigerian 6, 14, 122, 198–211
primitives, modern 81, 83
prose 18, 146–66
proberbs 21, 38, 131

Rabearivelo, Jean-Joseph 61
Rabemananjara, Jacques 53–4, 59
race/racial belonging 70–72, 73
racial ideology 85, 92, 97, 126
Regard du roi, Le (Laye) 151, 152, 162
religion 76–83, 100, 168
Renascent Africa (Azikiwe) 105
Richards, I. A. 16, 22, 25n

ABIOLA IRELE was formerly Professor of French at the University of Ibadan and is now Professor of African, French and Comparative Literature at the Ohio State University.